INVENTORY 98

 St. Louis Community College

Forest Park
Florissant Valley
Meramec

Instructional Resources
St. Louis, Missouri

CONDUCTORS
IN
CONVERSATION

CONDUCTORS IN CONVERSATION

Fifteen Contemporary Conductors
Discuss
Their Lives and Profession

**Interviews with
Jeannine Wagar**

G.K. HALL & CO.
Boston • Massachusetts

First published 1991
by G.K. Hall & Co.
70 Lincoln Street
Boston, Massachusetts 02111

10 9 8 7 6 5 4 3 2 1

Library of Congress Cataloging-in-Publication Data

Wagar, Jeannine.
    Conductors in conversation : fifteen contemporary conductors
discuss their lives and profession / interviews with Jeannine Wagar.
        p. cm.
    Includes index.
    ISBN 0-8161-8996-X
    1. Conductors (Music) – Interviews. I. Title.
ML402.W23 1991
784.2'092'2 – dc20   90-24997
                                                                      CIP
                                                                      MN

The paper used in this publication meets the minimum requirements of
American National Standard for Information Sciences – Permanence of
Paper for Printed Library Materials. ANSI Z39.48-1984.   ∞™
MANUFACTURED IN THE UNITED STATES OF AMERICA

With love to my parents,
Harold and Jean,
and to my aunt and uncle,
Mary and Armando

Contents

Foreword

There is a mystique about conductors. The glamour of the public image often masks the rigorous nature of the profession. To be a conductor is both difficult and demanding, and requires a life-long investment of enormous personal discipline and energy.

The qualities and skills of a conductor are those well-developed techniques and carefully honed abilities that enable talent to create art. Although the training occurs in many forms, the process of becoming a conductor must be purposeful; and sequential, not accidental.

In this book, Ms. Wagar demonstrates the rigor and sense of purpose of the notable conductors included. Present also is testimony to their commitment to music, to musicians, and to the role of the orchestra in our society. We are hereby allowed glimpses of the persons beyond the veil of mystique – real people whose talent and aspirations are nobly served by their technique and integrity. Through them our great art comes alive.

Here is some of the story of how great music happens; the rest is to be experienced and felt.

> – *Donald Thulean*
> *Vice President for Orchestra Services*
> *American Symphony Orchestra League*

Preface

The idea for this book of interviews was prompted by a desire to learn as much as possible about my chosen profession. Although my conservatory and university education had given me an extensive musical background, it did not provide enough insight into the realities of a conducting career. I felt that aspiring young conductors like me could benefit from a closer look at the profession we loved and for which we were preparing. I also felt that these interviews would be of great interest to any music lover.

My intention was to talk with a broad spectrum of international conductors from various backgrounds who would present different viewpoints on the conductor's art. These individuals have first-hand knowledge of the technical and practical aspects of a professional conducting career as well as its physical, mental, and emotional demands.

I sent out inquiries to approximately fifty conductors from varying generations and cultural backgrounds who held positions as music directors of professional orchestras in the United States and/or Europe. Letters were also sent to conductors working in Eastern Europe and the Soviet Union, although the political environment at that time prevented those conductors from responding positively. Most of the American and European conductors contacted were interested in participating in the book, although many interviews were impossible to arrange because of financial and time limitations. The final result is the fifteen interviews in this book. The balance of women and men conductors, unfortunately, represents the balance in the profession at this time, although I believe that within the next ten years we will see a more equal representation of women conductors attaining positions as music directors of major orchestras.

I chose questions that addressed some of the most pertinent issues in conducting today as well as some of the more technical concerns of the craft. I felt, for example, that discussions on early music performance practices and the current controversy over Beethoven's metronome markings were important because of the widespread effect musicological research is having on orchestral interpretations of music from the baroque to the classical and even romantic periods. Repertoire selection and the programming of twentieth-century music is another critical concern to the evolution of the modern orchestra and to its place in contemporary culture; is the orchestra a museum for dead composers or is it a vital, living expression of twentieth-century society? Technical questions were asked specifically with the young conductor in mind. Topics such as score study techniques, preparation of scores and parts, rehearsal techniques, and advice on professional careers are important to every aspiring conductor. Following are the areas discussed:

The background of each conductor

Views on interpretation and performance

Views on early music performance practices and the controversy over Beethoven's metronome markings

Views on twentieth-century music and criteria in judging new works

Repertoire selection as a music director and as a guest conductor

Rehearsal techniques as a music director and as a guest conductor

Differences in American and European orchestras and the differing concerns of conducting on both continents

Techniques for balancing orchestral sound in unfamiliar halls

Score study techniques

Viewpoints on memorization

Preparation of scores and parts

Gestural technique

Advice to young conductors

Each interview is followed by a brief biography and, for those conductors who have made recordings as orchestra leaders, selective discographies based on information provided by the conductors and current catalogs.

As the interviews progressed, I found it necessary to be flexible in adhering to the interview format I had established to accommodate differences in such areas as personality, training, experience, and orchestras and to allow for spontaneity. Consequently, the interviews evolved naturally and in ways that were unique to each conductor.

I now find that my original expectations have been more than fulfilled. Not only have I gained a considerable amount of knowledge about the workings of my profession, but I have also been personally enriched. The conductors I interviewed were an inspiration because of their total commitment to music and their generosity in sharing knowledge.

The art of conducting is the art of communication, not only to other musicians but to the general audience of music lovers. I hope these interviews will give this audience a glimpse into the mystery and mastery of the art.

Acknowledgments

I have been overwhelmed by the generosity and support I have received from so many people in the process of writing this book. So it is with heartfelt thanks that I wish to acknowledge the individuals who have helped make this project possible. First of all I would like to extend my grateful thanks to the conductors for their generosity in granting the interviews and for their time spent in editing and adding to their responses; to the artist's managements, namely Allied Artists, Columbia Artists, ICM Artists, and Shaw Concerts, for their assistance in arranging interviews and sending publicity, biographical materials, and photos; to conductor assistants Polly Barten, Pam Coutant, Odette Gelinas, Suzanne Hartin, Marcia Kimes, David Murray, Fiona Page, Marita Stepe, and Deborah Zudell-Dickey for their help in the process of scheduling and editing the interviews; to Stephen Lewis, president of Carleton College, and Roy Elveton, professor of philosophy and former dean of Carleton College, for their support and belief in this project; to the Carleton College Music Department for providing the use of a computer and laser printer; to my editors at G.K. Hall, Elizabeth Holthaus and Michael Sims, for their invaluable assistance and expertise; to my dear friends and colleagues Jean Alexis Smith, who helped me conceive the idea for the book, and Larry Archbold, Marcia Bauman, Monica DuClaud, and April Funke for their criticisms and comments on the manuscript; and finally to Francine Podenski and Dr. Nancy Trahms for their unflagging moral support.

"Music is revelation! The nature of music is revelation. It must say something, it must tell a truth that is human or divine or both. Just delivering notes, even if it's perfect, doesn't give this revelation at all. So when you ask what is performance, I think the answer I would like to give is this: It is a personal witness, it is the way the conductor sees its meaning or message. It is in his mind, and he has caught a glimpse of the composer's vision and gives it just as personally as if the composer would conduct it."

_____ Herbert Blomstedt

Herbert Blomstedt

JW: When did you decide to become a conductor and what course has your career followed?

HB: I didn't decide to become a conductor. I always knew that was what I wanted to do and I prepared myself for it very thoroughly for many years. However, I didn't follow the traditional path of becoming a conductor. For instance, in Germany you start as a piano accompanist at an opera house and progress by steps until you become an opera conductor. Only later do you begin to conduct symphonies. I wanted to go directly into concert conducting because opera was not part of my background. Therefore I had to wait and hope for opportunities partly because I was in Europe and not in America where the private initiative of a budding conductor is more likely to produce results.

JW: How long did you wait for opportunities and what direction did you take since you decided not to follow the operatic path to a conducting career?

HB: I had to wait a long time. I graduated from the Royal Conservatory when I was twenty-two but didn't have my debut concert until I was twenty-six! During those four years I was studying all the time and attended summer schools in America and Europe. Very occasionally I had a professional concert. When I graduated from the conducting school at the Royal Conservatory my teacher, Tor Mann, arranged for me to have a concert with a professional orchestra. It was the least prestigious orchestra in the Swedish province and the concert was not even to be in the town where the orchestra resided. It was to be in a much smaller town some thirty miles from where they regularly played. So, it was a nice experience but professionally it led nowhere. Two years later I got an invitation to conduct a studio performance with the Swedish Radio Orchestra. I did a Swedish baroque work and *Pulcinella* by Stravinsky. The program went very well but also led nowhere. No explosions went off! A year or two later I got another concert with the Swedish Radio Symphony. I did a Berwald symphony and recorded it for a radio production. One other experience during this time was very bad. My teacher, Tor Mann, was the music director of the same Radio Symphony and he invited me to audition during the last half hour of one of his rehearsals.

3

This symphony was identical with the Philharmonic of Stockholm as they had a contract to play twenty concerts a year for the radio station. I chose to conduct the *Haydn Variations* by Brahms, which I had studied at Salzburg and thought I knew very well. When I came to that rehearsal the musicians took their intermission. I was supposed to have the last half hour. My half hour never took place! The intermission was drawn out from 10 to 30 minutes. Finally the orchestra decided not to play to for me at all. They told me, "It's not in our contract to play under students." Well that wasn't very encouraging! These were my only conducting experiences during these four years. One public concert in the province, two recordings with the radio orchestra and this one very negative incident. Actually my lack of opportunities during this time was due partly to issues about my religious convictions. Everyone knew I was "crazy" and wouldn't rehearse on Saturdays which was considered impossible for this profession. Tor Mann, a great figure in the musical life of Sweden at this time, tried to joke this "problem" away. He really believed in me but couldn't convince the orchestras to give me the opportunities to conduct. So this period of time was frustrating and postponed the time of my debut. However, I'm not so sure that was bad. I got more time for preparation and when my chance finally came, I was in America studying at Tanglewood. I received an invitation to conduct a pair of subscription concerts with the Stockholm Philharmonic. Finally the message had gotten through. Here was someone with some talent that they wanted to explore.

JW: Why did they suddenly take an interest in you?

HB: I think the work I had done with the orchestras had left an impression and they decided to explore it. My debut concert was very successful and changed my life completely overnight. This was in 1954 when I was twenty-six. It was the first public concert in a musically important city that I did. I had a lot of years of preparation behind me. I chose pieces that I thought I knew very thoroughly and I had a firm belief, like a lot of young musicians, that I knew exactly how they should be performed. The program I chose also reflected the revolutionary kind of spirit I had. I chose to perform the Bach Second Orchestral Suite, which at that time did not exist in modern editions. It existed only in Max Reger's or Max Seyffert's arrangements with lots of slurs and dynamic markings. That was the only material available because it was long before the Peter's or the Baerenreiter editions came out. I had been very involved in the study of performance practice of baroque and renaissance music and while I was at the university I majored in musicology. I spent three years just in musicology while I was preparing for conducting. So, I was convinced I had a real message for the orchestra. "I'll show you how to play this." I didn't say this of course, but I completely edited the parts and took away all the slurs and hairpins and performed it the way I thought it should be performed. That was thirty-three years ago and I think for the general performance practice of baroque music at that time my performance was the "latest truth." And then I did the Beethoven Piano Concerto no. 1 (which was not my suggestion) and the Hindemith *Mathis der Maler* symphony, which was considered very modern music at that time. I think this kind of programming helped me in that enormous success. However, the press is usually favorable to young talent who are supposed to give something new. This was their chance to say that the old and regular was bad and that the new was wonderful. I had the great advantage of that type of thinking. I received rave reviews and my life totally changed!

JW: Did you get an orchestra immediately after that or did you continue guest-conducting?

HB: I got an orchestra very soon after my debut. However, the obstacle of the Saturday issue still had to be resolved. The provincial orchestra that I had my first experience with wrote me a letter saying they were looking for a music director. The letter was very short and simple. It said, "We have heard that you don't rehearse on Saturdays. Is that correct? Sincerely yours." Now I had the chance of my life. However, I had to say, "Yes, that's correct." They wrote a very nice reply but said, "We're sorry. It's impossible because we have our general rehearsal on Saturdays with our main concert on Sundays." After that there was a lot of talk in the musical circles about a talented young man who could not be used. A few weeks after that I got another letter from an orchestra south of Stockholm. A much better orchestra and very ambitious. They called and asked exactly the same thing. Again I had the chance to change my answer, but I couldn't and I had to say, "Yes, that's true. I don't rehearse on Saturdays." Well, they called and said we want to meet you and invited me for a couple of subscription concerts on a month's notice. I did them and had a wonderful time. The orchestra liked me and I was offered the position. However, the Saturday issue had to be dealt with. They finally agreed to change their general Saturday rehearsal to Sunday morning and we had the most wonderful collaboration for seven years.

JW: In retrospect do you feel this obstacle was to your advantage or disadvantage?

HB: I feel it was definitely to my advantage. These obstacles actually played a very important role in my life without me really knowing it at the time. Since my debut I have been kept extremely busy and had more work than I actually wanted. The Saturday issue, which prevented me from getting opportunities to perform at first, enabled me to develop more slowly and prepare myself for this career step by step. Some conductors start like rockets and then go steadily down. The first year they conduct the Berlin Philharmonic or the Chicago Symphony and ten years later they sit in the province.

JW: Is this because they don't have a background and enough repertoire behind them?

HB: Yes, it's mostly that. It is largely a repertoire problem. To get guest conducting engagements with important orchestras in the first year of your career is a great gift. However, if one doesn't have any repertoire built up and no experience it's almost impossible to stay at the top. These opportunities come largely from competitions. Everyone is curious about the first prize winner of the Karajan competition and I'm not so sure that's good. Winning a competition is one thing and it offers opportunities but it's difficult to use the benefits unless you have years of preparation behind you which most young conductors don't have. A conducting competition is not like winning the Tchaikovsky Piano Competition. A conductor is very different from a soloist. You can be a wonderful performer on the piano and on the violin and do ten concertos extremely well and that's all. You play them and you go. A conductor, however, has to work with musicians who many times are his superiors both musically and in experience. He comes young and the orchestras have played the works he conducts many times before with more experienced conductors. So how can a young conductor cope with that? You can do it once or twice but can you go for a whole year like that from one great orchestra to another? It's impossible. Your career can't go up from that. It can only go down.

JW: So you think it's much better to build a career slowly?

HB: Yes, definitely. I think I've been very lucky to go step by step at a pace I've really had no influence over. I'm often asked by journalists, "When did you decide to conduct in America? When did you decide to conduct the Dresden Staatskapelle?" I never decided those things. I was offered the opportunities and I said yes. Conductors, especially in the United States, are thought of as superambitious, power-hungry musicians who elbow their way up as fast as possible to the throne of glory. I would never have been a conductor if I had to build a career in that way. I'm not like that. I have created opportunities for myself only by trying to do a good job but I've never asked for any position except one. I applied for a position as an organist because I loved the organ and I graduated as an organist from the conservatory. I'm crazy about organ music to this very day. I asked for that position because I was getting quite "mature" and I wanted to start a family and thought I might go forever without getting a chance to conduct. So, I applied for this position but didn't get it which was very fortunate. However, I never applied for any conducting position. I never asked for a letter of recommendation and depended instead on other people to spontaneously say good things about my work. Actually, the word does go around if there is a talented student and he does a good job. I believe much more in this kind of development, at least with persons of my type of personality. I must say that I've been very lucky! My career has developed like a ladder going from step to step, from better orchestra to better orchestra at just the pace I needed.

JW: Don't you feel everyone's career development is personal and unfolds in different ways?

HB: Yes, let's look at composers. Let's compare Mozart and Schubert to Bruckner. Mozart and Schubert were already dead and had completed a fantastic life work at the age when Bruckner was still writing counterpoint exercises. Yes, everyone has a different pace and develops in different ways. I think it's good that it is like that. And even more so, I think it's important in the conducting profession to have as much maturity as possible before you start working because a conductor works with people! A composer works with paper and an instrumentalist works with his instrument. A composer can work for a year on a string quartet at his own pace. He doesn't hurt anyone and he can work on it until he thinks it's perfect. The same is true for the instrumentalist. A page and an instrument can take lots of mistakes but people can not. People will only take so many mistakes from a conductor before they will get frustrated.

JW: What about your current career? How many orchestras do you conduct and how many concerts per year do you do?

HB: I conduct about 100 concerts a year, which is a lot. When I was mostly active in Europe I did only seventy. However, since the San Francisco Symphony performs so much (they give four and sometimes five concerts every week) I am conducting around 100 concerts now. Of course, the San Francisco Symphony takes more of my time than any other symphony I have directed. This is partly because American orchestras work differently than European ones.

JW: In what sense do European orchestras differ from American orchestras?

HB: The music director in the States plays a much more decisive and influential role than in Europe. Here the orchestras depend much more on the music director for guidance and publicity and he has to O.K. even minor artistic decisions. Orchestras in Europe are generally more self-governing. There are even orchestras that don't have a music director and will never have one. For example, the Vienna Philharmonic doesn't have a music director and it has obviously worked quite well for them.

JW: So, of course, you as a conductor have to adapt to the different circumstances in which you are conducting, whether in Europe or the States.

HB: Yes, because every orchestra is a little different. Since American orchestras make more demands on my time than European orchestras I

7

spend more time with San Francisco than I did with the Dresden Staatskapelle. I also don't do very much guest-conducting. I would rather work with fewer orchestras more extensively. Currently I am music director of the San Francisco Symphony and honorary conductor of the NHK Symphony in Tokyo and I guest conduct a few other major symphonies in the United States and Europe.

JW: How do you conserve your energy with this tremendous schedule?

HB: This is a very interesting question. You'll get very many different answers to this. Personally I think it is a matter of life-style. I like people very much but I hate parties and I generally don't go out after concerts as many colleagues do. I think this has to do with eating habits. After a concert everyone is hungry because they don't eat before the concert. I eat the biggest meal in the morning at 7:00 A.M., a very good meal at noon and at 6:00 P.M. just a little. I eat this way every day, which means after a concert I'm not hungry and it gives me the opportunity to go straight to bed and I sleep immediately. However, if you're hungry and eat after the concert, your evenings get very drawn out and I'm sure that's not healthy with this type of schedule. The other answer is the Sabbath. Without the Sabbath I wouldn't be able to work as much as I do. It would be impossible for me to stop working with music because of the kind of love I have for it. Also, because of the ambition we have to be at the very top of our profession and to do the very best for our audiences and musicians, I would feel guilty if I were not preparing all the time. But it's a great relief to have a supreme command which says, "This is not the day to work. This is the day to recognize God's presence and to reflect and respond to it." Without that command I would be studying scores all the time and would burn myself out. [Igor] Markevitch, one of my most treasured teachers, did not understand this at all and even scolded me for it.

JW: When did you study with him?

HB: I came to him in 1950 when I was twenty-three and returned to him practically every summer for five years. He was a wonderful teacher but was very hard on me about this issue. Several times he needed help and wanted me to take over concerts with rehearsals on Saturday and was terribly angry when I wouldn't. However, twenty years later, when my career was doing very well and he was getting old, I conducted his orchestra at Monte Carlo. Of course, there was the same problem with the Sabbath which was finally resolved. Anyway, Markevitch came to my hotel room and told me that finally he understood. He told me, "The Sabbath has saved you. In reality that's the secret of your success. If you had not been a Sabbath keeper you would have worked yourself to death." That's what Markevitch did. He was seventy and almost burned out. So this is a very important answer to your question as far as I'm concerned. I think every conductor is different. For example there are people with almost photographic memories. Therefore they will have completely different study habits. However, the question of revitalization is absolutely necessary. The kind of music I like to make takes much psychic energy but it also stimulates me. The way I experience it is that after a concert I feel exhilarated and want to do it again. I never get tired of making music. When a work is rehearsed and played I never feel that it is finished, good-bye. I feel that there is so much more that I want to do in this bar and in that bar and on this note to make the whole more beautiful.

JW: I've watched you rehearse many times. I've watched you take a run-through of a passage and then go back and fix twenty or thirty details. It must be hard to keep all those places in your mind while you are conducting!

HB: I come to the rehearsals with an absolute vision of how I want the work to sound. The rehearsal procedure is making it sound the way I want it. At the same time the orchestra needs to feel that they are making the music, playing together, and that I don't compel them to play in a certain way. It feels natural for the musicians to make the music themselves and just look to the conductor for guidance. I have to organize the time. So much of what I want to achieve must be achieved in a limited amount of time. I could stop after each note, which would be completely unproductive. However, once I did that. I was conducting an American orchestra in the Brahms First Symphony. I stopped them after the first note which is something I had never done before. I said, Let's try again, it's only forte. But the trumpets said "BAH" and the timpani said "UGH"! I stopped three or four times after the first note and tried to get them to understand that this was not a loudness contest. This was music and they had to listen to each other. It changed the whole orchestra. After an hour they were completely different. Generally however, that's a very bad way to do it. You usually never achieve anything like that. Also at a rehearsal we have to feel we are making music! The musicians must feel that they are doing something that they like and that they are playing for me and at the same time I must learn from them. If you come to the rehearsal with a vision of exactly what you want to hear it's not hard to remember the details you want to change.

JW: How do you arrive at your vision of the music?

HB: Studying the score, listening to the score in your mind.

JW: Do you have a specific technique for score study?

HB: Everyone has his own method I guess. But I feel I must know the inner secrets of a score before I go in front of the orchestra.

JW: This takes years of study.

HB: Of course, and I'm not so conceited as to think that I know everything about a score even if I've performed the music many times. I'm always discovering new things and learning. But it's a mistake to postpone all this learning until after the rehearsal. You have to have a solid and detailed knowledge before coming in front of the orchestra.

JW: How many pieces do you add to your repertoire each year and at what point in your study of a score do you feel you are ready to conduct it?

HB: It depends on the kind of music it is and it depends on how much experience I have achieved. It was different thirty years ago than now. I'm sure it took me a month to learn a Haydn symphony at the beginning and now I can "learn" it in a couple of days. That doesn't say I'm ready to conduct it. I have my basic ideas and may even know the score by heart in a few days but it would be a serious mistake to think it was a part of myself in such a short time. Someone has said: "You only know the score when you can forget it," which means to forget about the technique and concentrate on the expression. It's part of you when you just do it without thinking how you acquired it. I think that's very true for music-making. A major piece of the central repertoire which I have never done before would take me several months and I would start a year or two in advance and go over details, lay it away and let it stay in my unconscious. Then I would take it up again bar from bar, movement to movement and would play the piece to myself sitting in my chair or walking in the woods or lying on my bed without the score. Then I would study it thinking through the music, choosing my tempos, choosing the balances and remembering what I want to hear in this bar or in that bar and trying to find the places where there might be problems. If it doesn't sound as I want I ask myself what I need to tell the orchestra to achieve the results I want? That means I'm preparing the score in advance with a sort of recipe of what I want and how to achieve it. I'm always thinking things like, "This bar must be played at the tip of the bow or the musician must not breathe in that bar," and so forth. I have to think about how to convey technically my vision of the music. This saves a lot of rehearsal time. However, sometimes I come to the actual rehearsal and change my mind based on what I hear. I sometimes imagine wrong things even though I've had lots of experience. Also, things change from orchestra to orchestra and from hall to hall or even from different times with the same orchestra. What works today may not work tomorrow. So there is always the possibility of new experiences because each performance reveals new aspects of the piece. I think it was Yehudi Menuhin who said, "Never perform a piece for the first time." A very clever saying. Absurd of course. It means that a first performance will never be valid. It might be wonderful but you will look at it very differently later, even the next day you will have second thoughts. A piece of music has so many facets, so many rich possibilities and the better the music is the more possibilities it contains. It's impossible to find them all out at once, especially for a conductor, because there are so many complicated aspects to consider.

JW: What about twentieth-century works? What are your criteria in selecting them for performance?

HB: This is a very difficult question to answer because there are so many different criteria. I think every conductor is acting within a specific situation unless he's one of those conductors that just guest-conducts everywhere. But if you are tied to an orchestra (which I think is the ideal situation), conductors should be the servants of that orchestra and have a loyalty to the composers of the community. So when I was the music director of the Danish Radio Symphony I played a lot of Danish music and with the Dresden Orchestra I played a lot of East German composers. It can't be any other way. It's very natural. Now I play quite a lot of American music which was unfamiliar to me before I came here. Some of the composers I'm playing now I had never even heard about. This is very nice and very interesting. But of course we don't perform every work that's written in the Bay Area. That would be impossible! Fortunately the San Francisco Symphony has wonderful people who help select the best. Dozens of scores are sent in and proposed.

JW: What role does the composer-in-residence have here?

HB: Of course he composes new works for us, but he also helps in selecting works by other composers. When the pile of scores comes down to half a dozen works or so, I select my preference. The composer-in-residence also changes periodically because each composer might favor styles that reflect his own personal taste as well as his own style. However, both he and the music director have to be open to many styles and has to try to be accepting and tolerant. I think the older the conductor is the more tolerant he becomes. When he is younger he tends to represent only his own generation. When he's older he has enough experience to see that every style has its value and can be very interesting and can say great things in different ways. I thought it was very interesting to hear Solti conduct the Corigliano Clarinet Concerto for instance. You generally would not associate him at all with this style. I think he did it very well. Also, take a conductor like Furtwängler, who is always associated today in everyone's mind with the German classics like Beethoven, Brahms, and Bruckner. The truth is that he did modern music all the time. However, he looked at it a little bit from above sometimes. I remember listening to him at a rehearsal in Salzburg when he conducted the Stravinsky *Symphony in Three Movements,* which was new at that time. It was written in 1945 and this was in 1951. I attended a rehearsal that ended with

11

the fugato. He rehearsed it and said very little, but while they were playing he remarked in German a little disdainfully, "so-called *fugue*." Though he certainly wasn't a Stravinsky type of conductor he performed it anyway and felt that it was his duty to do so.

JW: How do you conceive of performance? How do you prepare for a performance psychologically?

HB: The performance is just the realization of the vision the conductor has as it is fertilized through the work with the orchestra, through the playing of the orchestra and through the influence of the audience. That means every performance is unique because every audience is new and the disposition is different. But this only makes sense if the basic vision is there from the beginning. This is the way it should be and it should be so natural that it is synonymous with the conductor's personality. He may have asked himself during the course of his study and preparation, "How do I want this to sound? How do I want this to be?" By the time of the rehearsals and then performances the work should be synonymous with him. It should just flow naturally. I think that's the hallmark of a good performance. It has to be personal. Of course there are also technical considerations. Everyone hears if the horn misses the pitch or if the timpani make a wrong entrance. Though it should be as flawless as possible the flawlessness doesn't necessarily make a good performance. A good performance is absolutely personal though it needs to be as perfect a performance as possible technically. And here I think is the greatest test for any musician and conductor. His personality must be so in harmony with the piece through his internal disposition and his own discipline that he can act as an advocate of the piece. The composer writes music and puts it on paper. The music is absolutely lifeless unless it's performed. And the only way for a composition to live is through the musicians. It has to be extremely personal. At the same time it must be congruent and parallel to the composer's intentions. This is a great paradox as is so often the case with great truths. It must be absolutely personal and at the same time absolutely loyal to the intentions of the composer, it's creator. This is no small thing and is very difficult to achieve and requires great discipline and great knowledge and also the ability to abandon ourselves to the moment. We must be ready to sacrifice ourselves and at the same time to be ourselves completely. This is a typical quality of music as distinguished from other arts. In order to live it must be performed. And it must be just as personal as any personal saying. It's not just delivery, the result of the rehearsal or some exercises. Music is revelation! The nature of music is revelation. It must say something, it must tell a truth that is human or divine or both. Just delivering notes, even if it's perfect, doesn't give this revelation at all. So when you ask what is performance, I think the answer I would like to give is this: It is a personal witness, it is the way the conductor sees its meaning or message. It is in his mind, and he has caught a glimpse of the composer's vision and gives it just as personally as if the composer would conduct it. Yo Yo Ma was my soloist this week. He was very sick yesterday with a fever and bronchitis. Still he wanted to listen again to the Brahms First Symphony, which I was conducting. He said he was so happy to listen to a performance of this masterwork where the conductor was not the main thing. He was not listening to the conductor or seeing the performance. He heard the work itself and this is the paradox. A performance can only be personal when the person is forgotten. It should be as if the conductor didn't exist and the music spoke directly to him.

JW: What you are saying is to forget the ego and let the real music come through.

HB: And that has nothing to do with bloodless objective mechanized performance.

JW: Bernstein said something related to this. He said his greatest performances were when he didn't remember who he was or where he was.

HB: I think it's true. Bernstein is very often misjudged because he's such a showman. He doesn't try to be that way. He is that way. He's completely himself when he makes music. He's a very good example of what I'm saying. The music must be extremely personal. You must be exactly yourself otherwise there will be false overtones.

Biography

Herbert Blomstedt became music director of the San Francisco Symphony in 1985. Since then the partnership he and the orchestra have established has become recognized as one of America's most compelling artistic collaborations. That recognition has come in many forms – capacity concerts at Davies Symphony Hall, acclaim on tour, a major recording contract with London Records, and, for their recording of Nielsen's Fourth and Fifth symphonies, France's 1988 Grand Prix du Disque, and Belgium's Caecilia Prize.

Born in Springfield, Massachusetts, in 1927, Herbert Blomstedt moved with his family to Sweden in 1929. His mother, a pianist, gave him his first musical training. This led him to the Royal College of Music in Stockholm for studies in violin, piano, organ, theory, and conducting, and to the University of Uppsala for work in musicology. He continued conducting studies with the legendary Igor Markevitch, with Jean Morel at the Juilliard School, and with Leonard Bernstein at Tanglewood's Berkshire Music Center. Honors and accomplishments followed quickly: in 1953 the

Koussevitzky Conducting Prize; in 1954 his conducting debut (with the Stockholm Philharmonic) and first appointment as a music director (with Sweden's Norrkoping Symphony Orchestra); and in 1955 first prize at the Salzburg conducting competition.

Mr. Blomstedt has held positions as music director of the Oslo Philharmonic, Danish Radio Symphony, and Swedish Radio Symphony. In 1975, the musicians of the Dresden Staatskapelle, the world's oldest orchestra, invited him to become their music director and in ten years at its helm, he led the ensemble throughout Europe and in its first visits to the United States. He also dramatically extended the Staatskapelle's discography with recordings that include the complete symphonies of Beethoven and Schubert and, in an ongoing series, orchestral music of Richard Strauss. He has led various orchestras in recordings of 150 orchestral works, and his first set of the complete Nielsen symphonies, which he recorded with the Danish Radio Symphony in the early 1970s played a key role in making that composer's music known in the United States.

Mr. Blomstedt has led many of the world's greatest orchestras, including the Berlin Philharmonic, the Amsterdam Concertgebouw, the Boston Symphony, the Chicago Symphony, and the Philadelphia Orchestra.

Herbert Blomstedt Discography

Composer	Work	Orchestra	Soloists	Label	CD	LP	MC
Arnestad	Aria appassionata	Filharmonisk Selskaps		Philips		839254	
Beethoven	Leonore (complete)	Dresden Staatskapelle	Moser, Cassilly, Adam, Ridderbusch	EMI		157-02853-55	
Beethoven	Symphony no. 1	Dresden Staatskapelle		RCA		RL 30 418/440	
Beethoven	Symphony no. 2	Dresden Staatskapelle		RCA		RL 30 418	
Beethoven	Symphony no. 3	Dresden Staatskapelle		RCA		RL 30 418	
Beethoven	Symphony no. 4	Dresden Staatskapelle		RCA		RL 30 418	
Beethoven	Symphony no. 5	Dresden Staatskapelle		RCA		RL 30 418	
Beethoven	Symphony no. 6	Dresden Staatskapelle		RCA		RL 30 418	
Beethoven	Symphony no. 7	Dresden Staatskapelle		RCA		RL 30 418	
Beethoven	Symphony no. 8	Dresden Staatskapelle		RCA		RL 30 418	
Beethoven	Symphony no. 9	Dresden Staatskapelle		RCA		RL 30 418/440	
Beethoven	Symphony no. 9	Dresden Staatskapelle	Döse, Schiml, Schreier, Adam	Eterna			
Berg	Seven Early Songs	North German Radio Symphony	Lövaas	DG		413 797-1	
Berwald	Sinfonie singuliere	Swedish Radio Symphony		SRLP		1339	
Borup-Jorgensen	Marin	Danish Radio Symphony		Paula		16	
Brahms	Alto Rhapsody	San Francisco	van Nes	London	430 281-2		430 281-4
Brahms	Begräbnisgesang	San Francisco		London	430 281-2		430 281-4
Brahms	Gesang des Parzen	San Francisco		London	430 281-2		430 281-4
Brahms	Nänie	San Francisco		London	430 281-2		430 281-4
Brahms	Schicksalslied	San Francisco		London	430 281-2		430 281-4
Bruckner	Symphony no. 4	Dresden Staatskapelle		Denon	CD-7126		

Composer	Work	Orchestra	Soloists	Label	CD	LP	MC
Bruckner	Symphony no. 7	Dresden Staatskapelle		Denon	CD-7286	331/333	
Bäck	Fantasia on Dies sind die heiligen zehn Gebote	Swedish Radio Symphony		Bis			
Dvořák	Symphony no. 8	Dresden Staatskapelle		Eterna		ET 3039	
Grieg	Peer Gynt (complete incidental music)	Dresden Staatskapelle	Valjakka, Thalaug	Angel			4AM-34701
Grieg	Peer Gynt (incidental music)	San Francisco Symphony	Häggander, Malmberg	London	425 448-2		425 448-4
Gudmundsen-Holmgren	Chronos	Danish Radio Symphony		EMI		CC 063-38100	
Hindemith	Mathis der Maler	San Francisco Symphony		London	421 523-2		421-523-4
Hindemith	Symphonic Metamorphosis on Themes by Weber	San Francisco Symphony		London	421 523-2		421-523-4
Hindemith	Trauermusik	San Francisco Symphony		London	421 523-2		421 523-4
Höffding	Det er ganske vist	Danish Radio Symphony		EMI			C 063-38100
Kvandel	Symfonisk Epos	Filharmonik Selskaps		Philips		839254	
Lidholm	Poesis	Stockholm Philharmonic		SSD	SCD-1027	33160	
Lidholm	Ritornello per orchestra	Swedish Radio Symphony		SRLP		1339	
Lidholm	Skaldens Natt	Swedish Radio Symphony	Sörensson				
Lidholm	Three songs with string orchestra	Stockholm Philharmonic	Rödin	HMV		CSDS 1072	
Lidholm	Toccata e Canto	Stockholm Philharmonic		HMV		CSDS 1072	
Matthus	Piano concerto	Dresden Staatskapelle	Schmidt	Nova		885 105	

Composer	Work	Orchestra	Soloist	Label	CD
Mozart	A Berenice – Sol nascente, K. 70	Dresden Staatskapelle	Scovotti		
Mozart	A questo – or che in cielo, K. 374	Dresden Staatskapelle	Scovotti	EMI	165-46 531/533
Mozart	Adagio and fugue in c, K. 546	Dresden Staatskapelle		Eterna	ET-5015
Mozart	Ah se in ciel, K. 538	Dresden Staatskapelle	Scovotti	EMI	165-46 531/533
Mozart	Ah, lo previdi, K. 272	Dresden Staatskapelle	Moser	EMI	165-46 531/533
Mozart	Alcandro, lo confesso, K. 294	Dresden Staatskapelle	Scovotti		
Mozart	Andante for flute and orchestra, K. 315	Dresden Staatskapelle	Walther	Eterna	ET-3065
Mozart	Bella mia fiamma, K. 528	Dresden Staatskapelle	Moser	Eterna	
Mozart	Chi sa, chi sa, K. 582	Dresden Staatskapelle	Scovotti	Eterna	8 27 392
Mozart	Clarice, cara mia sposa, K. 256	Dresden Staatskapelle	Schreier	EMI	165-46 531/533
Mozart	Con ossequio, con rispetto, K. 210	Dresden Staatskapelle	Schreier	EMI	165-46 531/533
Mozart	Flute concerto no. 1, K. 313	Dresden Staatskapelle	Walther	Eterna	ET-3065
Mozart	Flute concerto no. 2, K. 314	Dresden Staatskapelle	Walther	Eterna	ET-3065
Mozart	Horn concerto no. 2, K. 412	Dresden Staatskapelle	Damm	Eurodisc	88 303 KK
Mozart	Horn concerto no. 3, K. 417	Dresden Staatskapelle	Damm	Eurodisc	88 303 KK
Mozart	Horn concerto no. 4, K. 447	Dresden Staatskapelle	Damm	Eurodisc	88 303 KK
Mozart	Oboe concerto in C, K. 314	Dresden Staatskapelle	Mahn	Eterna	8 26 559
Mozart	Divertimento in B-flat, K. 137	Dresden Staatskapelle		Eterna	ET-5015
Mozart	Divertimento in D, K. 136	Dresden Staatskapelle		Eterna	ET-5015

Composer	Work	Orchestra	Soloists	Label	CD	LP	MC
Mozart	Divertimento in F, K. 138	Dresden Staatskapelle		Eterna		ET-5015	
Mozart	Fra cento affanni, K. 88	Dresden Staatskapelle	Scovotti				
Mozart	Ma che vi fece – Sperai vicino, K. 368	Dresden Staatskapelle	Scovotti	EMI		165-46 531/533	
Mozart	Mia speranza adorata, K. 416	Dresden Staatskapelle	Moser	EMI		165-46 531/533	
Mozart	Misera, dove son, K. 369	Dresden Staatskapelle	Moser				
Mozart	Misero me – Misero pargoletto, K. 77	Dresden Staatskapelle	Scovotti	EMI		165-46 531/533	
Mozart	Misero, o sogno – Aura, che intorno, K. 431	Dresden Staatskapelle	Schreier	EMI		165-46 531/533	
Mozart	No. no. che non sei capace, K. 419	Dresden Staatskapelle	Scovotti	EMI		165-46 531/533	
Mozart	Non curo l'affetto, K. 74b	Dresden Staatskapelle	Scovotti				
Mozart	Or chi il dover – Tali e sotanti, K. 36	Dresden Staatskapelle	Schreier	EMI		165-46 531/533	
Mozart	Per pieta, non ricercate, K. 420	Dresden Staatskapelle	Schreier	EMI		165-46 531/533	
Mozart	Popli di Tessaglia, K. 316	Dresden Staatskapelle	Moser	EMI		165-46 531/533	
Mozart	Rondo for horn and orchestra, K. 371	Dresden Staatskapelle		Eurodisc		808 33 KK	
Mozart	Schon lacht der holde Frühling, K. 580	Dresden Staatskapelle	Moser	EMI		165-46 531/533	
Mozart	Se al labbro mio non credi, K. 295	Dresden Staatskapelle	Schreier	EMI		165-46 531/533	
Mozart	Si mostra la sorte, K. 209	Dresden Staatskapelle	Schreier	EMI		165-46 531/533	
Mozart	Symphony no. 38	Dresden Staatskapelle		Denon	CD-7146		
Mozart	Symphony no. 39	Dresden Staatskapelle		Denon	CD-7146		
Mozart	Symphony no. 40	Dresden Staatskapelle		Denon	CD-7022		
Mozart	Symphony no. 41	Dresden Staatskapelle		Denon	CD-7022		
Mozart	Va dal furor portata, K. 21	Dresden Staatskapelle	Schreier	EMI		165-46 531/533	

Composer	Work	Orchestra	Soloists	Label	CD	LP	MC
Mozart	Voi avete un cor fidele, K. 217	Dresden Staatskapelle	Scovotti	EMI		165-46 531/533	
Mozart	Vorrei spiegarvi, K. 418	Dresden Staatskapelle	Scovotti	EMI		165-46 531/533	
Nielsen	Andante lamentoso	Danish Radio Symphony		Seraphim		6097	
Nielsen	Böhmisk-Dansk Folketone	Danish Radio Symphony		Seraphim		6097	
Nielsen	Clarinet concerto	Danish Radio Symphony	Stevenson	Seraphim		6106	
Nielsen	Flute concerto	Danish Radio Symphony	Lemsser	Seraphim		6106	
Nielsen	Violin concerto	Danish Radio Symphony	Tellefsen	Seraphim		6106	
Nielsen	En Fantasirejse til Faeroerne – Rapsodisk Overture	Danish Radio Symphony		Seraphim			
Nielsen	Helios Overture	Danish Radio Symphony		Seraphim		6097	
Nielsen	Pan og Syrinx	Danish Radio Symphony		Seraphim		6098	
Nielsen	Saga-Drom	Danish Radio Symphony		Seraphim		6098	
Nielsen	Symfonisk Rapsodi (1889)	Danish Radio Symphony		Seraphim		6106	
Nielsen	Symphony no. 1	Danish Radio Symphony		Seraphim		6097	
Nielsen	Symphony no. 2	Danish Radio Symphony		Seraphim		6097	
Nielsen	Symphony no. 2	San Francisco		London	430 280-2		430 280-4
Nielsen	Symphony no. 3	Danish Radio Symphony		Seraphim		6097	
Nielsen	Symphony no. 3	San Francisco	Fromm, McMillan	London	430 280-2		430 280-4

Composer	Work	Orchestra	Soloists	Label	CD	LP	MC
Nielsen	Symphony no. 4	San Francisco Symphony		London	421 524-2		421 524-4
Nielsen	Symphony no. 4	Danish Radio Symphony		Seraphim		6098	
Nielsen	Symphony no. 5	San Francisco Symphony		London	421 524-2		421 524-4
Nielsen	Symphony no. 5	Danish Radio Symphony		Seraphim		6098	
Nielsen	Symphony no. 6	Danish Radio Symphony		Seraphim		6098	
Nielsen	Symphony no. 6	San Francisco Symphony		London	425 607-2		425 607-4
Nordal	Adagio for flute and strings	Swedish Radio Symphony	Marelius	HMV		CSDS 1087	
Nordheim	Canzona per orchestra	Filharmonisk Selskaps		Philips		839250	
Nordheim	ECO	Swedish Radio Symphony	Valjakka	HMV		CSDS 1086	
Norgard	Iris	Danish Radio Symphony		Caprice		54	
Norgard	Luna	Danish Radio Symphony		Danish		DMA-018	
Norholm	Concerto for violin	Danish Radio Symphony	Hansen	BIS		80	
Petterson	Violin concerto no. 2	Swedish Radio Symphony	Haendel	Caprice		1200	
Reger	Violin concerto	Swedish Radio Symphony	Haendel	Eterna			
Roman	Sinfonia no. 20	Swedish Radio Symphony		SRLP		1339	
Rosenberg	Symphony no. 2	Stockholm Philharmonic		SSD	SCD-1026	33160	
Rosenberg	Symphony no. 3	Stockholm		HMV		CSDS 1071	

Composer	Work	Orchestra	Soloists	Label	CD	LP	MC
Rosenberg	Symphony no. 4	Swedish Radio Symphony	Sædén	HMV		1059/60	
Rydman	Symphony of the Modern World	Swedish Radio Symphony	Sædén	HMV		CSDS 1089	
Sandström	Culminations	Swedish Radio Symphony		Caprice		1244	
Schubert	Symphony no. 1	Dresden Staatskapelle		Eterna		627649	ET-6001
Schubert	Symphony no. 2	Dresden Staatskapelle		Eterna		627649	ET-6001
Schubert	Symphony no. 3	Dresden Staatskapelle		Eterna		ET-5112	ET-6002
Schubert	Symphony no. 4	Dresden Staatskapelle		Eterna		ET-5112	ET-6002
Schubert	Symphony no. 5	Dresden Staatskapelle		Eterna		ET-5125	ET-6003
Schubert	Symphony no. 6	Dresden Staatskapelle		Eterna		ET-5125	ET-6003
Schubert	Symphony no. 7	Dresden Staatskapelle		Eterna			ET-6005
Schubert	Symphony no. 9	Dresden Staatskapelle		Eterna			ET-6004/5
Stenhammar	Interlude from "Sangen"	Stockholm Philharmonic		HMV		CSDS 1072	
Stenhammar	Sangen, symfonisk kantat	Swedish Radio Symphony	Sörensson	Caprice			
Stenhammar	Suite from "Chitra"	Stockholm Philharmonic		HMV		CSDS 1072	
Strauss, R.	Also sprach Zarathustra	Dresden Staatskapelle		Denon	CO-2259		
Strauss, R.	Don Juan	Dresden Staatskapelle		London	421 815-2		
Strauss, R.	Don Juan	Dresden Staatskapelle		Denon	CO-2259		
Strauss, R.	Ein Heldenleben	Dresden Staatskapelle		Denon	CD-7561		
Strauss, R.	Eine Alpensinfonie	Dresden Staatskapelle		London	421 815-2		
Strauss, R.	Metamorphosen	Dresden Staatskapelle		Denon	CO-73801		
Strauss, R.	Till Eulenspiegels lustige Streiche	Dresden Staatskapelle		Denon	CO-73801		
Strauss, R.	Tod und Verklärung	Dresden Staatskapelle		Denon	CO-73801		
Stravinsky	Le Sacre du printemps	Stockholm Philharmonic		Expo	Norr 1		
Weber	Clarinet concerto no. 1	Dresden Staatskapelle	Meyer	Angel	CDC-47351		

Composer	Work	Orchestra	Soloists	Label	CD	LP	MC
Weber	Clarinet concerto no. 2	Dresden Staatskapelle	Meyer	Angel	CDC-47351		
Weber	Concertino for clarinet	Dresden Staatskapelle	Meyer	Angel	CDC-47351		
Weber	Euryanthe Overture	Dresden Staatskapelle		Pilz	442058		
Weber	Konzertstück in f	Dresden Staatskapelle	Rösel	Eterna			
Weber	Piano concerto no. 1	Dresden Staatskapelle	Rösel	Eterna			
Weber	Piano concerto no. 2	Dresden Staatskapelle	Rösel	Eterna			
Wourinen	Golden Dance for Piano	San Francisco Symphony	Ohlsson	Nonesuch 79185-2			
Wourinen	Piano concerto no. 3	San Francisco Symphony	Ohlsson	Nonesuch 79185-2			

"When I was very young, I became absolutely fascinated with the sound of the orchestra. I remember that when my mother would take me to concerts, I would become entranced by just the sound. It was like entering into a magical world. I also figured out that when the person who stood in front of the orchestra came onto the stage, the magic began, and when he left, the magic ended. I knew as a child that I wanted to be part of that magical world, and that I wanted to be the person that stood right in the middle of it. So, from then on, it was very simple. I wanted to be a conductor, period."

Catherine Comet

Catherine Comet

JW: How did you decide to become a conductor and what course has your career taken?

CC: When I was very young, I became absolutely fascinated with the sound of the orchestra. I remember that when my mother would take me to concerts, I would become entranced by just the sound. It was like entering into a magical world. I also figured out that when the person who stood in front of the orchestra came onto the stage, the magic began, and when he left, the magic ended. I knew as a child that I wanted to be part of that magical world, and that I wanted to be the person that stood right in the middle of it. So, from then on, it was very simple. I wanted to be a conductor, period.

What's interesting to me now though, is that even after the hundreds of concerts I've given, the magical feelings have never left. They come during that time before a concert when I'm alone backstage. When the orchestra is on the stage and the concert master has gone to tune them up. I suddenly get the same feeling of magic that I felt as a little girl. I think, "Well, the magic is about to begin."

JW: Where and when did you begin your musical training? Who were your teachers?

CC: I studied piano at the conservatory in Paris when I was very young. Even though I already knew that I wanted to be a conductor, I started with the piano because you had to be twenty-one to enter the conducting classes. I studied a lot of music along with harmony and counterpoint. Then Nadia Boulanger took me on when I was twelve years old. She always believed that I would become a conductor. We did a lot of score analysis and then I auditioned for Juilliard because you didn't have to be twenty-one to get into a conducting program.

JW: That's where you met Leonard Slatkin?

CC: Oh, yes. We were in classes together.

JW: You were actually his assistant in St. Louis for three years under the Exxon Conducting Program. How was that?

CC: I was really very lucky to be the Exxon assistant in St. Louis with Leonard. I learned a lot from him and was able to ask him lots of questions. He's also a real master at programming. He influenced me a great deal.

JW: What is your philosophy of programming as the music director of both the American Symphony and the Grand Rapids Symphony?

CC: Well, it's to cover as much of the repertoire in every possible corner that you can. Don't limit your program to only one period. Make them diversified. Programming is very much like making a dinner menu for your guests. You want to serve a little bit of everything and yet not too much. You want the people to leave the table satisfied but not full. So I'm trying to balance and to challenge the orchestra at the same time. We do music of all periods, baroque, classical, romantic and twentieth century. We also make sure that over a cyclic period of three or four years that we cover the Beethoven and Brahms symphonies. They are like a credo to the musicians. So, you see, programming can really be fascinating. You spend an enormous amount of time on it. It's always on your mind. For instance, I'm constantly thinking of future programs, of how different pieces of music fit together, how certain pieces complement or oppose each. It's like a giant puzzle.

JW: What is the difference in your programming when you guest conduct?

CC: Well, first of all you can be told that a given person will be your soloist and will be playing a certain piece. You then have to build a program around that concerto; a program that makes sense with that particular work. Also, the music director of where you are conducting has to make the final decision because he is looking at his entire season as well as at the three or four year cycle of the orchestra. Also, the music director or your management can tell you that they would like music of this or that period, this or that composer, or that you will have access to a very large number of extras and how would you like to use them? They give you certain parameters to work with and you have to function inside of those parameters. But it is really the music director that makes the final decision. You need to give them different proposals and they will choose what they want and what will be the best for the orchestra. I do the same when I look at a guest conductor's program.

JW: What is your criteria in programming twentieth-century music?

CC: I try to do music that I believe in and feel strongly about. That way I feel I can do a good job and really serve the composer. There are some wonderful composers, though, that I don't feel compatible with. It would be very unfair then for me to do their music. So, I suggest them to a guest conductor if I believe they are good and important enough to be performed. But I wouldn't do it myself.

Also, my first priority is to program American composers. American orchestras are made of American musicians, they have an American audience and are supported financially and emotionally by an American community. Therefore I strongly believe that the orchestras should play American music and that the audiences should hear it. To play it is to bring it to life. It shouldn't be left on a shelf somewhere. Now you don't always have to program a premiere. You have basically 100 years of symphonic music to choose from. Of course, a piece written in 1900 isn't exactly contemporary. I have also done a lot of contemporary music from many different countries but I would always give my first priority to an American composer. Here in Grand Rapids and with the American Symphony, I do an American work on every concert. And I don't just do five-minute pieces to do my duty. I program large pieces as well.

JW: How do you find your audiences reacting to it?

CC: I find my audiences are very involved and are reacting just fine. Some pieces they like and some pieces they don't like, but at least they react. They are curious about it. Composers have been coming very often to Grand Rapids to talk to the audience and to talk to the community. They become known that way. You know the composer is really a very important person. Our community at this point is very much aware of composers as well as their own composers. Some like the music and some don't, but at the very least they are reacting and are thinking about it. It's really nice to be stopped in the supermarket the day after a concert and to be asked questions about certain pieces. That's what it's all about.

JW: That's wonderful to be able to generate that kind of enthusiasm. A lot of orchestras are currently having problems with programming contemporary music.

CC: Well, I'm not really aware of that type of problem here. Now some people will say, "I won't come to the symphony anymore unless you play Muzak because I come to the symphony to relax." Well, I can't argue with that type of person. Everyone is free to come for whatever they want to come for. We are not like a health club though, where we make sure that everyone can relax and have a good time. We do not play Muzak! If people need to go home and sit in their easy chairs and turn the radio on to relax and sooth them without having to think, they should do just that. However, we don't do that. That's not what an orchestra is about. We will never do that. We give quality experiences instead. It's like the difference between going to a museum and really looking at, not just seeing, the masterpieces of art versus just turning the TV on and absorbing the images mindlessly. So, people going

27

to a concert make a certain choice by just going to the concert. However, I do try to balance my programs out.

JW: What is your viewpoint on early music performance practices? What do you think of what Roger Norrington is doing?

CC: I'm fascinated with what he and others are doing. I would really love to take a week or ten days to just observe and study with him. Now I'm not saying that I would play non vibrato, use baroque bows and instruments without clefs with my orchestra. But nevertheless, you hear and see from the score that the structure and phrasing would be really clarified enormously or brought to a totally different light if original instruments were used.

JW: Do you follow Beethoven's metronome markings?

CC: Well, to begin with, I've been as involved as any conductor with the Beethoven symphonies. Beethoven symphonies for a conductor are like books you have next to your bed at night. So, yes, I've been very involved in this controversy which I believe is really wonderful. I've learned a lot from working as the associate conductor in Baltimore with David Zinman, who believes very strongly in Beethoven's metronome markings. I think, though, that in the end your own personal taste will decide which direction you will go. I also believe that your personal taste should come from the score and from the knowledge that you accumulate through the years about the period, the composer and all the music of that composer. You discover a lot by reading what the composer's influences were, and by studying the composer's entire output, not just their symphonic repertoire. You study their piano music, chamber music, vocal and choral music. You get as close as you can to what the composer meant. You always try to serve the composer the best way that you can.

JW: Would you consider using original instruments in the future?

CC: Well, I would have to study a lot to do that. I just don't have the time right now. But like I said, if I had time I would really like to spend a week or ten days with conductors who are doing this. I'm particularly fascinated with what Mr. Norrington is doing. I find his recordings a real lesson. I found his recording of the *Symphonie fantastique* particularly enlightening because I grew up with Berlioz's book on orchestration. Actually one of the first books I bought when I was very young, seven or eight years old, was Berlioz's treatise on orchestration. It really is a passionate book. He is so passionate about the different sounds of the instruments. So I often wondered, even as a child, what a trombone or horn of his period sounded like. Now we can hear it and with musicians who are technically much better than they were a hundred years ago. It's really incredible.

JW: How do you study a score?

CC: Well, first of all, it takes hours and hours. Score learning is basically about score analysis. You go as deeply as possible. You need to be able to reconstruct from scratch what the composer originally did and then put it back together again. You have to look at the larger perspective as well as the single components that comprise the work. To do this takes a lot of time and I find that I either lie in bed with the score if my back is hurting or sit at a table and analyze, analyze, and analyze for hours. Then you think that once you have spent maybe 200 hours on a score that you have learned it. Well, that's not true, because if you happen to do it again two years later you realize how much you missed the first time and you have to start all over again. It just takes an immense amount of hours. You really work a lot in this business. More than the audience would ever imagine. I really believe (and I think that most conductors would agree on this) that only one percent of our work is done at concerts. Four percent of our work is done at the rehearsals. The remaining 95 percent is done by the hours and hours you spend at home with the score.

JW: Have you ever had to learn things overnight?

CC: Not too often, but yes. In that case, you use the techniques that you have accumulated over the years. For instance, by now I can read a score rather quickly because I've spent so many years doing it. But you can't really give an in-depth approach to that score because you would only have the fifteen hours during the night to learn it.

JW: So you would stay up all night?

CC: Oh, yes, I would use the night to learn it.

JW: How did Nadia Boulanger go through a score with you?

CC: By analysis. She was such an influence on me. Even now when I am studying a score, I have the feeling that she is in the room looking at it with me. What made her so extraordinary was that she really classified things for you. I was very young, twelve years old, when she took me on. She would always put questions to you. She led you to find solutions. "Why did the composer use that chord here? Is this particular chord important? Why didn't he go somewhere else that would have made a standard solution according to the laws of harmony? Why is this line like this and what does the orchestration do to the style at this certain point?" Why? Why? Why? She would always ask a lot of questions like this. She would make you come up with possible answers. Or sometimes she would ask me to play a certain two measures and to try it in different ways. She'd ask me, "Which way do you like the best? And how does it make sense to the performance of the whole?"

I was just fascinated taking lessons with her as a kid. After those lessons I was told to take the bus and to go back home because like every teenager you were supposed to be home around 5:30. Well, I would just walk the streets of Paris and completely forget about the bus. I'd keep asking those questions over and over in my head and think that maybe I was getting closer to some answers. I'd get home late and my mother would be very upset.

JW: What a wonderful experience to have studied with her! How much detail do you go into? For instance, do you analyze every chord in a score or just the important points?

CC: I analyze every chord, of course. Who doesn't? You analyze a score both vertically and horizontally. You analyze horizontally for the lines that are working together and vertically so that you can feel the tension. Both are very important.

•••••

JW: What type of rehearsal techniques do you use?

CC: Well, you know it's rather simple. You have to clarify what you want with a minimum of words and with the minimum of time. We are serving the music but at the same time we are serving the musicians too. They are the ones who are playing. The conductor doesn't play. You could put a curtain in back of the conductor and still hear the music. It's the orchestra that is playing. So, you have to make sure that the score is really clarified by the musicians. You have to bring your ideas and your approach to the musicians and as quickly and as effectively as possible.

JW: Do you do run-throughs and then begin work on the details?

CC: It depends on the score. But to a certain extent, run-throughs are very important. You try to make sure that the orchestra knows how the music unfolds as a whole. But nevertheless, you have to work on details. You don't really go to a rehearsal with a preconceived plan. Instead, you react to what you hear and compare it to what you hear in your head.

JW: So, rehearsals are spontaneous?

CC: Well, you come in with a perfect image, a photographic negative, so to speak, of how the piece should go and the orchestra gives you the actual photo.

JW: You are in the forefront of women conductors today. In the course of your career, have you encountered any opposition because you were a woman?

CC: Well, first of all, there were many women before me. But personally I haven't encountered any opposition, but I've never been a man so how could I really know if I had or not?

JW: As a woman how do you balance your personal life with such a demanding career?

CC: Just the way a woman singer, or pianist, or violinist does. I do it the way any woman artist would do it with this kind of schedule. I'm not the only one in the world. How does a movie actress who works from 5 A.M. until midnight balance out her life? So, I work at home as much as I can and my family is very supportive of what I am doing.

JW: But you are gone a lot now?

CC: Yes, more and more. But I take a lot of planes. Planes do exist, you know. I never liked flying, because the flights are always late and they lose your luggage a lot, but they are very useful. I am certainly a big airline traveler. I know airports very well.

•••••

JW: How would you advise a young conductor to break into the profession?

CC: Well, I don't know how a conductor makes it. That is something that has always been something of a mystery to me. You have to study a lot and be ready because somehow everybody gets chances. But you have to be ready for it when it comes. Of course, these chances never happen at the perfect moment with six months notice. They just sort of happen suddenly and you really have to be ready for them. You can find yourself on the podium and from then on everything goes very fast. Especially compared to the endless hours of studying. Chances come like a big bang. You have one hour and that is it. So study as much as you can even though it can be frustrating because you may not have the chance to conduct the scores you are studying immediately. But nevertheless, we have so much to learn and to accumulate in repertoire and in knowledge. The more you study the better you will be. Conducting is a crazy profession. Don't do it unless you are really crazy also. Many people have come to me and said, "Well I'm thinking about a career as a conductor." I reply that if they are just thinking about it they should forget it. It's not a profession to recommend to children. It's not one of those good "safe" professions of law or medicine. To be a conductor you have to be obsessed with music. Somehow that's really crazy and conductors are really crazy too. And then in the final analysis, you never really know why a concert works or doesn't work. You ask yourself what made a particular concert go so well. "Maybe I walked on the left side of the street," or "Maybe I wore a certain dress," or "Maybe I touched the wall in a particular spot before I walked on stage." Then you try to reconstruct all of these event before your next time and the concert doesn't work. So you really never know why. It's a mystery!

Biography

Catherine Comet, recently named music director of the American Symphony Orchestra, will complete her fourth season as music director of the Grand Rapids Symphony at the end of the 1989-90 season. In her first season, ASCAP awarded Grand Rapids first prize for regional orchestras for adventuresome programming in contemporary American music, and in her second season, the orchestra was awarded third prize.

As a corecipient of the 1988 Seaver/N.E.A. Conductors Award, administered by the New World Symphony, Catherine Comet was awarded a cash career development grant that will provide access to a wide variety of artistic resources, opportunities to work with and observe master conductors, travel and supplies, all designed to enhance her potential for artistic development and personal achievement. The award was designed to recognize exceptionally gifted America conductors who are in the early stages of significant careers.

Associate conductor of the Baltimore Symphony from 1984-86, Catherine Comet conducted that orchestra in numerous concerts including community development concerts, Music for Youth concerts, family concerts, special concerts, and subscription performances. As Exxon/Arts Endowment Conductor of the St. Louis Symphony from the 1981-82 season through 1983-84, she conducted concerts annually in the subscription, chamber orchestra, pops, and summer classical series. Under her direction, the St. Louis Symphony Youth Orchestra won first prize at the 12th International Youth and Music Festival in Vienna in July of 1983.

Prior to her appointment at St. Louis, Catherine Comet was conductor and music director of the University of Wisconsin-Madison Symphony and Chamber Orchestras and before that, conductor of the Ballet Company of the Theatre National de l'Opera de Paris. A native of Paris, born on December 6, 1944, Ms. Comet studied at the Conservatoire National Superieur de Musique and at the Juilliard School in New York. Her principal teachers included Igor Markevitch, Pierre Boulez, and Jean Fournet.

Recent appearances include performances with the Philadelphia Orchestra, the San Francisco Symphony, the Minnesota Orchestra, the Toronto Symphony, the National Symphony of Washington, D.C., the

Cincinnati Symphony, the Buffalo Philharmonic, the American Symphony, the St. Paul Chamber Orchestra, the Vancouver Symphony, the New Orleans Symphony, the Winnipeg Symphony, the West Australian Symphony in Perth, and the American Composers Orchestra.

In the summer of 1990, she was chosen to serve as the United States' resident conductor for the American/Soviet Youth Orchestra in their second tour of Europe, the Soviet Union and the United States. Catherine Comet is married to Michael Aiken, currently provost of the University of Pennsylvania. They have one daughter, Caroline.

Catherine Comet Discography

Composer	Work	Orchestra	Soloists	Label	CD
Colgrass	Light Spirit	St. Louis Symphony		NW	318

"What you get in a rehearsal and what you get in a concert are two different things. I'm also different. In rehearsal, I'm concentrating on everything that goes wrong and where all the problems are. At night at the concert, I try to conduct in a way to prevent the problems. I try to do something inspirational; I try to make dramatic events happen and to give inspirational performances. Rehearsing is a necessary, sometimes pleasurable experience. It is a necessity. However, our profession doesn't consist of rehearsing, it consists of performing!"

—————————————————————————————————————— Dennis Russell Davies

Dennis Russell Davies

JW: I understand you began your career as a piano major at Juilliard. What led you to become a conductor and then the music director of the St. Paul Chamber Orchestra at such a young age?

DRD: I was a piano major at Juilliard when I met Luciano Berio. I became his assistant and started studying conducting as a second major. Through him I began to have the chance to do some conducting outside of the student level. Also, when I was twenty-four, a position opened up in a community orchestra in Norwalk, Connecticut. I became the music director there for four seasons as well as assistant conductor to Berio of the Juilliard Ensemble. The Juilliard Ensemble was a very professional group which consisted of a combination of students and faculty.

Through Luciano I got to meet some very important musicians and composers such as Pierre Boulez and Bruno Maderna and made a very good impression on them. At the same time I had also begun to see that though I was a good pianist I wasn't ever going to be winning the Moscow Tchaikovsky Competition. Some of the gifts I had were much more suited to conducting; so, I began to lean more in that direction. Also, I wasn't "leaning toward conducting" in the sense of wishing I could do it because I *was* doing it, I *was* working. I also got a graduate assistant position at Juilliard and did a lot of teaching and conducting with one of the student orchestras. Basically though, I was just treading water because who the hell would be interested in a twenty-five-year-old conductor! Nobody would, period. In the conducting profession you are working with people who are generally very well trained, have a great deal of experience, and work regularly with prominent and experienced conductors. It was originally through my work in new music that I received my first important opportunity. However, through a fluke I got one of the guest conductor shots with the St. Paul Chamber Orchestra during the season they were looking for a conductor. Something told me that was the place I would be. They were in desperate straits at that time and I was the best candidate for the ticket.

JW: Well, you are still something of a cult hero in the Twin Cities. Everyone remembers what you did for the St. Paul Orchestra! I've also heard so many positive things about your approach to programming. What were your goals then?

DRD: Well I had been fascinated by American music for many years. When I was eighteen I heard my first performance of a piece by Charles Ives. Actually, one of my teachers brought in a recording in one of my classes at Juilliard. I thought, "What is this? Why haven't I heard this before?" It was like hearing something I'd known for a long time. It was a very moving experience because I had thought that the only good music was European music; I had always thought that I'd go to Europe to study. Suddenly the whole horizon of American music opened up for me; that was the first spark. Then, through Luciano and other composers, I became fascinated with the whole avant-garde who were composing new music while still performing, listening to, and playing old music; they weren't shutting off the old music. For me that was an eye-opening experience. Two things then occurred to me. One, was that American music was the key to building an American audience. Two, was that performing chamber music was the key to building an orchestra as an instrument. It also occurred to me that key people of the press weren't going to come to hear the St. Paul Chamber Orchestra if we were going to program yet another performance of Mozart, Haydn, or Beethoven. They would be perfectly justified in staying home. The problem was how to get the public and the press to come hear a struggling young orchestra. So we decided to program new works by major composers; the press was then forced to come; they couldn't ignore it. We also organized a couple of trips to New York and were able to get the orchestra talked about outside of St. Paul. Actually after the orchestra was talked about in New York, Minneapolis finally began to recognize us and this was a major accomplishment! We also had the advantage of being the only full time Chamber Orchestra in the United States and we used that for publicity.

My programming philosophy was to focus on one or two composers. I would feature a twentieth-century composer with a well-known composer from the past whom I was committed to such as Mozart, Haydn, Beethoven, Bach, or Schumann. My first season in St. Paul focused on Ives and Corelli. My second season focused on Haydn and John Cage; in fact Cage came several times during that season. It really helps the publicity to have the composer present! Then I wandered away from having just two composers and began to program three or four modern composers. The word got out that new music was actually being performed in St. Paul and composers began to grab on to us. It was as though we were a life raft for the art!

JW: Don't you think there is more contemporary music being performed now than in the past? Most orchestra seasons are programming quite a lot of new music.

DRD: Yes, I have to say as I look around the States now that it seems better than when I left for Europe. When I left in 1980 the situation was rather bleak; now it seems as though the composer-in-residence programs have had a very enlightening effect on orchestral programming! I find that very encouraging. But for me when I started out, it was essential to find a way to put the orchestra in the public eye and you have to do that through the media. At the same time I believe very strongly that music is a preservation of the past and a cultivation of the future.

JW: Your programming for the Cabrillo Festival certainly expresses this philosophy.

DRD: Yes, you can also look through the Bonn programs and I don't think you will see much difference in the concepts, just different names.

JW: Do you use the same programming philosophy when you are conducting opera or the symphonic repertoire as you do when you are conducting chamber orchestra programs?

DRD: Basically, yes. The chamber orchestra is not any different than a symphony orchestra except for the number of people involved and the core repertoire. You need as big a support staff for a chamber orchestra as for a symphony. You need to raise as much money as possible, which is always a struggle.

JW: That's certainly true, but opera is a different world, isn't it?

DRD: Yes. The only opera work I've done has been in Europe, mostly in Stuttgart. Stuttgart has always had a very progressive reputation in terms of opera. We were able to do five or six new productions a season out of which at least two were twentieth-century works and one was likely to be a world premiere. That was the sort of basic programming premise!

JW: That's really exciting. I wish that could happen more here in the States. What's the difference between European and American audience response to progressive programming?

DRD: The audience in Europe is more experienced. That's really the only difference. I actually think the audiences here are more open! However, there is a great deal of fear in the administrations of all these large organizations because they are so dependent on the box office sales and on corporate support. You just cannot run an artistically responsible program when the main consideration is the box office. You should see to it that the house is full without pandering to the most elementary tastes of the public. You can give the public a good selection of things that they know and love while at the same time seeing to it that their horizons are expanded. This way you have a chance to build an audience that's growing and not one that is dying off. You absolutely need to get younger people to come while providing for the needs of your older audience.

JW: Well, you certainly had the image in St. Paul to attract a younger audience!

DRD: Yes, I was a true child of the sixties. I wore long hair and drove a motorcycle. St. Paul used that image as a contrast to Skrowaczewski's elegant and Central European image. The motto of the St. Paul Chamber Orchestra that year was, "Come hear Minnesota's other great orchestra." That was very clever promotion.

JW: So there was a lot of competition between the two orchestras then.

DRD: Yes. At the time the Minnesota Orchestra didn't want to acknowledge the existence of the chamber orchestra. So the publicity photos of me on the motorcycle, a "regular American guy," really helped us.

JW: Did you consciously work on that image or did you just represent yourself as who you were?

DRD: Well, I'm a product of my time and where I'm from. I grew up in the midwest and lived there until I was eighteen; after that I moved to New York to go to school and lived there until I was in my late twenties; then I lived in Minnesota for eight years and in 1980 started living in Europe. So, I'm a product of all of this, my time, my generation and my upbringing. I can hold my own, serve in intellectual circles, I'm in the international scene. At that same time I'm a baseball fan and love to go to ball games. I love to play softball and that is something I have in common with a pretty large cross-section of the American public. That's interesting for many people in the United States because so many times their symphony orchestra conductors might as well be from the moon, culturally speaking.

JW: Well, I definitely believe American orchestras could benefit from American conductors. I hope symphony boards and managers move more in this direction instead of always looking for European or Oriental imports. American conductors should serve American orchestras!

DRD: I agree. We still have European chauvinism in the States. We didn't have an American music director in any of the major orchestras in the States until Leonard Bernstein made his debut with the New York Philharmonic. Leonard personified the exception; he was the exception that made the rule possible. He was a great conductor, a great musician and nobody else was going to have a chance. If they couldn't have Leonard they would take somebody from Europe. Loren Maazel was another exception (though he is an American born in Europe with the European culture). Only recently Leonard Slatkin jumped in and made St. Louis into a major orchestra. Unfortunately, in general I don't think the situation is changing at a major level. I'm not going to wait; I have things to do!

JW: Why do you think we have this type of situation here in the States?

DRD: Because for the last forty years the art of classical musical has always been associated with European soloists and conductors. Also, societies have a fascination for the exotic such as the American interest in not only European but Oriental conductors. I benefit from this same fascination by being an American in Germany. Unfortunately, young German conductors have similar difficulties as their American colleagues.

JW: What is your experience in Germany? What is it like to be an American conductor in Germany and how has it affected your repertoire and your musicianship? How has it affected you personally?

DRD: It's expanded my repertoire a great deal. I've also learned first-hand some of the advantages of the Central European tradition. One of the reasons there are so many successful European conductors is that they are very good. They are very good and have a certain experience, generosity, and ability to inspire. It's something many of my American colleagues haven't learned.

JW: What do you mean by generosity?

DRD: Generosity of the beat, the ability to stimulate and mold a phrase in the classical and romantic repertory.

JW: This is very interesting. Why do you think this is the case? Is it their cultural heritage, their training, or their educational system that makes the difference?

DRD: I think it has to do with their musical training and their experience. Simply that. It's a matter of hearing certain music played in a certain way for a long time. There's a lot less emphasis in Europe on technical proficiency. A lot of the European-trained conductors are technically inferior to the Americans, yet they are musically a great deal superior. How you beat, how you conduct, whatever your physical mannerisms are, is a great deal secondary to the musical results that come out! For instance, my predecessor in Stuttgart, the Swiss conductor Silvio Varviso, has a reputation of being a very weak rehearsal conductor. I was told all of this when I came to Stuttgart. I went to the opera house on one of the first nights I was there and found him conducting *Così fan tutte*. Now I had thought I was a very good Mozart conductor. Well, I've never heard a more wonderful sounding *Così* in all my life. I was told he couldn't rehearse it to save his life but he could *perform* it!

41

There he was standing and smiling in a certain way, raising his hand, making everyone feel good and they played like gods for him! I thought of my own conducting and how I crossed every *t* and dotted every *i*. In my rehearsals I usually spend a lot of time fixing everything the way I want it performed. By the performance, everyone knows exactly what to do and how I want it and yet my performance may not be half as good as what Varviso gets by just coming in and performing without a rehearsal. When he conducted in Bonn last month, I went down to see him do a performance; I sat down in the pit because I had such a nice time watching him. I couldn't begin to imitate the way he conducts; I wouldn't know where to begin. So I tell young conductors to go and take a look at someone like Varviso. A lot of them come back and say, "Yeah, but. . . ." There is no "but"! If he hadn't been conducting, it wouldn't have sounded that way. This attitude is symptomatic of the way Americans tend to think. The American educational process with its emphasis on technique has lost something musically. I think that by living and working in Europe for the last twelve years, I've been able to integrate this different approach to music.

JW: That's very interesting. Now I understand that you were only the second American conductor to conduct opera in Bayreuth. What was that experience like?

DRD: Yes, I was the second American and the second-youngest conductor to conduct in Bayreuth. I was there for three seasons. (The first American and youngest conductor was Thomas Schippers.) I was thirty-four and was extremely self-confident at that time in my career. A little bit of that self-confidence came from being naive, being very convinced of my own abilities without really knowing what was out there! I conducted the *Flying Dutchman* and did one hell of a job, but really, it wasn't easy! I was conducting a very proud group of musicians who know their Wagner tradition and know how they think it should be played. Here I was with hair past my shoulders in blue jeans and a T-shirt just being myself. I wasn't doing it to offend anybody but at the same time I was very conscious of not conforming. I felt, for instance, that the "tradition" didn't always conform to the score as I understood it. It was a great experience which wasn't easy for anybody. I have come to learn a great deal from this tradition though at that time I was fairly skeptical about it.

JW: Why were you skeptical about it?

DRD: Because I had come from a different tradition, a different way of playing and hearing. I was very proud of just going to the score and performing what I saw there. In Europe, though, there are different languages. The longer I worked in Germany the more I began to listen to what was actually going on there; certain instruments are played very differently. The oboe, for instance, sounds drastically different in Germany; it's a much softer and more expressive sound; it doesn't have the carrying power of the American sound; they have a whole different concept of the instrument. The French are somewhat in the middle; their oboe playing is more like the Americans. I've come to love the German oboe sound. It's so expressive.

JW: You mentioned that you conducted Flying Dutchman *in Bayreuth. What was your approach to that score? You knew that the orchestra knew it cold and had done it many times before. What did you feel you had to bring to the production?*

DRD: Well, there are a lot of tempi changes that are done because it is the tradition to do them. They aren't in the score and I made a point of playing only what I found in the score. Also, Wolfgang Wagner, the grandson of Richard, had very thought-provoking ideas and was very supportive. He gave me access to the original orchestration of *Flying Dutchman,* which hadn't been used since the premiere. We took out all the changes that had been made in the parts and played the original score. The musicians thought they were coming in to play their beloved *Flying Dutchman* the way they knew it well and were completely outraged at the changes. They almost rioted! I worked so hard in those rehearsals.

JW: I also heard that you once became the target of an anti-American demonstration when you were conducting Mahler in Bonn. Can you tell more about that?

DRD: No, that's a very long and involved story that has to do with the selection process in my becoming the music director and all of that.

JW: Can you tell me more about how you approach a score? Do you have a method of analysis that you use? How do you learn it?

DRD: I just read it.

JW: Do you have perfect pitch?

DRD: Yes. And I don't worry about analysis. I think if there's a formal question, it usually becomes clear. I try at first to become involved in the technical questions such as "Who's doing what when?" Then I try to hear what the sound of the score is like. Questions about the general piece usually become apparent to me during the rehearsal if it's a brand-new work. If it's a traditional piece I have a pretty good concept before I rehearse it. I also sing through the parts a lot when I'm away from the score, while I'm walking or jogging. You do have to sit down at your desk and do a certain amount of work, but at the same time you can only do a certain amount of that. Another process of learning takes place while you do your other activities.

JW: Do you memorize your scores?

DRD: Not consciously. I always conduct with a score.

JW: Is there a reason for that?

DRD: Yes, because it's very useful to have the score. My function as a conductor is to inspire and to facilitate the performance of a work of art. If the fourth horn is a bar off in a very complicated passage I want to be able to fix it immediately. After conducting a work several times in performance having the score becomes perhaps less important, but I enjoy having it and feel more comfortable having it to refer to. It's otherwise not an artistic question; I have a huge amount of work to do and I just don't have the time consciously to memorize everything. I'm not conducting to make a show; I'm there to make the musicians feel at ease so they can do their work. I know how I feel when I'm playing and someone is conducting from memory. It is a show that often has little to do with the end artistic product. There are very few pieces in the repertory that benefit from conducting by memory. *Rite of Spring* is probably one of them.

JW: Don't you think that it hurts the performance to have the conductor buried in the score?

DRD: Of course it does. Knowing the score and memorizing it are two completely different things. For example, one must know the score well enough to give the musicians eye contact. Any good conductor always uses positive eye contact and breathes with the musicians. Those are the two major things a conductor has to do. However, there are some scores where I don't look up for a minute; I make sure that the musicians know they are going to get every beat where they need it, especially in changing metric patterns. What difference does it make to the performance if I would take the extra two or three weeks to memorize it? I would rather use that time reviewing new scores or practicing. Incidentally, when I play a piano concert I always play without the score. I don't question that there are people who have more ability or a better ability in this area. But I personally don't find that it's an artistic question.

•••••

JW: How long does it take you to learn a score?

DRD: Sometimes two days, sometimes overnight, depending on the size of the piece and what is involved in it, and sometimes several months. However, you know, I'm forty-six now and am getting to the point where I have a significant repertoire. I've always done so many unusual things. I have to say the size of my repertoire is really astonishing. So with a lot of experience under my belt it is much easier to learn new works. I built a tremendous foundation during my St. Paul Chamber Orchestra years. I did so much Mozart, Haydn, J. C. Bach, J. S. Bach, and Schubert. You know that most symphony conductors do very little of the basic classical repertory. The first season I was in Stuttgart I programmed all of the Schubert symphonies. They had never heard all of them! You can as a young person bring certain insights to that music. Many of these composers were younger than I am when they died!

JW: What do you think about conducting technique? Do you or did you practice your gestures?

DRD: I'm physically very gifted that way. I also had excellent training with Jean Morel and Jorge Mester at the Juilliard School. The emphasis was always that the conductor should be as clear as possible. For me, you know, it's the tool of the trade. On top of a clear technique, musicality begins to play a role. Opera training for conductors is really the best. You have singers on the stage, lighting and stage directions, you have orchestra musicians sitting in the pit reading music they probably haven't seen in three months. All they want is to know where the downbeat is. If they see you doing something the way you saw someone else doing it on television you are in serious trouble!

JW: You mentioned earlier that you had a specific approach to rehearsal technique. Can you elaborate a little on that?

DRD: Basically, I think the conductor has to know what the piece should sound like before he walks into the room. Then you have to listen to what it is you are actually getting back from the orchestra; you have to be able to make quick judgments. You need to ask yourself, "Is what I am hearing what I want?" It is the same when I play the piano; when I play a Steinway with a very sweet tone, there is a limit to how loud the piano will play. I have to scale everything to that dynamic range. It's the same thing with an orchestra. Successful conducting involves having an ensemble play the very best it can play. To do that you have to be able to hear what they are actually doing. So many of my colleagues shut their ears the minute their arms go into motion. It's difficult to conduct! It's very easy to sit still and listen; it's much harder to listen when you are moving. In terms of rehearsing, I've always worked very exactly. I've always been able to penetrate right to the heart of a problem. It's been the same with my own practicing; when I'm playing a piece I can go right to the two bars that will make that page work. As a pianist I can deal with those two bars and I do the same as a conductor. Sometimes you really have to work on certain problems, such as intonation. If you have someone who continually plays sharp or flat it's very useful and helpful to the general morale of the ensemble if you can help the player in a positive way. They are glad to know if they are sharp or flat! Musicians hear a great deal but a conductor should be able to hear more because you are the only one without an instrument under your ear! I also try to gauge where and when I should correct something that goes wrong. If I hear a mistake and look in a certain direction and get a hand wave the mistake has been taken care of; if it happens again I comment. When you stop you should have three, four, or five different things to say; that way you don't waste the orchestra's time; that's the kind of memory a conductor should develop. You should remember a catalog of things so that when you do stop you can mention several things that could be improved. The musicians really appreciate that technique because there is nothing harder than to stop and start mid-phrase, mid-movement without playing anything to completion.

You can, however, get involved in doing too much detail work. One of the things that opera experience has done for me is to free me from a good deal of the over exactitude of rehearsing. You know "the best-laid plans of mice and men" don't always turn out as planned! I can work and work to the last detail and then in the final analysis realize that my orchestra and I are only human; something is always going to go wrong. On the other hand, when I'm conducting opera in Germany we'll have a dress rehearsal two or three days before the premiere and I'll think, "My God, this is never going to work," and it works. During my first season in Stuttgart we did a new production of *Tristan and Isolde*. During my second season we programmed a revival of it. I was supposed to have an orchestra and a stage rehearsal but I got sick and couldn't do them; so, we just did it without a rehearsal. We hadn't played *Tristan* in four or five months and it turned out to be the best performance of the whole season. The musicians came in, concentrated, and knew what they had to do. I saw that and said, "There is something going on here that I'd better get involved with." The stage manager was always complaining because of the rehearsal requirements of some conductors and directors. He would say "This opera house is not a rehearsal stage, it's a performing institution. We are supposed to *perform*, not rehearse!" The truth is that the best way to make progress on a piece is to play it in public.

Recently I was at Ravinia with the Chicago Symphony. We were doing the Mahler Fifth Symphony, which is a signature piece for them. I was given two rehearsals that turned out to be during an incredible heat wave. After my first rehearsal I told them to go home and that we would just perform it at the concert. They were so relieved! Of course they played the hell out of it. I would never have had the confidence to do that sort of thing had I not had significant theater experience. The Chicago Symphony knew I had the confidence in them and they in return had the confidence in me that I could conduct the piece. You know the conductor has to have the courage of his own convictions and the ability to transmit those convictions at the right moment. You are a performer; you are not somebody who dots *i*s and crosses *t*s; you are somebody who has to inspire and to stimulate; you need to be able to change at the spur of the moment if it is called for. Another experience with the Mahler Fifth was when I did it for the first time in the States with the Cincinnati Orchestra. I went in and we started playing. They were wonderful. I was thinking, "What am I rehearsing for? This piece is ready to go." A couple of things went wrong in the scherzo, but I didn't stop. We just repeated the movement and everything went much better. Things usually get better the second time through. Musicians are very intelligent people!

What you get in a rehearsal and what you get in a concert are two different things. I'm also different. In rehearsal, I'm concentrating on everything that goes wrong and where all the problems are. At night at the concert, I try to conduct in a way to prevent the problems. I try to do something inspirational; I try to make dramatic events happen and to give inspirational performances. Rehearsing is a necessary, sometimes pleasurable experience. It is a necessity. However, our profession doesn't consist of rehearsing, it consists of performing!

•••••

JW: Well, you seem to lead a very balanced life for a conductor.

DRD: Yes, I try to keep in shape. I walk a lot and jog. Of course in Germany everybody's always outside. I enjoy sports. I enjoy competitive sports. I follow them as a spectator a great deal. When I jog I just let my mind wander. It's a wonderful stress antidote. Most important for me is a stable family life. My wife, Renate, is a strong and helpful partner, and I have five children between the ages twenty-four and four. Balancing family and career considerations is perhaps the most difficult and yet most rewarding task that a conductor faces.

Biography

Dennis Russell Davies currently holds three music directorships and performs as guest conductor with major orchestras on both sides of the Atlantic. In his fourth year as general music director of the city of Bonn, West Germany, he is also principal conductor and cofounder of the highly regarded American Composers Orchestra and music director of the Cabrillo Music Festival. He was recently appointed music director of the Brooklyn Academy of Music and principal conductor of the Brooklyn Philharmonic, effective for the 1991-92 season.

Mr. Davies served as general music director of the Stuttgart Opera from 1980 to 1987. From 1972 to 1980 he was music director of the St. Paul Chamber Orchestra, leading the ensemble to international recognition through increased touring activities and recording projects. In addition, he was principal conductor/classical music program director of the Saratoga Performing Arts Center (summer home of the Philadelphia Orchestra) from 1985 to 1988. His operatic engagements in the United States have included performances with the Chicago Lyric Opera, the Houston Grand Opera, and the Santa Fe Opera. In Europe, he has conducted at the Netherlands Opera, the Paris Opera, and the Hamburg Opera. He has also conducted at the Wagner Festival in Bayreuth, the second American ever invited to do so.

Born in Toledo, Ohio, in 1944, Dennis Russell Davies studied piano with Berenice B. McNab. He attended the Juilliard School where he studied piano with Lonny Epstein and Sascha Gorodnitski and conducting with Jean Morel and Jorge Mester. Mr. Davies first attracted public attention in 1968 when he and Luciano Berio founded the Juilliard Ensemble.

A champion of contemporary music, he has presented the works of such composers as William Bolcom, Philip Glass, Hans Werner Henze, Heinz Winbeck, and Arvo Pärt. Throughout his career, he has collaborated with a wide range of musicians, including Laurie Anderson, Keith Jarrett, Duke Ellington, and Elliott Carter.

Dennis Russell Davies Discography

Composer	Work	Orchestra	Soloists	Label	CD	LP	MC
Bach, J.C.	Sinfonia in g	St. Paul Chamber		Nonesuch		71324	71324-4
Bolcom	Commedia	St. Paul Chamber		Nonesuch		71324	
Bokom	Open House	St. Paul Chamber	Sperry	Nonesuch		71324	
Cage	Seasons	American Composers		CRI		S-410	
Copland	Appalachian Spring (suite)	St. Paul Chamber		ProArte	CDD-140		PCD-140
Copland	Clarinet concerto	St. Luke's	Blount	MM	60162	20162	40162
Copland	Music for Movies	St. Luke's		MM	60162	20162	40162
Copland	Music for the Theatre	St. Luke's		MM	60162	20162	40162
Copland	Quiet City	St. Luke's		MM	60162	20162	40162
Dvořák	Bagatelles (5)	Beethovenhalle Bonn	Casleanu, Kurkowski, Brunnert	MM	MMD-60180H	MMD-60180H	
Dvořák	Serenade for Winds	Beethovenhalle Bonn		MM	MMD-60180H		
Glass	Akhnaten	Stuttgart State Opera		CBS	M3K-42457		M3T-42457
Harrison	Elegiac Symphony	American Composers		MM	MMCD-60204		MMC-40204
Haydn, M.	Symphony in G	St. Paul Chamber		Nonesuch		71324	71324-4
Hovhannes	Lousadzak	American Composers	Jarrett	MM	MMCD-60204		MMC-40204
Hovhannes	Symphony no. 2, Mysterious Mountain	American Composers		MM	MMCD-60204		MMC-40204
Ives	Three Places in New England	St. Paul Chamber		ProArte	CDD-140		PCD-140
Mozart	Cassation in D, K62a	St. Paul Chamber		Nonesuch		71323	71323-4
Mozart	Symphony no. 33	Beethovenhalle Bonn		MM	MMD-60175T		
Mozart	Symphony no. 34	Beethovenhalle Bonn		MM	MMD-60175T		
Overton	Pulsations	CRI Chamber Ensemble		CRI		298	
Pärt	Cantus	Stuttgart Radio Symphony		ECM	817764-2	817764-1	817764-4

Composer	Work	Orchestra	Soloists	Label	CD	LP	MC
Phillips	Canzona 3	Juilliard Ensemble		CRI		S-286	
Rhodes	Divertimento for Small Orchestra	St. Paul Chamber		CRI		S-361	
Schubert	Symphony no. 5	St. Paul Chamber		Sound 80		102	
Stokes	Continental Harp and Band Report	Louisville		Louisville		760	
Stokes	On the Badlands – Parables	St. Paul Chamber		CRI		S-415	
Thorne	Symphony no. 5	American Composers		CRI	CD-552		
Trimble	In Praise of Diplomacy and Common Sense	CRI Chamber Ensemble	Frisch	CRI		298	
Wuorinen	Two-Part Symphony	American Composers		CRI		S-410	

"The baton is not a beautiful instrument. If you are too clear, the orchestra doesn't sound good. If people rely totally on you for cues, they don't listen to each other. If you are not clear in a musical way, it is also wrong. I think ideal conducting is when beating becomes less and less important. The conductor's only job should be imprinting his ideas about a piece on the orchestra during rehearsals and performances. Technically, he shouldn't be too necessary. In an ideal situation, the orchestra should be able to play without the conductor. There must be someone, though, who imprints the spirit of the piece on the entire group of musicians. You cannot have 75 to 90 persons' ideas on a work. Music-making is done together, but the imprint has to be done by the conductor."

_____ Christoph von Dohnányi

Christoph von Dohnányi

JW: What are the main differences in the conducting profession in this country compared to Europe?

CvD: First of all, there is quite a difference in sound, which I think is partly a matter of the halls. Orchestras such as the Vienna Philharmonic and the Berlin Philharmonic have very unusual and beautiful halls to perform in. Few orchestras in this country have the same quality halls as the European orchestras have. The exceptions are Symphony Hall in Boston, Carnegie Hall in New York, and Severance Hall here in Cleveland. The hall is an important part of an orchestra's sound; it's quasi their instrument. So when we perform at home it's like playing on our own expensive and rare violin. When we are on tour we are usually using a less familiar instrument. So some of the European orchestras, using this analogy, "play" high quality instruments at home and are, once they are on tour, reaching out for their "sound" in other halls.

Also, you usually get more rehearsal time in Europe. Unfortunately the European orchestras are also getting less and less rehearsal time so that it's almost the same now there as here. The normal rehearsal time for the Berlin Philharmonic is three rehearsals of 2 1/2 hours, which is really very little. In the earlier days and with other European orchestras the music had more time to develop and the music-making itself was better. You could concentrate more on the real music instead of just technique. The American orchestras though, at this point, have an advantage because, generally speaking, their technique is better than the European orchestras. For instance, with [the members of] the Cleveland Orchestra you don't need to rehearse much technique; you can start making music earlier with them than with most other orchestras.

JW: Do you think the Cleveland Orchestra has a greater technique than the Berlin Philharmonic?

CvD: They have a different type of technique; they are faster readers, much faster than the Berlin Philharmonic. But the Berlin Philharmonic also has its specialized repertoire, which it plays probably better than most other orchestras in the world; if the musicians don't know a piece though, they take

53

much longer than the Cleveland Orchestra; they aren't used to reading as much music as we do.

JW: Do you rehearse the Berlin Philharmonic differently than the Cleveland Orchestra?

CvD: Technically things come together much faster here; however, music-making in Berlin is very special! They are tremendously trained in pure sound production.

JW: Do you program differently in Europe than you would in Cleveland?

CvD: Not at all. Why would I choose a different repertoire? The world is so small now; it only takes a few hours to go back home.

JW: Many conductors say that programming here in the States is more difficult than in Europe because our system relies so heavily on ticket sales. Do you agree with this?

CvD: I put together very interesting programs here in Cleveland, though of course sometimes one might have problems selling them. We are willing to take that risk. We have to have a balance in the programming and to perform certain pieces, even though that may risk having fewer people in the audience. I mean, as long as we survive everything is O.K. I would not be interested in performing a repertoire to just please an audience; I would also not be interested in performing a repertoire just to displease an audience. You have to have a balance of this. Of course, the more concerts you have in your subscription season the more flexibility you have in programming. I also try to make clear to people that in spite of what they may think, they probably understand nineteenth-century music less than they understand twentieth-century music. For example, the way the public understands Beethoven is not proven to be right. Don't you think it would be much more difficult to agree on different subjects with someone from the nineteenth century than it would be to deal with someone from our century?

JW: Of course.

CvD: Beethoven's music wasn't meant only to be enjoyed the way we are enjoying it now. First of all, if Beethoven were alive today he would be composing in contemporary styles and, of course, would support contemporary music.

•••••

JW: What do you think of all the new performance practice ideas? What do you think of the Roger Norrington performances?

CvD: Norrington is a very interesting man who, in my opinion, has an interesting approach. I don't know very much about it yet and would like to hear more. I'm very skeptical of using the "correct" metronome markings in a stubborn way, especially since there is not one contemporary musician who writes the right metronome markings! The metronome was invented in Beethoven's time, 150 years ago, and composers today still can't use it correctly! I just performed a piece by Michael Tippett which cannot be performed with his metronome markings; Stravinsky never used his own markings literally and neither did Schoenberg. I think the only real reservation I have in Norrington's case is that he is not very flexible. There are very motoric movements in Beethoven that shouldn't be flexible, but there are movements that should have flexibility, such as in the slow movements and in the minuets and trios. Both Schindler and Czerny wrote about the flexibility in Beethoven's own performances! And think of Mendelssohn being quasi a contemporary artist of Beethoven, raving about the flexibility in the tempi of an artist like Franz Liszt.

The old instruments Norrington uses are interesting to hear, but my concern is that this music is somehow going to be owned by all these "specialists." Many conductors rarely perform Bach now and I'm afraid that will begin to happen with Mozart, then Beethoven, Brahms, and Mahler! However, then maybe there will be a chance for contemporary music because the older music will be left to "specialists." Still, it's good to have a man like Norrington around. People can discuss him and like or dislike what he does. Some of the things he does, such as taking almost all the repeats, may be historically correct, but for us is musically questionable. We know that Beethoven was performed in many different ways throughout the nineteenth century.

JW: Do you retouch scores?

CvD: If it's necessary I will make small changes. However, I almost never change an orchestration. In the *Eroica* I add one horn, but I don't use it many times! If I recorded it again I might rethink my previous retouchings. I might support the woodwinds instead of adding the trumpet in the coda. It's a matter of personal decision. If you think Beethoven would have added it, you should do it. I think we should have that freedom. It's a matter of experience also. You need to have worked a lot on the composer in order to make intelligent decisions. A lot of people, for instance, have never done a Schumann symphony without retouching it. I think you need to hear it first the way in which it was written before you can make those kinds of decisions. It has become an accepted idea that Schumann was a bad orchestrator, and that's not necessarily true. Schumann was a wonderful musician. We need to take what he originally wrote more seriously! I recorded all the Schumann symphonies without retouching any of them, except for changing some dynamics.

•••••

JW: What are your criteria in programming twentieth-century works? How do you judge a twentieth-century work you are looking at for the first time?

CvD: Unfortunately we don't do enough twentieth-century works, though we perform more than some orchestras. Also, when we think of the twentieth century, we need to realize that it's not so modern. The twentieth century is about to come to a close! Mahler and Debussy are twentieth-century composers!

I usually do only the pieces I believe in. Sometimes, though, I do perform works I believe in but have some reservations about. If I believe in them, I feel people deserve to be able to listen to them and to judge the works themselves. Felix Mottl, when conducting Brahms, was sometimes rather happy if people did *not* like the music, since he believed more in Wagner, for instance. The important thing is that I believe in the piece, and if I do, I feel the work deserves to be heard. "Liking" a piece might not be the most important criterion.

JW: Is it true that you feel very close to the Second Viennese School?

CvD: I've performed a lot of that music because I feel you cannot approach the music of our day without understanding or knowing the music of the Second Viennese School.

JW: Why do you think the public has never really embraced that music?

CvD: Look at Schoenberg's face. He was not a man the public could embrace. There were many great artists that the public could never embrace. To me that's not so important.

JW: I agree with that; however, many composers have lost an audience. Contemporary music has suffered because there has virtually been no audience for it! Now composers are trying to reach the public again. What is your opinion about that?

CvD: This is not quite true. Music of our day somehow, since it is young, needs to be supported like a child, but not spoiled. We know that children grow up with stronger personalities if they are not spoiled, and believe me, we are not in danger of spoiling contemporary music in the States. On the contrary! There was a time in Germany, however, when anything contemporary – good or bad – was supported. Contemporary music became a spoiled child!

My belief is that it is O.K. for composers to have a difficult but not impossible time. The social structure should guarantee them the possibility of being heard. Also, it is up to the artist to write without consideration of public appreciation or to consider the public as a partnership. Schoenberg was well aware of this. He wrote his music knowing he would be alone and without the support of the public. He just couldn't go on with tonality and had to make the break and sacrifice himself because of it. Many of his works are self-portraits. They are an analysis of his decision to go on, but in a different direction. He was trying to build the art form of the next century. Schoenberg sacrificed a lot of his life because of this decision! His friends Alban Berg and Anton Webern even had to collect money to support him because Schoenberg had alienated his support system and the public.

Now if a composer just says to society, "Please support me because I'm different," you have to be very careful. (There are very few Schoenbergs!) Society needs to support them without spoiling them. You have to be careful with every decision. On the other hand, there are composers like Philip Glass that cater to the public's needs and are making a living with their music. There is nothing wrong with that. They do well without any support.

JW: Do you think serialism is dying out as a compositional style?

CvD: Twelve-tone music will never be very popular; it just isn't the "public's" music. Webern once said though, that "the time will come when people will whistle my melodies." (In Germany there is an expression, "If they whistle it, they appreciate it.") Now I don't think that Webern was really thinking about being a popular composer, though I think he did have a premonition that his music would be appreciated at a later time. For me and for many he was the greatest of all; he came closest to our way of thinking and to the philosophy of our century. Maybe there will be a time when the public will look at twentieth-century music and Webern will play a real major role.

JW: Do you find the audiences more conservative here or in Europe?

CvD: It's about the same. Some people think Vienna is very conservative, but it's very easy to program contemporary music there. They even have a music organization of young and very open people called the "Jeunesse musicale." This organization has got about 100,000 members in Austria.

•••••

57

JW: How do you approach a score by Webern?

CvD: I analyze it, of course. I might also listen to a recording for comparison purposes. Usually I'm reluctant to listen to recordings because unless you know a piece extremely well, the recordings can preoccupy you and influence your own performance. In any case, I first study and then listen to other peoples' work in recordings.

JW: How do you approach a score of the standard repertoire?

CvD: The classical repertoire is easy to analyze. It starts becoming difficult with the late Romantics. In Bruckner, for instance, you have to know exactly what is going on; you have to find the style. It is a much more forward-thinking style than Brahms or even Mahler. After analyzing, the musical problems start.

JW: How would you tell a student to find the style of Bruckner?

CvD: You have to read a lot of Bruckner scores and study them. You also have to see how he was influenced by other composer's works and in turn find out how he influenced composers that followed him. It's difficult, for instance, to imagine composers like Stockhausen or Ligeti without Bruckner! I need to know the connection between composers and their style of composing.

JW: How long do you study a score before you perform it?

CvD: If it is a great score, again and again. I don't even know when I first started to study Beethoven's Ninth. Performing a work for the first time is only starting a work. You learn a work by both studying and performing it. I read and study many scores at the same time. I don't read them at the piano anymore because I don't play well enough now, but I have a good ear so I can picture how scores sound in my mind; I'm sometimes very surprised at the first rehearsal when the real sound occurs – how close you can come with your inner ear and imagination to the reality of sound!

•••••

JW: Do you ever practice a gestural technique?

CvD: Not really. You think about it, but you don't need to practice. I do not like bar lines. In fact, I actually don't like conducting as far as just beating is concerned. The baton is not a beautiful instrument. If you are too clear, the orchestra doesn't sound good. If people rely totally on you for cues, they don't listen to each other. If you are not clear in a musical way, it is also wrong. I think ideal conducting is when beating becomes less and less important. The conductor's only job should be imprinting his ideas about a piece on the orchestra during rehearsals and performances. Technically, he shouldn't be too necessary. In an ideal situation, the orchestra should be able to play without the conductor. There must be someone, though, who imprints the spirit of the piece on the entire group of musicians. You cannot have 75 to 90 persons' ideas on a work. Music-making is done together, but the imprint has to be done by the conductor. In earlier days I over-emphasized things like technique and correct intonation. I'm spoiled here in Cleveland because I don't have to work very much on intonation or technique; I can start much earlier with pure music-making. We don't even talk too much about technique – cueing is not the same matter as conducting. Our orchestra has, as most of the American orchestras, a very extensive repertoire. If I were conducting in Vienna and gave a cue to the orchestra in a piece they know quasi by heart, such as *Rosenkavalier*, they would laugh at me!

Biography

Music director of the Cleveland Orchestra since the fall of 1984, Christoph von Dohnányi first conducted the orchestra in December 1981, assumed his responsibilities as music director designate in 1982, and became music director with the 1984-85 season. Mr. Dohnányi has recently taken the orchestra on its second tour of Europe. They made their first European tour in 1986 and performed throughout Japan and Taiwan in October 1987.

Born in Berlin in September 1929, Christoph von Dohnányi began to study the piano at the age of five. After World War II he undertook the study of law at the University of Munich and, in 1948, also entered the Musikhochschule there. He soon won the Richard Strauss prize for composition and conducting – and withdrew from his law studies.

There followed a period of study with his grandfather, Erno Dohnányi, at Florida State University, and studies of conducting at Tanglewood during the period Leonard Bernstein was serving on its faculty. Upon his return to Europe, in 1952, Christoph von Dohnányi was offered a position coaching and conducting at the Frankfurt Opera under Georg Solti; he was later named artistic and musical director of the company. He has also served as director of the West German Radio Symphony Orchestra in Cologne and from 1978 to 1984 served as artistic director and principal conductor of the Hamburg State Opera.

Mr. Dohnányi has conducted at the world's great opera houses, including Covent Garden, La Scala, the Vienna State Opera, in Berlin, Paris, and Munich, at the Salzburg Festival, and, in this country, at the Metropolitan Opera, the Lyric Opera of Chicago, and the San Francisco Opera. He was also invited by Wieland Wagner to conduct at Bayreuth.

Mr. Dohnányi has been guest conductor of many of the world's leading orchestras, including the BBC Symphony Orchestra, the New York Philharmonic, the Israel Philharmonic, the Philadelphia Orchestra, the Tonhalle Orchestra of Zurich, and the Chicago Symphony Orchestra; he is a regular guest conductor with the Berlin Philharmonic, the Vienna Philharmonic, and the Orchestre de Paris.

Christoph von Dohnányi Discography

Composer	Work	Orchestra	Soloists	Label	CD	LP	MC
Bartók	Concerto for Orchestra	Cleveland		London	425 694-2		425 694-4
Beethoven	Leonore Overture no. 3	Cleveland		Telarc	CD-80145		
Beethoven	Overtures	Cleveland					
Beethoven	Symphony no. 1	Cleveland		Telarc	CD-80187		
Beethoven	Symphony no. 2	Cleveland		Telarc	CD-80187		
Beethoven	Symphony no. 3	Cleveland		Telarc	CD-80090	DG-10090	
Beethoven	Symphony no. 4	Cleveland		Telarc	CD-80198		
Beethoven	Symphony no. 5	Cleveland		Telarc	CD-80163		
Beethoven	Symphony no. 6	Cleveland		Telarc	CD-80145		
Beethoven	Symphony no. 7	Cleveland		Telarc	CD-80163		
Beethoven	Symphony no. 8	Cleveland		Telarc	CD-80198		
Beethoven	Symphony no. 8	Cleveland		Telarc	CD-80091	DG-10091	
Beethoven	Symphony no. 9	Cleveland	Vaness, Taylor, Jerusalem, Lloyd	Telarc	CD-80120	DG-10120	
Brahms	Symphony no. 1	Cleveland		Teldec	8.43479		
Brahms	Symphony no. 2	Cleveland		Teldec	8.44005		
Brahms	Symphony no. 3	Cleveland		Teldec	8.44134		
Brahms	Symphony no. 3	Cleveland		Teldec	243 711		
Brahms	Symphony no. 4	Cleveland		Teldec	43678		
Brahms	Tragic Overture	Cleveland		Teldec	243 711		
Brahms	Variations on a Theme of Haydn	Cleveland		Teldec	8.44005		
Bruckner	Symphony no. 9	Cleveland		London	425 405-2		425 405-4
Busoni	Piano Concerto	Cleveland	Ohlsson	Telarc	CD-80207		
Dohnányi	Piano Variations on a Nursery Song	New Philharmonia	Wild	Chesky	CD-13	CR-13	
Dvořák	Piano Concerto	Vienna Philharmonic	Schiff	London	417 802-2		417 802-4

Composer	Work	Orchestra	Soloists	Label	CD	LP	MC
Dvořák	Scherzo Capriccioso	Cleveland		London	414 422-2		
Dvořák	Slavonic Dances, opp. 46, 72	Cleveland		London	430 171-2		430-171-4
Dvořák	Symphony no. 7	Cleveland		London	417 564-2		417 564-4
Dvořák	Symphony no. 7	Cleveland		London	421 082-2		
Dvořák	Symphony no. 8	Cleveland		London	414 422-2		
Dvořák	Symphony no. 8	Cleveland		London	421 082-2		
Dvořák	Symphony no. 9	Cleveland		London	414 421-2		414 421-4
Dvořák	Symphony no. 9	Cleveland		London	421 082-2		
Lutoslawski	Concerto for Orchestra	Cleveland		London			
Mahler	Symphony no. 1	Cleveland		London			
Mahler	Symphony no. 5	Cleveland		London	425 438-2		425 438-4
Mendelssohn	Die Erste Walpurgisnacht	Cleveland		Telarc	CD-80184		
Mendelssohn	Symphony no. 1 in c	Vienna Philharmonic		London	421 769-2		
Mendelssohn	Symphony no. 2 in B-flat	Vienna Philharmonic	Ghazarian, Gruberova, Krenn	London	421 769-2		
Mendelssohn	Symphony no. 3 in a	Cleveland		Telarc	CD-80184		
Mendelssohn	Symphony no. 3 in a	Vienna Philharmonic		London	417 731-2		
Mendelssohn	Symphony no. 4 in A	Vienna Philharmonic		London	417 731-2		
Mendelssohn	Symphony no. 5 in d	Vienna Philharmonic		London	421 769-2		
Mussorgsky	Night on Bald Mountain	Cleveland		Teldec	244920-2		
Mussorgsky	Pictures at an Exhibition	Cleveland		Teldec	244920-2		644152
Schubert	Symphony no. 8	Cleveland		Telarc	CD-80091	DG-10091	
Schubert	Symphony no. 9	Cleveland		Telarc	CD-80110	DG-10110	
Schumann	Piano Introduction & Allegro Appassionato in G	Vienna Philharmonic	Schiff	London	417 802-2		417 802-4
Schumann	Symphony no. 1	Cleveland		London	421 439-2	21 439-1	421 439-4
Schumann	Symphony no. 2	Cleveland		London	421 439-2	421 439-1	421 439-4
Schumann	Symphony no. 3	Cleveland		London	421 643-2	421 643-1	421 643-4
Schumann	Symphony no. 4	Cleveland		London	421 643-2	421 643-1	421 643-4

Composer	Work	Orchestra	Soloists	Label	CD	LP	MC
Tchaikovsky	Polonaise from Eugene Onegin	Cleveland		Telarc	CD-80131		
Tchaikovsky	Symphony no. 6	Cleveland		Telarc	CD-80131		

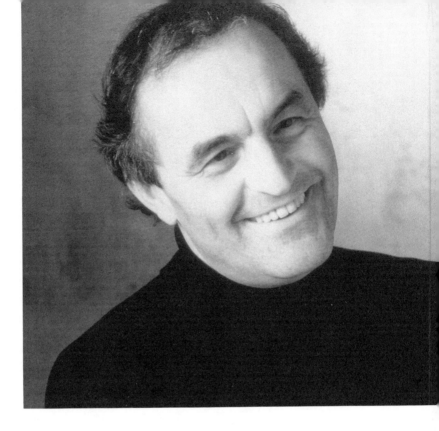

"We can't imitate them [the older school of conductors] now because they lived in
a certain time, and we live in a later time. Our pulse is different. When I see a
movie made fifty years ago, it strikes me how slowly the plot moves. It was obvious
that the public had to be told the plot slowly in order for them to understand and
follow the film. Today, perception is much faster because we are spoiled by all the
new technology. We see so much, we hear so much, and are able to perceive
things at a much faster rate. Because our perception has changed, the way of
making music has changed. This is the great thing about music. It goes along with
the times; it's a living art; it's not stagnant. You can't say that this is the right or
wrong way; it moves with the times in which it is performed."

Charles Dutoit

Charles Dutoit

JW: How did you start your career as a conductor?

CD: I grew up in Switzerland and was exposed to all types of concerts and music. My decision to become a conductor was based on these early experiences. I decided to become a conductor when I was twenty-one and was fortunate to be given chances to conduct almost immediately. There weren't many decently gifted conductors in Switzerland then so I was singled out and people began to give me opportunities. My problem was that I was given too much to do at once and I wasted years just trying to survive! I didn't have the repertoire and I wasn't ready for all of the opportunities that came my way. I had to earn a living though, and I was struggling with financial problems. I had to keep taking everything that came along. I survived, fortunately! I worked very, very hard and was helped by many people around me.

When the point came in my career to break into a higher level I wrote letters and sent brochures like everybody else does without anything happening. Finally I had a manager who talked to Herbert von Karajan. It was the greatest thing he ever did for me. My break came precisely because I was conducting Stravinsky's *Rite of Spring* for the first time, the same year Karajan was and Karajan heard (through my manager) that there was this young kid doing the same. My concert was successful and Karajan wanted to meet me and asked if I would come to Vienna. My manager immediately replied, "Of course, anytime, you know he has nothing to do!" At that point Karajan invited me to conduct Manuel de Falla's *Three-Cornered Hat,* a new production in the Vienna opera. At the time I had never been in an opera house in my life and had never conducted outside of Switzerland! There I was in the Vienna Opera, super-exposed and over-exposed. Karajan was there for the performance and I fortunately had great success with the orchestra. I stayed on for two years in Vienna and also did a few ballets. I was asked to do more operas but I wasn't prepared and couldn't do them.

During that period I studied a lot, organized concerts with friends, and did a lot of modern music for small chamber works like Stravinsky's *Soldier's Tale, Les Noces,* and *Octet.* Eventually everything went well. This is not a recipe for success though. I have been very fortunate and I'm sure a few people that have had more talent than I have been less fortunate. Many people have chances, though, but if you aren't prepared or aren't talented enough you won't get to go on. Conducting requires so many things and you need to be prepared in many different ways. You also need good health and a good emotional balance. You have to be very natural in the way you impose yourself on the orchestra. You can't be too heavy-handed when dealing with the musicians. I've learned a lot through the years and I've worked very hard. It's only been in the last eight years that I have felt that I know my profession well. At this point I can deal with any situation in the world today, with any orchestra. I finally have enough experience to deal with anything that comes my way. It took all those years of experience to get to this point. I think that it really takes around twenty years to learn this profession after you start conducting! Maybe some people think I did things better fifteen or twenty years ago. Maybe I had a certain freshness that came from inexperience. But today I know why I do certain things. I don't conduct only from my instincts but from my experience and knowledge. It has taken twenty years to gain this!

JW: What steps should a young conductor today take to break into the professional conducting world? Is a manager important at the beginning?

CD: I have answered or at least tried to answer this question a hundred times. Obviously, every young conductor is preoccupied with the situation. Managers are what they are, period. They can be important in a certain moment, but most of them do absolutely nothing. When you see artist's management's rosters listing 200 conductors you have to ask what it means. It means that they keep all of these conductors under their control. If anything happens, for instance, if the conductor gets a guest conducting job on his own, the orchestra will have to go through the agent or manager. To have a manager is certainly not an answer to a career, though they can be important at certain times.

I think that instrumentalists are in a better position. At least they can audition. Young artists like Midori and Joshua Bell played for a few conductors when they were young and were the best pupils of important teachers in New York. From there they could just go and see Isaac Stern or someone else of his calibre and arrange a concert. This creates a kind of a sparkling atmosphere around them and they begin their careers. Everybody knows they are good; they don't have to talk with anybody. They just go and play and that's it. Everything else will be taken care of for them!

A conductor's position is just the opposite. He must have experience in order to conduct a major orchestra or any orchestra for that matter. He must have experience in order to make the concert work and to be remembered. A conductor also needs to be rebooked before people begin to take him seriously. Now how does a conductor gain this experience if he is not given opportunities? This is the dilemma! I think I am very supportive of young conductors but I can't book them if they don't have experience! More than that, I can't book them unless they have some sort of reputation. We have to sell a big season and ticket sales are very important to us. Unless we attract an audience with known artists we will not be able to make it financially. I simply couldn't afford to invite a young person with no experience to guest conduct my orchestra. A conductor needs to be able to impose his interpretation on an orchestra and that takes experience! Some young conductors just let the orchestra play and try to find their own way by following them. They learn nothing this way. This is the reason I am totally against the way some young people are pushed too early and go straight to the top without having the experience of struggling.

JW: That sort of thing happens a lot right now. After Bernstein and Michael Tilson Thomas, orchestras and management are looking for young charismatic geniuses. Unfortunately, how many Bernsteins do you find in one, two, three, or four generations?

CD: That's right. I feel frustrated and wish I could have a better answer to this problem.

JW: Do you think assistantships help young conductors?

CD: Well, I have an assistant. When I arrived in Montreal the principal viola player was interested in conducting. This young man worked with me for a couple of seasons. He knew my rehearsal technique and what I was doing to build the orchestra. Little by little I gave him work. I would give him rehearsals when I knew he knew what I wanted and would not waste time. So, he prepared the orchestra for me for two or three years and became associate conductor. I gave him many opportunities to conduct and he was well accepted by the orchestra. He eventually became music director of the Edmonton Symphony.

I replaced him with another musician from my orchestra, the first bassoonist, who was also interested in conducting. He stays in the orchestra because he is cautious, though I'm sure if he finds a position elsewhere he will go. So far it's good for him and he is doing well. He's very talented and I give him a lot of work. An assistant for me is not somebody who goes around carrying my briefcase. He has got to work and I give him a lot of work. He's the one who rehearses when I am caught somewhere in an airport; he's the one who will help me rehearse when we have sectionals. He does a lot of run-out concerts and of course has to know all the repertoire in case I'm not feeling well. But in ten years I've never canceled a concert, so he's not very worried. He also reads a lot of contemporary scores with the composer-in-residence for me. I simply don't have time to look through everything that is sent. He's also trying to organize a youth orchestra.

The situation in the States, though, is tough. Tanglewood and places like that are nice providing you make it to the two top conducting slots! Otherwise you will never be seen. It also helps to actually play in the orchestra at times. I played for Karajan. I played both the violin and viola.

JW: What do you look for in a young conductor?

CD: It's hard to judge talent. How can you tell if someone has what it takes to make it? I don't know. A young talented conductor may be given the opportunity to conduct the New York Philharmonic as a replacement like Bernstein did. He may go on to be a great success or he may break his neck and finish his career before it begins! Young conductors need reasonable opportunities and good advice. I think I give both to my assistants in Montreal. For instance, if I am invited to conduct in South America I will let my assistant go ahead and prepare the orchestra for ten days before I arrive. He knows exactly what I want. In exchange, I will also make sure to give him some concerts. For instance, out of eight concerts scheduled in Montevideo, Uruguay, and Buenos Aires, Argentina, he will conduct at least two. He is very happy with this arrangement. Now I would not push him with the Boston Symphony because he is not quite ready to face an orchestra like that. I want him to gain experience little by little. One day things will open up for him.

It's very strange in the States. It's much better to have an orchestra in South America or in Mexico for awhile than to be in the States unless you are at the top. A conductor's start in this country is very peculiar. You always have to belong to a certain class and it's very difficult to climb steps in a healthy way. Don't you agree with me?

JW: Absolutely.

CD: You know I have refused to conduct here until recently. I knew that in the States you either hit the front page or get lost in the middle. It's a hard profession everywhere, but it is especially hard here. So, I didn't come!

•••••

JW: What's your method of score analysis? Some conductors I've interviewed have told me they don't have a method. They are able to read through a score and learn it in that way.

CD: Of course there is a method! People without methods obviously don't conduct many scores in a year. When I was a kid, I didn't have a method. Finally I learned one and then didn't have the experience to use it. It took me months and months to study a score. Today it takes me a hundred times less because I feel I have done it all my life by now.

There is a method that is purely analytical. I mean every intelligent musician and soloist should study scores. Usually a violinist or a pianist will start by reading through the music to get it in their fingers or mind and then if they are thoughtful performers will begin to analyze the structure. In general, soloists are less analytical than conductors because conductors don't play the music they study. I mean we can try to play scores on the piano but I think it's a terrible habit to get into. It prevents you from imagining the world of sounds which is in the score. You can become very lazy playing through the score on the piano! It's a practical instrument if you rehearse with a soloist for an opera, but if you think you are studying a score by playing through it you are wrong. The piano first of all is not even an orchestral instrument. An orchestra is not a piano reduction! If I had students I would definitely tell them that it is counterproductive to use a piano.

JW: Do you have perfect pitch?

CD: Yes, but that is not even relevant. With or without perfect pitch you have to live with what you see and have to be able to imagine how a score sounds. You need to analyze the forms and find out how a movement is constructed. You have to do exactly the reverse of what the composer did. He started from nothing and built something. The conductor starts with the finished product and needs to break it down. Find the structural skeleton of the work; how the movement is divided into parts; what happens within these parts. You have got to know where the work is going and what the structural high and low points are. You need intellectual control of the material in order to let your emotions and sensitivity take over.

Conducting should always be controlled by the brain in a way which enables you to put the shape of a movement into context. Otherwise you would easily distort the work by your emotions, letting yourself go too far. You may find this sort of interpretation all through the nineteenth century where performers tended to just express themselves freely, not caring what was actually written in the score. Today we tend to be a bit stricter about interpretation. We try to have a more honest approach. Felix Weingartner and Arturo Toscanini were the forerunners of a more honest approach. This was in contrast to Artur Nikisch, Richard Wagner, and others who were more egocentric in their interpretations and took many liberties with the music. Today we have a new breed of conductors developing like Roger Norrington and Christopher Hogwood who are trying to change that post-Wagnerian school of conducting and are rethinking performance practices. They are rethinking Beethoven and putting Beethoven back into his own time period. Even the *Eroica*, though written in a style more romantic than classical, was written in the early nineteenth century. It should be played with the style of that time, the possibilities of that time and not with the style and possibilities of the 1890s. It shouldn't be played like Wagner with a sort of

Götterdämmerung sound. Currently we have a conflict between these two schools of thought and it's good that this conflict exists. It's very healthy; it's healthy that conductors are rethinking and reviewing these things a bit. It's wonderful to hear a new and fresh approach to the music. Conductors like Norrington are dedicating their lives to these new concepts. It's good to hear and to use ancient instruments. The public and the press also think it's very interesting. On the other hand we also have a lot to learn from the older school of conductors like Wilhelm Furtwängler. We can't imitate them now because they lived in a certain time, and we live in a later time. Our pulse is different. When I see a movie made fifty years ago, it strikes me how slowly the plot moves. It was obvious that the public had to be told the plot slowly in order for them to understand and follow the film. Today, perception is much faster because we are spoiled by all the new technology. We see so much, we hear so much, and are able to perceive things at a much faster rate. Because our perception has changed, the way of making music has changed. This is the great thing about music. It goes along with the times; it's a living art; it's not stagnant. You can't say this is the right or wrong way; it moves with the times in which it is performed.

JW: Would you ever retouch a Beethoven symphony?

CD: Not now. I used to use the retouchings that Weingartner published in his book on the Beethoven symphonies. I thought that he was a great master regarding Beethoven and what he said was very interesting. Today I'm a little more careful. I don't think that retouchings are necessary, not even in places where Beethoven ran out of notes for instruments of his day such as in the coda of the first movement of the *Eroica* or in the scherzo of the Ninth Symphony. If Beethoven had had the use of our modern instruments he probably would have written those places differently, but he didn't and that is important to remember. His orchestra would have sounded very differently than our modern ones!

JW: What do you think about all this clamor over observing his metronome markings?

CD: Well, it's always interesting to hear his music with his metronome markings. I must say that I don't have a clear opinion about them. I think they are too fast and if I do them at that speed the music doesn't make sense to me. When I hear David Zinman or Norrington using those tempos I find them interesting. Actually the first conductor to use those markings was [René] Leibowitz, a disciple of [Arnold] Schoenberg. He made his first recordings of the Beethoven symphonies with Beethoven's markings about thirty or forty years ago. Everybody thought he was crazy at that time. Not only was he a disciple of Schoenberg; he was also a French Jew and for those reasons didn't have much credibility with the public. He made very little impact by playing Beethoven in tempo at that time in history!

I am very struck by Norrington. He is a great friend of mine whom I like very much. He's a wonderful musician and he's not a fanatic. We have had long discussions and though he defends and fights for his point of view he always says, "I am not trying to convince you, this is just the way I feel about these things."

JW: I have listened to his recordings of the Beethoven symphonies and find them very illuminating.

CD: When I first heard these tempos I thought, "Gee, that's not possible." After awhile I got used to them and they make more sense to me now. I couldn't use them myself because I've heard them differently all my life and maybe I just don't have the courage to try to force myself to try another approach. On the other hand I must say that I have changed a lot of things. My approach to seventeenth-century music has been very different in recent years. When I was a kid and a member of a chamber orchestra we used to play Bach in the old style. We used phrasings from the nineteenth century and as you know, the musicians of the nineteenth century were not aware of the traditions of the seventeenth or eighteenth centuries. The nineteenth century just didn't have access to the type of research we have today. So they played this music in a nineteenth-century fashion that distorted it. Now we can play more in the context in which this music was composed. I do a lot of baroque music myself and I invite many early music specialists to conduct my orchestra. I want my orchestra to be aware of these things. Performance styles will keep changing and it is an educational experience to know what is going on. So you see I am very open about these new directions. What I hate is the attitude that there is no other way to perform this music! Fortunately some of the conductors who have had that attitude in the past are changing now and becoming much more flexible.

I had the strangest experience last December when I conducted the Concertgebouw in Amsterdam. You know that [Nicholas] Harnoncourt has conducted them for ten years now in early music performances. I had programmed Mozart's Symphony no. 29, Glazunov's Violin Concerto, and Elgar's *Enigma Variations.* When I got the parts from them for the Mozart, I realized that they were Harnoncourt's parts with all of his bowings and phrasings. I saw his whole life and everything that he believes in front of me on that score. But I just couldn't use those parts. I told the orchestra, "Listen my friends, I'm in a very strange situation because I obviously admire Harnoncourt very much and I'm not in a position to argue with his approach. But I can't use his parts; we'll have to use other parts. I have to do this symphony my way." They said, "O.K., but forgive us, we haven't played a Mozart symphony with another conductor for ten years." It actually took me one or two rehearsals to make the orchestra relapse into the "old-fashioned way" of playing Mozart. I think that is unhealthy. How could they let one conductor do only one style of performance practice for ten years with such a great orchestra?

JW: Could we go back to score analysis for a moment? After finding the structure of a piece do you do a harmonic analysis? Do you analyze each chord or do you just find the general harmonic tendencies?

CD: I don't go through and analyze each chord unless I'm learning a new work. I have worked with the classical repertoire now for thirty years so that when I do a new Mozart symphony, for instance, I don't need to analyze it the way I used to. I have done so much Mozart that nearly everything I would find in a new symphony is predictable. You know, once you speak twelve languages you can speak fourteen very easily. So, if you have done 17 piano concertos by Mozart, you can easily learn 22 or 23. You learn the style and that allows you to work very fast. So far we are only talking about the technical approach. What you get out of the music is a whole different story! For this you need time to think and time to look at the score again and again. You need to flirt with it without analyzing it. Once the analysis is done it is done forever. I don't mean memorization though. When I go back to a piece I need to memorize it again.

JW: Do you have a technique for memory?

CD: Yes, analysis of the score is the key. Let me give you an example. In 1974 I met that wonderful Korean violinist, Kyung Wha Chung. She was going to perform with me in Switzerland and was very nervous because she was going to play the Violin Concerto by Alban Berg for the first time. She just couldn't memorize it. She told me, "I have never used music before in my life when I perform, but I can't seem to memorize this concerto. I just don't want to bring out my music stand for a twenty-three-minute piece." Well, I told her that I didn't think it was shameful to use the music and that I personally prefer to conduct 100 different scores with the music rather than ten without the music. I told her though, if she really wanted to memorize it I would show her how to analyze the structure and that I was sure it would help a lot. Finger memory should be controlled by the mind, especially in this piece. She worked with me for a couple of days. I happened to know the piece extremely well and had an analysis of the score with me which I showed her. We started working on the series that the concerto was built on; we looked at the way it started with the four violin open strings; the way the theme was constructed with the tritone at the end which was also the beginning of the Bach Chorale in the last movement. I told her, "In that theme you already have the material for the entire concerto including the Bach Chorale." For some reason she didn't know that. It hadn't been clear to her before. We worked from both the orchestral score and the violin part putting in numbers on the notes that corresponded to the original series. We even worked with colored pencils. We also discovered a mistake in her part that she had always played, a B flat that was wrong because it wasn't the right note in the series. She saw that every note had to make sense. Berg, though far from being dogmatic, controlled the compositional material from his intellect. There is nothing improvised about that piece! After two days of working in this way she had memorized the concerto and never used the score again. This is a perfect example of how analysis helps your memory. She had never done that type of analysis before because nobody had asked her or shown her how to do it. It's easy to memorize a Mozart concerto but when you start performing new music that uses new techniques and new forms you need to analyze it in detail to discover what is going on. After this experience Kyung started to work with the Bartók Violin Concerto in the same way.

Many people think that Stravinsky's *Rite of Spring* is difficult to memorize. Actually the *Rite* is the easiest piece in the world to conduct from memory. There are all these very simple little ABA forms or ABACA forms. The only thing that is dangerous is if you lose your concentration and do a wrong beat. You have to know the rhythmical themes and how they are constructed. If you work intelligently you should not have a problem. If you don't use an analysis technique then the *Rite of Spring* is impossible to memorize!

JW: I worked for several days just on the B section of Danse Sacral. *I finally figured out a rhythmic analysis of that part.*

CD: Well, that section isn't easy, but if you don't go through and find the secrets you will never be able to memorize it. If you try to memorize by ear the score will not deliver its secrets. It will only help you keep the beat going. But if you know how the beat is related logically to the music the form becomes completely clear. Mind you, one has to be careful in the *Rite*. Also, if you are studying that piece try to look at the original version. Many of the rhythms are different. The 1921 version was rearranged by Ernest Ansermet who was my mentor. A lot of measures were changed. Unfortunately the original score is not published. My dream would be to play the *Rite of Spring* with the original parts.

JW: Don't you have a recording with the Montreal Symphony of the original version?

CD: It's not the original 1913 version but the 1921 version. Most of my colleagues use the 1945 or 1951 version. I use the 1921 version which is not the original but is the closest I can come to it. You know that in the original most of Stravinsky's rhythms were not written 3 plus 2 but were notated in

5/4. Musically it makes more sense and it's too bad that the conductors of the time had problems beating those rhythms. They changed certain things to make it easier to conduct. They didn't change the actual rhythmic patterns (the 3 and the 2 are always in the same order) but instead of having a bar in 5 or in 7 they rewrote it in bars of 3 plus 12 plus 12 or 3 plus 12. Even Bernstein, and mind you I am not in a position to criticize him, changed a few bars to facilitate beating the rhythms.

JW: Do you ever rebar Petrouchka?

CD: Never.

JW: A lot of conductors rebar the 5/8 section at the very end of the fourth tableau [rehearsal no. 243] by putting two bars together and conducting the quarter notes in 5/4.

CD: No, that section should be conducted in one! It destroys the rhythm to conduct the quarter notes. By the way, did you know that Stravinsky even rebarred the first movement? Instead of subdividing the 5/8's he rebarred them in measures of 2 plus 3 or 3 plus 2 [rehearsal no. 20]. I do those measures all in one. The orchestras are a bit surprised the first time, because by now they are used to the new version. There is really no problem with these Stravinsky rhythms if you just forget about them and dance with the music. They need to be controlled by your brain at first but afterwards you can forget them. They are highly danceable rhythms. The problem with our western society is that we are not ready to dance in five. All of our folklore is in two, three or four. If you go to Russia or better yet to Greece or the Balkans, the mountains around Romania, you will see that all of the folk dances are in 5, 7, or 11. It is no problem for them to dance to music with 11 beats!

Most modern conductors have no real problem now with these rhythms, but it was still a big mystery thirty years ago. I saw Herbert von Karajan conduct the *Rite of Spring* for the first time when he was fifty-six years old! It was a big challenge even for him because he had grown up on Beethoven and Brahms. I've known Karajan all my life and used to play in his orchestra when I was a kid and as a student when he was teaching. I know the man pretty well. He has the most unbelievable quality of concentration. He hardly moves when he conducts! He also conducts everything by memory including all of the Wagner operas! And so after watching him conduct *Parsifal* without a score I saw Karajan walk up on the podium with the score to *Rite of Spring* and I could see that he was very nervous. Imagine, even in the early sixties there were still very few conductors conducting the *Rite.*

JW: Now everyone studies that score.

CD: Yes, and now a good orchestra can play it in two rehearsals!

JW: It's amazing don't you think?

CD: We have mastered the language because we have done a lot of twentieth-century music by now. Conductors in the nineteenth century could barely beat in five. The famous movement in 5/4 in Tchaikovsky's *Pathetique* caused a lot of problems for some conductors. Pierre Monteux and Ansermet were among the few that could handle these new problems.

JW: Did you ever talk to Monteux about his first performance of the Rite?

CD: No. I heard him talk about it but I never asked him about it because I was sure he had to answer that kind of question all of his life. I do know he got a lot of rehearsals, fifty I believe, because the orchestra just couldn't play it; nobody could play it. So by having fifty rehearsals he had time to master the piece himself. But I can picture the first time Monteux looked at the score to the *Rite*. He must have thought it looked like Chinese. Ansermet was always at ease with these new developments. He had a very natural approach to these rhythms. He was a champion of new music and performed most of these works for the first time right after Monteux in the early twenties. Ansermet also did a lot of premieres, you know. He premiered the 1918 version of *Firebird*, *L'histoire du soldat* in 1918, and *Les Noces*, which was written in 1917 but orchestrated in 1921 or 1922. He also did performances of Bartók and Hindemith. Those conductors were surrounded by great composers. They were really spoiled! When I was a kid in Geneva I used to hear a premiere nearly every week conducted by Ansermet. Each week something new was coming, something by Britten, Bartók, or Stravinsky! It was very exciting. The public was dying to hear the latest piece by Stravinsky or other people such as Arthur Honegger or Bohuslav Martinu. A tremendous amount of music was composed and heard during that period of time and unfortunately that sort of enthusiam is not happening today. Today's public is not dying to hear the latest contemporary piece! We are not as free today as we used to be. The expectation for new music is not there. Instead there is resistance. Maybe this will change. I hope so, the twentieth century has given a lot.

JW: What are your criteria in judging a twentieth-century work?

CD: There are no criteria.

JW: Which twentieth-century repertoire do you program in Montreal?

CD: I feel that it is my responsibility to perform as much new music as possible. I wish I could do more than I do. There are so many composers now and each week I receive several scores from different parts of the world. Since I am in Canada many of the scores are written in Canada. I try to choose the best, at least what I consider to be the best for performance. I also try to give performances of works that don't have my approval. My approval is not that important. So even if I don't like a score that much I will try to do it because I feel that the composer deserves a little bit of attention. He deserves to hear himself and to inform the public of his presence. This is part of my duty as a music director.

There are so many different styles now that it is nearly impossible to establish a criteria for performing new works. I've always made it a point to try to stay open to different trends and to listen to as much contemporary music as possible. I stayed open to post war serialism, though around 90 percent of that music has now disappeared! But being open to that music also gave me the opportunity to meet composers like Krzysztof Penderecki and Witold Lutoslawski. They are examples of great composers that actually made it through the compositional jungle of the twentieth century and wrote good pieces. I also remember hearing Pierre Boulez for the first time when Boulez was better known as a personality than for his music. People would talk about Boulez and his music without ever having heard any of it. That was typical of the period. Everybody had known that Boulez had written *Le marteau sans maitre.* Everyone had heard the names of his famous pieces and would even talk about them when they hadn't actually heard them! Finally I had the opportunity to hear Boulez conduct some of his works. Afterwards I performed a lot of his music because I respected him so much.

I also got involved with the Society of Contemporary Music in Montreal. Together with the Montreal Orchestra, we organized festivals around many composers, which were very successful. We invited Olivier Messiaen, Penderecki, Lutoslawski, Iannis Xenakis, and other composers to come.

The year I invited Xenakis to come for a conference we were thinking of doing a performance of *Metastaseis B* and his last piece, *Imprints.* I had heard the premiere of *Metastaseis B,* conducted by Hermann Scherchen as a kid in Geneva. Xenakis thought this was a great idea and proceded to help me organize the whole thing. Now Xenakis loves to impress people with his élan. He's really a mathematician who when describing his music writes formulas all over the blackboard. He loves to talk about things nobody understands to create a little bit of mystery around his work. I can say these things about him because he's a good friend of mine. Anyway, at the conference in the middle of a complex description of one of his works, I caught him by asking a candid question, "What kind of music would you like to have on the same program with your own music?" He was completely stuck! He finally said Brahms and I asked why and he said because he liked Brahms! Now personally I can't imagine Brahms and Xenakis on the same program, but I thought it was a very funny answer. Here was this great man in the middle of his world of abstractions having a difficult time talking about standard repertoire! We had a great time at that conference. I made a point to ask him to come down to earth and talk to us simple citizens.

Later in the evening at the concert when I saw those huge Xenakis scores on my stand, it occurred to me that I just couldn't do this to my public. I thought, "Here they come after a hard day's work and what are they going to hear? *Metastaseis B* by Xenakis." I recalled my early days in Geneva and remembered that even though I was open and was a music student I had been shocked by this music. I decided that I had to talk to my audience (which is something I normally don't do because I need to talk to them in two languages). I turned around on the stage and said, "Ladies and gentlemen, we are going to play two pieces by Xenakis, who is a very important composer of the postwar period. I have to tell you not to expect something which you are familiar with. There is no melody, there is no harmony, there is no counterpoint. You will hear nothing that you would normally associate with music. It's a different world of sound with things hanging here and there. Forget everything you know and try to be interested in it. This music expresses the stress, anxiety, and happiness of humanity in the 1980s. You don't have to like this music but please try to be open." On top of that I told them that the pieces were short and that the composer was in the audience.

The audience reaction was fantastic. They were extremely receptive, concentrated, and gave Xenakis a standing ovation. He had a tremendous success. First of all, the orchestra played extremely well and he was terribly happy with the performance. After that experience we invited Henri Dutilleux, another important contemporary composer, and did his Violin Concerto, which was written for Isaac Stern. We have done a lot of pieces by contemporary composers. We just did *Notations* by Boulez and tried to invite him to come and conduct the work but he was too busy. He would have such a great time in Montreal because the orchestra is so good at playing this type of music.

JW: There are so many different stylistic trends at the moment? Do you think we are finally finished with postwar serialism?

CD: Absolutely. It was like communism. Composers had all of these theories and idealogies that are dead now. This language has been explored, used, overused, and is finished. I don't know what the language of tomorrow is going to be.

JW: What do you think about minimalism? Do you think it is a reaction to the overly intellectual serialists?

CD: Partly, yes. I think it will come and go and right now it is the fashion. Compositional languages are like painting movements. They come and go and who knows what will be next. You see some serious composers like Lutoslawsky who will outlast the fashion trends. From the very beginning he has championed new things. He was one of the very first composers to write music with clusters and to develop new techniques for writing music. I make

79

a point to invite people like this to conduct in Montreal. I want this music played regularly so that my orchestra will be comfortable with all the new styles. Lutoslawski is a great composer. He is a major figure of our time and on top of being a musician who writes beautiful music, his technique of composition is really striking. He knows exactly what he wants and the music is perfectly written to achieve those effects.

JW: Would you choose repertoire differently in the States than you would in Canada?

CD: No.

JW: Would you program differently as a guest conductor?

CD: Of course. When I guest conduct here in the States I always deal with the music director. In Europe it is different. If you are in London they will want you to program traditional programs because they are so preoccupied by the box office sales. I don't even try to do something unusual. Usually they will ask for something they know me by through the recordings I have done in Montreal. In Montreal I have personally conducted 900 scores in ten years. We've done nearly everything: all the Beethoven, Brahms, Bruckner, and Mahler symphonies as well as the French repertoire. We have a huge repertoire. When I go to Berlin though, they will never ask me for Beethoven or Brahms. They have many people who do that. They will ask me for Berlioz, Bartók, or Hindemith.

JW: I have never heard a better [Berlioz] Symphonie fantastique *than when I heard you do it here with the Montreal Symphony.*

CD: Well, you know, it was actually a rehearsal. We were in the first week of our tour and had played three programs in a row. In each city we were playing pieces for the first time. The program with *Symphonie fantastique* was played first here in Minneapolis. Afterwards we went to Chicago and New York where we were better rehearsed. Before the tour I had been gone for two-and-a-half months and had come back for only one week to rehearse the orchestra. I had very little time for the Berlioz. Even the soloist was playing here for the first time. But the orchestra is good and we play that kind of music well. We have nice winds, no?

•••••

JW: Do you have a technique for achieving a good balance in new halls?

CD: Well, we are a little bit old fashioned in this way. We have a very understanding general manager, Zarin Mehta [Zubin's brother], who is a great musician though he doesn't read a note. He will always help me in

80

arranging an acoustical rehearsal in new halls for fifteen minutes before concerts. I consider myself spoiled in this respect because many major orchestras in this country have contracts that don't allow for that! For instance, I heard the Boston Symphony at the Concertgebouw. The Boston Symphony Orchestra, one of my favorite orchestras, was struggling with the acoustics of the hall! They were performing the Mahler Ninth. The Concertgebouw hall has a rich and creamy sound and the musicians were struggling to hear each other. Now of course this struggle was at a very high professional level and most of the audience wouldn't have been able to tell. But nevertheless, they were struggling and I think it is wrong that orchestras of that quality should have to deal with that sort of thing. They should be allowed a little rehearsal in the hall in which they will be performing! It's really counterproductive not to allow that. This type of situation is basically the fault of the music unions in the States. Unfortunately, they don't seem to care about artistic issues anymore.

When I balance my own orchestra in new halls I make sure that my orchestra is never noisy. We can be very powerful but I make sure that the sound is always rich. I sometimes feel that in certain bright halls our brass can be overwhelming. They are aware of it and I cannot change that very much. For instance Avery Fisher Hall in Lincoln Center is very difficult because it's very bright. If the brass and percussion start to overplay the sound is immediately very vulgar. But we have been in so many halls and since I personally know most of the halls in the world today, I usually know in advance what to say and what to ask for. For instance, I might say, "Let's be careful here and let's try to give as much warmth as we can because this hall is dull." Or sometimes during the concert I'll ask the orchestra to sustain the notes longer if the hall is too dry.

When I guest conduct other orchestras I have to get used to their particular sound and particular hall. When I am in Avery Fisher Hall with the New York Philharmonic for example, I always tell them that I know the hall isn't very good and that we will try and cope with the difficulties. One has to rebalance the orchestra there. When I guest conduct the Concertgebouw in Amsterdam it takes me awhile to get used to their rich sound. The Concertgebouw has 100 years of experience with their rich sound, heavy repertoire, and rich, warm hall. I had very interesting experiences when I toured with them because of this. They are used to their rich and warm hall which influences their own sound so much. Their sound is an actual osmosis between them and their hall. When we played in other cities they would immediately try to recreate their sound and of course that's not possible if the acoustics won't support it. You have to adapt to the new environment which changes the sound of the orchestra.

My theory is that all great orchestras belong to their halls. The sound of the Concertgebouw is the sound of their hall and of their orchestra. It is the same with the Vienna Philharmonic, Boston Symphony, New York Philharmonic, and Philadelphia Orchestra. Philadelphia was educated in a certain environment and their sound was the combination of their hall, their conductor, and their repertoire. It was the same thing for Chicago and Cleveland. When I hear the tremendous Cleveland orchestra, I hear the tremendous schooling they had under Szell and Maazel. Their hall supports that training. New York's sound was built in Carnegie Hall. One tends to forget that because they have been playing for twenty-five years in Lincoln Center. But New York developed their sound in Carnegie Hall under Mahler and Toscanini and Carnegie Hall was the best hall in America at the time.

Biography

Charles Dutoit was appointed music director or the Orchestre Symphonique de Montreal in 1977. Under an exclusive long-term contract with London/Decca since 1980, Mr. Dutoit and the OSM have produced over thirty recordings, winning a total of twenty international awards such as the Grand Prix de President de la Republique (France), the Prix mondial du disque de Montreux, the High Fidelity International Record Critics' Award, the Amsterdam Edison Award, and the Japan Record Academy Award. Charles Dutoit's numerous other recordings have been produced on the Deutsche Grammaphon, Philips, CBS, and Erato labels.

Born in Lausanne, Switzerland, on October 7, 1936, Charles Dutoit received formal musical training in violin, viola, piano, percussion, composition, and conducting at the Lausanne and Geneva conservatories. After winning First Prize in the conducting class at the Geneva Conservatory, he continued conducting studies with Alceo Galliera at the Academie Musical Chigiana and with Charles Munch at the Berkshire Music Center in Tanglewood. In 1964, Mr. Dutoit was invited by Karajan to make a debut with the Vienna State Opera. This led to a debut at London's Festival Hall and the beginning of a collaboration with the Royal Philharmonic Orchestra, the London Synphony, the London Philharmonic, and the Philharmonia. Charles Dutoit was named music director of the Bern Symphony in 1966, a post he held until 1978. He has also held the positions of music director of Goteborg Symphony and the National Symphony Orchestra of Mexico.

In addition to his schedule in Montreal, Charles Dutoit conducts many of the world's major orchestras, including the Boston Symphony, the New York Philharmonic, the Phildelphia Orchestra, the Cleveland Orchestra, the Chicago Symphony Orchestra, the Israel Philharmonic, the Berlin Philharmonic, and the Amsterdam Concertgebouw. He has also been named artistic director and principal conductor of two summer festivals: the

Phildelphia Orchestra's concert series at the Mann Music Center in Phildelphia, and at the Saratoga Performing Arts Center in Saratoga Springs.

Charles Dutoit holds honorary doctorates from both the Université de Montreal and the Université de Lavai. In 1982, he was named "Musician of the Year" by the Canadian Music Council. In 1988, the same organization awarded Mr. Dutoit the Canadian Music Council Medal in recognition of his contribution in Canada.

Charles Dutoit Discography

Composer	Work	Orchestra	Soloists	Label	CD	LP	MC
Bartók	Concerto for orchestra	Montreal Symphony		London	421 443-2		421 443-4
Bartók	Music for strings, percussion, and celesta	Montreal Symphony		London	421 443-2		421 443-4
Berlioz	Grande symphonie funèbre et triomphale	Montreal Symphony		London			
Berlioz	Harold in Italy	Montreal Symphony		London			
Berlioz	Rob Roy Overture	Montreal Symphony		London			
Berlioz	Romeo et Juliette	Montreal Symphony		London	417 302-2		
Berlioz	Symphonie Fantastique	Montreal Symphony		London	414 203-2		
Bizet	Carmen Suite no. 1	Montreal Symphony		London	417 839-2		417 839-4
Bizet	Carmen Suite no. 2	Montreal Symphony		London	417 839-2		417 839-4
Bizet	Jeux d'enfants	Montreal Symphony		London	421 527-2		
Bizet	L'Arlésienne, suite no. 1	Montreal Symphony		London	417 839-2		417 839-4
Bizet	L'Arlésienne, suite no. 2	Montreal Symphony		London	417 839-2		417 839-4
Chabrier	España	Montreal Symphony		London	421 527-2		
Chabrier	Joyeuse Marche	Montreal Symphony		London	421 527-2		
Chaminade	Flute concertino	Royal Philharmonic	Galway	RCA	AGL1-5448		AGL1-5448
Chausson	Poème for violin	Royal Philharmonic	Chung	London	417 118-2		
Chopin	Piano concerto no. 1	Montreal Symphony	Bolet	London	425 859-2		425 859-4
Chopin	Piano concerto no. 2	Montreal Symphony	Bolet	London	425 859-2		425 859-4
Debussy	Images	Montreal Symphony		London			
Debussy	La mer	Montreal Symphony		London			
Debussy	Le martyre de St-Sebastien	Montreal Symphony		London			
Debussy	Nocturnes	Montreal Symphony		London			
Debussy	Prélude à l'après-midi d'une faune	Gothenburg Symphony		Bis		LP-301/3	
Debussy	Prélude à l'après-midi d'une faune	Montreal Symphony		London			

Composer	Work	Ensemble	Soloist / Conductor	Label			
d'Indy	Symphonie sur un chant montagnard français in G	Philharmonia	Entremont	CBS		MT-37269	
d'Indy	Symphonie sur un chant montagnard français in G	Montreal Symphony		London			
Dukas	Sorcerer's Apprentice	Montreal Symphony		London	421 527-2		
Elgar	Enigma Variations	Montreal Symphony		London			
Elgar	Falstaff	Montreal Symphony		London			
Falla	El amor brujo	Montreal Symphony	Tourangeau	London	410 008-2		
Falla	Three-cornered Hat	Montreal Symphony	Boky	London	410 008-2		
Falla	Three-Cornered Hat three dance	Montreal Symphony		London	417 748-2		
Fauré	Flute fantaisie	Royal Philharmonic	Galway	RCA	AGL1-5448		AGL1-5448
Fauré	Pavane	Montreal Symphony		London	421 440-2		421 440-4
Fauré	Pelléas et Mélisande	Montreal Symphony		London	421 440-2		421 440-4
Fauré	Piano Ballade	Philharmonia	Entremont	CBS		MT-37269	
Fauré	Requiem	Montreal Symphony	Te Kanawa, Milnes	London	421 440-2		421 440-4
Franck	Symphonic Variations	Philharmonia	Entremont	CBS		MT-37269	
Franck	Symphony	Montreal Symphony		London			
Franck	Variations for piano	Philharmonia	Entremont	Odyssey			YT-39778
Gershwin	An American in Paris	Montreal Symphony		London			
Gershwin	Cuban Overture	Montreal Symphony		London			
Gershwin	Porgy and Bess: Symphonic Picture	Montreal Symphony		London			
Gershwin	Rhapsody in Blue	Montreal Symphony	Lortie	London	411 708-2		
Gounod	Faust, ballet music	Montreal Symphony		London	417 553-2	417 553-1	
Holst	The Planets	Montreal Symphony		London	417 553-2		416 553-4
Honegger	Mouvement symphonique 3	Bavarian Radio Symphony		Erato	ECD-88171		
Honegger	Pacific 231	Bavarian Radio Symphony		Erato	ECD-88171		

Composer	Work	Orchestra	Soloists	Label	CD	LP	MC
Honegger	Pastorale d'été	Bavarian Radio Symphony		Erato	ECD-88171		
Honegger	Rugby	Bavarian Radio Symphony		Erato	ECD-88171		
Honegger	Symphony no. 1	Bavarian Radio Symphony		Erato	ECD-88171		
Honegger	Symphony no. 2	Bavarian Radio Symphony		Erato	ECD-88178		
Honegger	Symphony no. 3	Bavarian Radio Symphony		Erato	ECD-88045		
Honegger	Symphony no. 4	Bavarian Radio Symphony		Erato	ECD-88178		
Honegger	Symphony no. 5	Bavarian Radio Symphony		Erato	ECD-88045		
Ibert	Divertissement	Montreal Symphony		London	421 527-2		
Ibert	Flute concerto	Royal Philharmonic	Galway	RCA	AGL1-5448		AGL1-5448
Lalo	Cello concerto in D	Philharmonia	Lodéon	Erato	ECD-55042		
Lalo	Symphonie espagnole for violin	Montreal Symphony	Bell	London	411 952-2		
Lalo	Symphonie espagnole for violin	Montreal Symphony	Chung	London			
Mendelssohn	Fair Melusine Overture	Montreal Symphony		London	417 541-2		417 541-4
Mendelssohn	Hebrides Overture	Montreal Symphony		London	417 541-2		417 541-4
Mendelssohn	Midsummer Night's Dream, incidental music	Montreal Symphony		London	417 541-2		417 541-4
Mendelssohn	Piano concerto no. 1	Bavarian Radio Symphony	Schiff	London	414 672-2		
Mendelssohn	Piano concerto no. 2	Bavarian Radio Symphony	Schiff	London	414 672-2		
Mendelssohn	Ruy Blas Overture	Montreal Symphony		London	417 541-2		417 541-4
Mendelssohn	Violin concerto	Montreal Symphony	Chung	London	410 011-2		

Composer	Work	Orchestra	Soloists	Label	CD	LP	MC
Mussorgsky	Pictures at an Exhibition	Montreal Symphony		London	417 299-2	417 299-1	417 299-4
Offenbach	Gaité parisienne	Montreal Symphony		London			
Paganini	Le Streghe, Variations	London Philharmonic	Accardo	DGG	413 848-4	413 848-4	
Paganini	Violin concerto no. 1	London Philharmonic	Accardo	DGG	415 378-2	413 848-4	
Paganini	Violin concerto no. 2	London Philharmonic	Accardo	DGG	415 378-2		
Paganini	Violin concerto no. 3	London Philharmonic	Accardo	DGG	423 370-2		
Paganini	Violin concerto no. 4	London Philharmonic	Accardo	DGG	423 370-2	419 482-4	
Poulenc	Flute sonata	Royal Philharmonic	Galway	RCA	AGL1-5448		AGL1-5448
Prokofiev	Symphony no. 1	Montreal Symphony		London	421 813-2	421 813-4	
Prokofiev	Symphony no. 5	Montreal Symphony		London	421 813-2	421 813-4	
Rachmaninoff	Piano concerto no. 2	Montreal Symphony	Bolet	London	421 181-2	421 181-4	
Ravel	Alborada del gracioso	Montreal Symphony		London	410 010-2	410 010-4	
Ravel	Boléro	Montreal Symphony		London	410 010-2	410 010-4	
Ravel	Boléro	Montreal Symphony		London	414 406-2		
Ravel	Daphnis et Chloë	Montreal Symphony		London	400 055-2		
Ravel	Daphnis et Chloë Suite no. 2	Montreal Symphony		London	414 406-2		
Ravel	La Valse	Montreal Symphony		London	414 406-2		
Ravel	La Valse	Montreal Symphony		London	410 010-2		410 010-4
Ravel	Le tombeau de Couperin	Montreal Symphony		London	410 254-2		
Ravel	Ma mère l'oye	Montreal Symphony		London	410 254-2		
Ravel	Pavane pour une infante défunte	Montreal Symphony					
Ravel	Pavane pour une infante défunte	Montreal Symphony	Rogé	London	414 406-2		
Ravel	Piano concerto in D for the left hand	Montreal Symphony		London	410 230-2		
Ravel	Piano concerto in G	Montreal Symphony	Rogé	London	410 230-2		
Ravel	Rapsodie espagnole	Montreal Symphony		London	410 010-2	410 010-4	410 010-4
Ravel	Tzigane	Royal Philharmonic	Chung	London	417 118-2		
Ravel	Valses nobles et sentimentales	Montreal Symphony		London	410 254-2		
Resenberg	Symphony no. 6	Gothenburg Symphony		Bis		LP-301/3	

Composer	Work	Orchestra	Soloists	Label	CD	LP	MC
Respighi	Feste Romane	Montreal Symphony		London	410 145-2		
Respighi	Fountains of Rome	Montreal Symphony		London	410 145-2		
Respighi	Pines of Rome	Montreal Symphony		London	410 145-2		
Rimsky-Korsakov	Capriccio espagnole	Montreal Symphony		London	410 253-2		410 253-4
Rimsky-Korsakov	Scheherazade	Montreal Symphony		London	410 253-2		410 253-4
Rodrigo	Concerto de Aranjuez for guitar	Montreal Symphony	Bonell	London	400 054-2		
Rodrigo	Concerto de Aranjuez for guitar	Montreal Symphony	Bonell	London	417 748-2		
Rodrigo	Fantasia para un gentilhombre	Montreal Symphony	Bonell	London	417 748-2		
Roussel	Bacchus et Ariadne	Orchestre de Paris		Erato	ECD-75348		MCE-75348
Roussel	Suite in F	Orchestre de Paris		Erato	ECD-75348		MCE-75348
Roussel	Symphony no. 1	Orchestre National de France		Erato	ECD-88225		
Roussel	Symphony no. 2	Orchestre National de France		Erato	ECD-88226	NUM-75284	MCE-75284
Roussel	Symphony no. 3	Orchestre National de France		Erato	ECD-88225		
Roussel	Symphony no. 4	Orchestre National de France		Erato	ECD-88226	NUM-75284	MCE-75284
Saint-Saëns	Carnival of the Animals	London Sinfonietta	Rogé, Ortiz	London	414 460-2		414 460-4
Saint-Saëns	Danse macabre	Philharmonia		London	414 460-2		414 460-4
Saint-Saëns	Havanaise for violin	Royal Philharmonic	Chung	London	417 707-2		
Saint-Saëns	Introduction and rondo capriccioso	Royal Philharmonic	Chung	London	417 118-2		
Saint-Saëns	Le rouet d'omphale	Philharmonia		London	414 460-2		
Saint-Saëns	Phaéton	Philharmonia		London	414 460-2		
Saint-Saëns	Piano concerto no. 1	Royal Philharmonic	Rogé	London	417 351-2		
Saint-Saëns	Piano concerto no. 2	Royal Philharmonic	Rogé	London	417 351-2		
Saint-Saëns	Piano concerto no. 3	Royal Philharmonic	Rogé	London	417 351-2		

Composer	Work	Orchestra	Soloists	Label	CD	LP	MC
Saint-Saëns	Piano concerto no. 4	Royal Philharmonic	Rogé	London	417 351-2		
Saint-Saëns	Piano concerto no. 5	Royal Philharmonic	Rogé	London	417 351-2		
Saint-Saëns	Samson et Dalila, Bacchanale	Montreal Symphony		London	421 527-2		
Saint-Saëns	Symphony no. 3	Montreal Symphony	Hurford	London	410 201-2		
Saint-Saëns	Violin concerto no. 1	Montreal Symphony	Bell	London	411 952-2		
Saint-Saëns	Violin concerto no. 1	Montreal Symphony	Chung	London			
Saint-Saëns	Violin concerto no. 3	Montreal Symphony	Bell	London			
Satie	Trois Gymnopédies	Montreal Symphony		London	421 527-2		
Stenhammer	Piano concerto no. 1	Gothenburg Symphony	Mannheimer	Sterling	1004		
Stenhammer	Late Summer Nights	Gothenburg Symphony	Mannheimer	Sterling	1004		
Stravinsky	Firebird	Montreal Symphony		London	414 409-2		414 409-4
Stravinsky	Fireworks	Montreal Symphony		London	414 409-2		414 409-4
Stravinsky	Le sacre du printemps	Montreal Symphony		London	414 202-2		
Stravinsky	Petrouchka	Montreal Symphony		London	417 619-2	417 619-1	417 619-4
Stravinsky	Scherzo fantastique	Montreal Symphony		London	414 409-2		414 409-4
Stravinsky	Song of the Nightingale	Montreal Symphony		London	417 619-2	417 619-1	417 619-4
Stravinsky	Symphony in C	Suisse Romande		London	414 272-2		
Stravinsky	Symphony in three movements	Suisse Romande		London	414 272-2		
Stravinsky	Symphony of wind instruments	Montreal Symphony		London	414 202-2		
Suppé	Overtures (7)	Montreal Symphony		London	414 408-2		
Tchaikovsky	1812 Overture	Montreal Symphony		London			
Tchaikovsky	Capriccio italien	Montreal Symphony		London			
Tchaikovsky	Hamlet	Montreal Symphony		London			
Tchaikovsky	Nutcracker, suite no. 1	Montreal Symphony		London			
Tchaikovsky	Piano concerto no. 1	Montreal Symphony	Bolet	London	421 181-2		421 181-4
Tchaikovsky	Piano concerto no. 1	Philharmonia	Devoyon	RCA	60010-2-RG		60010-4-RG
Tchaikovsky	Piano concerto no. 1	Royal Philharmonic	Argerich	DGG	415 062-2		413 161-4
Tchaikovsky	Slavonic March	Montreal Symphony		London			
Tchaikovsky	Symphony no. 4	Montreal Symphony		London			
Tchaikovsky	Symphony no. 5	Montreal Symphony		London			

Composer	Work	Orchestra	Soloists	Label	CD	LP	MC
Tchaikovsky	Violin concerto	Montreal Symphony	Chung	London	410 011-2		
Thomas	Raymond Overture	Montreal Symphony		London	421 527-2		

"I feel that a Beethoven symphony is as important to us today as it was for Beethoven's contemporaries. I'm afraid that if you put his symphonies in too much of a historical costume, you will put them out of context for today's listeners. I'm afraid it will become a little bit like going through a museum. 'Now you enter the eighteenth-century room!' Beethoven shouldn't only be heard in this historical context. What he has to say is so transcendental. He addresses the deep questions of humanity in the most basic way. His problems are still our problems! His music affects audiences in Tokyo in much the same way as it does in Moscow or in the States. I'm afraid that if you put him into a wig, the audience won't be able to hear the transcendence of his work."

_____ Gunther Herbig

Gunther Herbig

JW: What are the main differences between European orchestras and American orchestras?

GH: You certainly expect me to talk about the different musical aspects, but I think the main difference is the economic structure upon which an orchestra is financed. You know that in Europe (with the exception of England) orchestras, opera companies, and ballet companies are almost completely subsidized by the government. In the United States government funding hardly exists at all! In the States the budget of an orchestra is made up from box office, private, and corporate sponsorship. A very small percentage of the funds come from government sources. That means that the emphasis in the States is much more on earning the money to support your orchestra. In Europe you don't have to worry about that as much because the support is already a given! You know that the government will subsidize your orchestra the following year so you don't need to worry about it. Why is this so important? It means that in the United States you have to attract people to your concerts. With the exception of places like New York, Boston, Chicago, or San Francisco, most North American orchestras are in places where the musical culture has not penetrated society in the same way as in central Europe. This means that you have to make an enormous additional effort to attract people to your concerts; this limits the possibilities and the freedom you have in programming. You have to program works that attract an audience. For example, if you program a lesser-known Prokofiev piano concerto such as the Second Concerto, you will have to balance it with a Tchaikovsky symphony to attract enough people. If you program the Prokofiev Concerto with another contemporary composer (you see Prokofiev is still considered contemporary!) you would find you couldn't attract enough audience; there would be a lot of empty seats. Last week we programmed an early Haydn symphony, the Schubert Mass no. 5, and the Berg Violin Concerto. The Haydn and the Schubert had never been performed in this city before! You would think this would be a very interesting program for the audience with familiar composers. Well, our ticket sales were down!

JW: I'm surprised that Detroit is that conservative.

GH: It is very conservative in that sense. So you understand that the economic situation here determines how you program. The programs you design are less interesting and less adventurous than those you would do in Europe. In Europe the box office is not of the same importance and yet at the same time you have an audience that is musically, relatively speaking, highly sophisticated (varying of course from city to city). So you see the whole artistic life of an orchestra is finally decided by this initial and fundamental question. "What is the financial base?" If you depend heavily on the box office you also have to give as many concerts as possible with many different programs. This limits the rehearsal time. In the States you usually get four two-and-a-half-hour rehearsals. In Europe you get five, six, or more three-hour rehearsals! Again the limited rehearsal time affects your programming choices. It is not easy to perform an unknown difficult contemporary work in this country. So, all of these things make the orchestral life and the artistic product of a European orchestra and an average American orchestra very different.

JW: Did you find that you were able to achieve much better artistic results in Europe than in the States?

GH: Yes, certainly in the long-term building of an orchestra and an audience, because of the greater artistic freedom of programming. In each simple concert it's a toss up, depending on the orchestras' quality and the actual circumstances.

JW: Why did you come here? What was your motivation?

GH: Well, there is another aspect. The financial security that European orchestras enjoy does not propel the orchestras to always be at the absolute limits of their capacities. In the States you have musicians of fantastic musical quality. They are the highest professionals; they have been forced to be that good; and to achieve high results in a very short time. Each musician knows that he or she has to produce at the top level of their ability every moment and this produces excellent musical results. In Europe the tension to produce excellence is not as great. If one concert is not as good as it should have been you know that your budget won't be withdrawn! England is more like the States because the English government also does not subsidize the orchestras. The musicians there mainly make their income from their recordings, the film industry, and from the box office. There is very little rehearsal time with English orchestras!

Let us assume that two orchestras, one European and one American, are about the same quality. The American orchestra would start on a higher level in the first rehearsal than a European one. However, most American orchestras tend to have the feeling that technical perfection is the important goal. They might not see that you have to go beyond the notes to express the deeper meaning of the music. On the other hand, European orchestras would start rehearsing at a lower level and the rehearsal process might be more cumbersome but they tend to see the musical goals as more important than just the technical perfection of the notes. So, it's a toss-up. Sometimes, you get the same end results from different approaches.

•••••

JW: What is your approach to score study?

GH: I must admit that my way of studying scores through the years has become more and more simple and primitive. It has now reached the point where I read through each instrumental line horizontally. I start reading the double basses for a length of perhaps 32 measures. I read it just as a musical line, as a musician would read his part. Then I go to the cellos; I see what they are doing with the double basses; I read everything, every dot on the notes, every little accent as if I am playing the line very slowly. I go through the entire score in this manner. So you see this is very simplistic and primitive, but I am learning the work the way the orchestra learns the work. I see immediately what a player is confronted with and where the traps are. I read it trying to think how I would play it. I immediately start thinking about what kind of bowings I have to put in, what kind of phrasing should I try. It's an incredibly simple process, but it's a process that guarantees that not a detail has escaped my eyes.

JW: Do you study at the piano? Do you play through the individual lines?

GH: No, I haven't touched a piano for years. I am married to a pianist but I personally don't even have a piano in my room where I study.

JW: What other instruments do you play?

GH: As a child I studied cello, flute, and piano. Later as part of my training as a conductor in Germany I studied many different instruments. I had two years on each instrument of the orchestral family. I played horn for two years, I played percussion and violin and even had one year of singing lessons. This is very helpful for a German conductor because opera is one of the main paths into the conducting profession in Germany. So, it is very good if you have at least a basic idea of when singers need to take breaths.

Well, back to score study. So, slowly in this rather painstaking manner, I begin to see the whole picture. I see which instrument or instruments have the important lines; I see the technical problems; then the whole harmonic structure begins to come out and I get a feeling for where the musical

95

phrases are; whether they are in two plus three measures or four plus four measures. I see how the microcells connect to the whole organism.

JW: That's a very interesting approach. Many conductors analyze a score beginning with the macro to the micro instead of the reverse process which you just described.

GH: Yes, starting with the macro has the advantage of being much quicker. My method is very simple but very time consuming. I feel though, if I look at the totality first I easily might overlook the details. You have to be honest with your self. Now this method won't work all the time for someone who needs to learn repertoire rapidly or who conducts forty-eight to fifty weeks a year with 80 to 100 works to learn like I do. I have to make compromises. For instance, tonight I am conducting the Prokofiev Second Piano Concerto. I didn't take the time to approach it in this detailed manner as I would have done with the Ninth Symphony of Mahler. With enough experience you learn to "learn" scores rapidly. You have to ask yourself, "Where can I save time? Where can I cut corners and where don't I dare cut them?" So I have to choose when to be meticulous and thorough and when to take the short cuts.

JW: How many of the 80 to 100 works you conduct a year are new works? How many are you doing for the first time?

GH: At my age there are many, many repeats. There are pieces I have conducted 150-160 times, such as the Brahms symphonies. When you have conducted a work that often things go quicker. You still have a lot of details in your mind and a simple glance lights up the memory. On the other hand if I haven't conducted a work for six or seven years I might find that I do have to start very much from the beginning again. For instance, tonight I am conducting the Tchaikovsky Sixth Symphony. A conductor of my age should know that piece very well; however, I haven't conducted it for a few years and it took me around fourteen hours to prepare it again. When I first learned the work I learned it in tremendous detail. Look at my score; I have written everything in. Here are all the harmonies, all the phrasings, the rhythmic and motivic analysis, interpretation considerations and details of bowing. Here, for example [1. Movement, letter A], Tchaikovsky wants all the first violins *divisi.* Instead I made the decision to let all of the first violins play in unison; I give the *divisi* to the second violins; this way you get more of a crescendo here. I don't regard this as altering the score because I haven't done anything to change the instrumental color. I have only increased the crescendos and climaxes. When you have worked on a score in such detail, you can "relearn" it relatively quickly. I always use the same score to study with. It would take hours to copy these details into another score!

Now if I were learning a Mahler symphony from scratch I would begin at least one year before the performance. I would study that score as much as possible during that year whenever the daily pressure was not too great. I would look at the atmosphere surrounding the piece. I would find out when it was written and what Mahler's personal situation was at the time; I would find out what else was being written in Europe and in general would want to know the whole artistic, intellectual, and political environment of the piece. The historical component is a very important aspect of learning scores by people like Bruckner or Mahler. Then I would slowly start to read my way through the score. I would go through every harmony, every detail line by line.

When I can read the technical aspects of the score very fluently the next most important moment comes. "What does the music want to say? What does it want to express? What is the message of this or that bar, phrase, or scale?" This is the most interesting part. This is the process in which individualism comes in. You cannot know exactly what the composer actually meant in a certain phrase; you can only make a knowledgeable guess. You can only say, "I felt that he wanted to say this or that." Your interpretive decisions have immediate repercussions on other details. If you decide, for instance, that a chord should be played *sforzato*, you need to decide what type of *sforzato* you need. There are at least a dozen different ways to execute a particular one. It can be played with a hard blow, it can be played with a soft attack with expressively warm pressure from the bow; it can be very short with a sudden drop; it can be long and singing, diminishing slowly. We know that the composer wanted a certain type of *sforzato* and we have to make an intelligent decision on which one. We then have to determine what we think this *sforzato* chord expresses. What is the context of the chord? "If it is a D major chord at the end of a march in D major should it be played differently than if it is a diminished seventh chord in the middle of a development section?" We need to consider all of these things before we make a decision. So you have to find out, first of all, what you think is the meaning of the piece. You then start from the skeleton and try to find out parameter by parameter the meaning of the work as a whole. You need to have a very vivid imagination. You should decide what the piece means, imagine the sound, and then from your professional experience work to achieve this vision. You should ask yourself questions like, "Should the strings play at the frog or the tip, should they play up bow or down bow." This is the creative aspect of the conductor's work. When you come into the first rehearsal you will know what to ask for because, first of all you know the score, second of all you have decided what it should express, and because of your training and experience you will know how to ask for it.

•••••

JW: Do you prepare your conducting gestures?

GH: I don't prepare the gestures; I don't think about gestures. What I try for is to have the music and my interpretation of the music vividly clear in my imagination. If my mind is clear then I hope that my gestures will convey what I try to express. Some conductors have the advantage of being very gifted in this way. Every gesture they make conveys completely what they want. They need less rehearsal time with the orchestra because they are able to show every nuance of their interpretation. Others can't do this as well but it is important to realize that this has nothing to do with the quality of the conductor. There were great conductors in the past and today that are relatively unimaginative in their gestures yet are able to give great performances of the music. Karajan, for instance, conducts in more or less a straight 4/4 or 3/4 meter. There isn't much variety and yet he is very able by other means, to convey his image of the work to the orchestra.

I also think it's important to modify your gestures to the needs of the orchestra. What I mean is that if the orchestra plays a piece for the first time they may need some extra gestural help from the conductor! If there are changing meters and difficult rhythmic structures, a clear beat becomes important for the quality of the performance. If you have a piece the orchestra knows inside and out your gestures can concentrate on conveying the psychological waves, the up and downs of what the music has to say. Instead of having to beat time (though within any work there are measures where you have to be very clear) you can mold the shape of the phrases. You have to know when the orchestra needs a very clear beat and when the gesture has to step back a little.

•••••

JW: What is your opinion about the musicological research on performance practices?

GH: I think all of this research is very valuable. It adds an additional dimension to the works we know so well. I'm sure that this influence will permeate and penetrate the style of performing these works in a very broad way. However, performances on original instruments would be extremely unpractical in a modern symphony's normal subscription concert week, primarily because of the financial restraints we have discussed. An average subscription concert might start with a contemporary work followed by a Tchaikovsky piano concerto and end with a Beethoven symphony. Where would the rehearsal time come from to prepare performances with old instruments? Those type of performances are for specialized groups to do. I find these performances very interesting, especially the importance of the articulation, but I'm a little bit hesitant to completely endorse performances like this because it puts the whole work into a historical category. I feel that a Beethoven symphony is as important to us today as it was for Beethoven's contemporaries. I'm afraid that if you put his symphonies in too much of a historical costume, you will put them out of context for today's listeners. I'm afraid it will become a little bit like going through a museum. "Now you enter the eighteenth-century room!" Beethoven shouldn't only be heard in this historical context. What he has to say is so transcendental. He addresses the deep questions of humanity in the most basic way. His problems are still our problems! His music affects audiences in Tokyo in much the same way as it does in Moscow or in the States. I'm afraid that if you put him into a wig, the audience won't be able to hear the transcendence of his work.

JW: What about Beethoven's original metronome markings? What is your opinion about them? Also, what is your attitude about retouching the symphonies?

GH: Well, we try to acknowledge every note, dot, and accent in Beethoven's music. We try not to change anything. I don't retouch the symphonies the way Weingartner recommends in his book *[The Beethoven Symphonies]*. I do quadruple the woodwinds in symphonies three, five, seven, and nine. I use, in some works, two extra horns just to balance today's larger string sections which are necessary for our larger halls. We must not forget that the *Eroica* was first performed in Vienna in a palace that had only about 140 seats. Now we perform this work in a hall with 3000 seats. We have to admit that a certain augmentation has taken place. In my judgment you need to also augment the woodwinds to compensate for the larger number of strings. If you reduce the orchestra to its original size you should go back to the original size of the halls which is impossible to do today because of economic reasons and our broad democratic musical life. The proper interpretation of Beethoven's metronome markings is a little more controversial. We know they are by Beethoven; we know that he sat at the piano and dictated the metronome markings to his nephew; we know that he started doing this about the time of his Eighth Symphony and that he went back and remarked his other works. There is a story though about a British conductor who asked Beethoven for his metronome markings. Beethoven sent him a letter with different markings than he had published in his scores! I have never seen this letter but there is that story going around. Another consideration that we must make is that Beethoven only marked the beginning of movements. We know from descriptions of how he played and conducted that he didn't think in the same strict way in which we do today. There was more flexibility in tempos throughout one movement. He was relatively free in this way, at least as Czerny described the performances. He didn't have the same attitude toward "classical" that we have today. Today we try to force the second theme into the same tempo of the first theme. Beethoven took much more liberty. For example, I'm absolutely certain that in the adagio of the Ninth Symphony Beethoven didn't think the tempo was the same throughout that movement. How can the tempo be the same when the music goes first in half notes, then in eighth notes, then in six, then suddenly in triplets. No, Beethoven took more liberty. But we are educated to think, "Well, he marked the beginning and this must hold for the entire movement except when he makes special marks for the second subject." I don't think his markings are as strict as people say they are. If you relax some of his tempo markings they begin to make sense again. However, if you use the same tempos for the variations that you do at the beginning of the movement the music makes no sense to me at all. Now some of his markings are very easy to achieve. But some are simply beyond what is technically possible. For instance at the beginning of the last movement of the Ninth he writes a recitation for celli and the double basses. He uses, strangely enough, the French word *mais*, but in tempo. Musically the metronome mark makes no sense at all. Some of his marked prestos are not technically possible even for todays musicians; think how much more difficult they would have been for the musicians of that time. So, it's a difficult question because on the one hand they are his metronome marks and on the other hand you cannot do something which destroys the logic of the music or goes beyond the technical abilities of your players. I think it's more important to ask what the message of a passage is. The message is lost many times because of all these historical considerations. But nevertheless, the research on ornamentation, articulations, and use of the bow is extremely valuable and make us rethink our approach. Also, we have to remember that we hear music today with the ears that heard Wagner, Bruckner, and Mahler. For us an adagio is certainly different than an adagio in the eighteenth century. Bruckner and Mahler's adagios are endless and wide and have stretched our sense of tempo. This of course influences how we hear a Beethoven adagio. We might find an eighteenth-century adagio quick and superficial if we give it the tempo which was regarded as an adagio then. I'm also sure that many fast movements in the baroque age were not played as quickly as we play them now. I think we have a different feeling of speed today. Our transportation is by car and plane instead of by foot and on horseback. That must certainly change our concept of speed! The same is certainly true about noise level. What was noisy for Mozart's contemporaries would not be loud for us today. We are used to today's traffic and today's amplified music. We have a different feeling of what is soft and what is loud. In performing for our audiences you need to take into consideration the environment in which they live. Another interesting question is to ask why Haydn wrote 106 symphonies. It was because people at that time didn't want to hear the same piece a second time; whenever Haydn's prince held the next festivity he would expect a new symphony or a new opera.

100

JW: I guess the music business then was like the film industry today.

GH: Yes, exactly. They wouldn't want to go hear the works they knew already!

Of course, that attitude has changed dramatically. Our audience comes in and knows what they want to hear. They want to hear mainly the pieces that they know.

JW: Why did this attitude about classical music change? Why doesn't a modern audience want to hear new works?

GH: Well, it's a process that I think is relatively easy to understand. Let's say around 1800, the composer still expressed the basic feeling of his society. People who listened to that music could immediately understand what the composer was saying; they could follow him emotionally and they understood and by understanding the music they enjoyed the music. During the nineteenth and twentieth century composers have become much more individualistic. Each one is speaking in his own individual language, which is not always easily understood by the masses. If you look at the operas of Mozart's time you will find they are about things that everybody could identify with. They are about love, betrayal, and reconciliation. Or for example, in Beethoven's *Fidelio,* you have a plot about high moral issues in which the hero and heroine are prepared to sacrifice their lives for love and for a cause beyond themselves. These emotions, though lofty, are very common and everybody can either look up to them or identify with them to some extent. Opera subjects during the nineteenth and twentieth century became much more elitist. In Wagner's *Tristan* the hero and heroine are caught in a love and death situation in which the couple dies. In this death lies the redemption of the soul. Mozart would never have written a subject like that. In his operas the couple may hate each other for a minute but they will become lovers again.

JW: Do you feel that the subjects become more elitist because of the discovery of psychoanalysis and the unconscious? Art tended to become an individual's inner spiritual search instead of an outer expression of society.

GH: Yes, definitely; It has to do with the growing sense of the individual. The individual during the nineteenth and twentieth century drifted more and more apart from society in general. The artist saw himself opposed to society instead of being part of society. In the Middle Ages you felt part of society in whatever class you were in. If you were a knight or a peasant or a serf or a king, you realized that you had been put in your place within society by God; you accepted this and played your part within that society. In the nineteenth century the sense of individualism developed though audiences could still identify, to a certain extent, with transcendental subjects like *Tristan and*

Isolde. Take it one step farther, though, and you find operas like *Wozzeck* or *Lulu* in which no sound and healthy human being could identify with the hero.

The same analogy is possible if you look at symphonic music. The musical language became much more individualistic and complex with Bruckner and Mahler. Compare those symphonies with Mozart and Haydn symphonies! Look at the lieder Beethoven and Schubert dealt with (though both composers were also becoming more individualistic) and compare them with what Mahler wrote. They could never have imagined something like *Kindertotenlieder*! Then look at the last piano works of Brahms, opus 118 or 119. These pieces are so introverted that they weren't meant for the concert hall anymore. They are pieces for one individual to play for his own personal self-expression. Finally the extreme was reached when direct communication between the composer and a large crowd or audience was no longer possible. This was true especially after World War II when composers were using and developing compositional techniques that made the music less and less accessible to the common person. Finally, composers themselves began to realize that they had separated themselves from their audience and that the audience is gone and has drifted away. It's very encouraging to see that many composers are again trying to find a language which is understandable and can communicate with modern audiences! There is still resistance from the audience because of what happened in the past. We get very nasty letters about contemporary music that say, "Why torture us and subject us to such unkind treatment." I personally think that this type of resentment will be overcome with time. The audience needs to realize that twentieth-century music can have something to say that touches them in a real way.

JW: I think the minimalists have been able to reach a large audience. I noticed that you programmed a John Adams piece. What do you think about minimalism?

GH: Well, minimalism is somewhat like jumping from a burning skyscraper to save yourself. Obviously it is a reaction to the over-complicated musical languages that had been developed in the last fifty years. They simply flipped over into the opposite extreme of oversimplification. Maybe they thought that by going back to such a basic and primitive musical language they could make immediate audience contact.

JW: Well, I think they did. Philip Glass, Terry Riley, and John Adams are extremely successful!

GH: Yes, they are reaching an audience, with the power of monotony like in primeval ritual dances. But I don't think they can hold an audience in this way for a long time. I don't think repeating an A major chord 140 times will remain interesting. It has helped to close the gap between the audience and the contemporary composer.

JW: What are your criteria in programming twentieth-century works?

GH: Well, they must be well crafted and technically interesting to begin with. But the most important thing is that the music expresses something to me. I must be able to see an emotional stream going through it that I can identify with; only then can I make it an interesting experience for the audience. If it is only a mathematical process no matter how well composed, I will hesitate to perform it because I really have nothing to say with it. I have performed too many of those pieces already. It's like dropping an apple: it falls and nothing happens; the audience doesn't like it and it is not performed a second time.

Biography

Gunther Herbig was born to East German parents in a small town in Czechoslovakia on November 30, 1931. He began his musical training with Hermann Abendroth at the Franz Liszt Academy in Weimar. He continued his studies with Hermann Scherchen and was one of only a few students chosen for intensive study with Herbert von Karajan with whom he worked for two years. In 1972 he became general music director of the Dresden Philharmonic Orchestra and from 1977 to 1983, before coming to Detroit, was the music director of the Berlin Symphony Orchestra.

In addition to his music directorship with the Detroit Symphony, Gunther Herbig holds the post of music director designate with the Toronto Symphony Orchestra during the 1989-90 season. He has taken the Detroit Symphony Orchestra on tour several times to the major east coast concert halls, and in early 1989 led the orchestra on a European tour.

Because of his many commitments in East Germany, Gunther Herbig's first opportunity in the West came later in his career. It was only in 1984, when he vacated his position as music director of the Berlin Symphony Orchestra, that Mr. Herbig was able to find the time to guest conduct regularly in the United States and in Western Europe. The major orchestras in New York, Chicago, Boston, Philadelphia, London, and Paris have invited him to appear with them frequently.

Gunther Herbig Discography

Composer	Work	Orchestra	Soloists	Label
Beethoven	Creatures of Prometheus (complete)			Eterna
Beethoven	Ein Ritterballett			Eterna
Beethoven	Symphony no. 3			Eterna
Brahms	Ein deutsches Requiem			Melodiya
Brahms	Symphony no. 1			Eterna
Brahms	Symphony no. 2			Eterna
Brahms	Symphony no. 3			Eterna
Brahms	Symphony no. 4			Eterna
Brahms	Tragic Overture			Eterna
Brahms	Variations on a Theme by Haydn			Eterna
De Falla	Nights in the Gardens of Spain		Czapski	Eterna
Dessau	Orchestra music no. 4			Eterna
Eisler	Orchestral works			Eterna
Francaix	Concertino for piano and orchestra		Czapski	Eterna
Franck	Symphonic Variations for piano and orchestra		Czapski	Eterna
Hartmann	Symphony no. 5			Eterna
Hartmann	Symphony no. 6			Eterna
Haydn	Piano concerto in D		Roesel	Eterna
Haydn	Piano concerto in G		Roesel	Eterna
Haydn	Symphony no. 4			Eterna
Haydn	Symphony no. 5			Eterna
Haydn	Symphony no. 6			Eterna
Haydn	Symphony no. 7			Eterna
Haydn	Symphony no. 8			Eterna

Composer	Work	Orchestra	Soloists	Label	CD
Haydn	Symphony no. 9			Eterna	
Haydn	Symphony no. 10			Eterna	
Haydn	Symphony no. 93			Eterna	
Haydn	Symphony no. 94			Eterna	
Haydn	Symphony no. 95			Eterna	
Haydn	Symphony no. 96			Eterna	
Haydn	Symphony no. 97			Eterna	
Haydn	Symphony no. 98			Eterna	
Haydn	Symphony no. 99			Eterna	
Haydn	Symphony no. 100			Eterna	
Haydn	Symphony no. 101			Eterna	
Haydn	Symphony no. 102			Eterna	
Haydn	Symphony no. 103			Eterna	
Haydn	Symphony no. 104			Eterna	
Haydn	Funeral Music			Eterna	
Lutoslawski	Livre pour orchestre			Eterna	
Lutoslawski	Paganini variations for piano and orchestra		Czapski	Eterna	
Mahler	Ruckert Lieder		Lorenz	Eterna	
Mahler	Symphony no. 5			Eterna	
Mendelssohn	A Midsummer Night's Dream			Eterna	
Millöcker	Der Bettelstudent (excerpts)	Leipzig Radio Symphony	Schreier, Vogel	Philips	422 143-2
Mozart	Cassation, K. 100			Eterna	
Mozart	Cassation, K. 62			Eterna	
Mozart	Cassation, K. 63			Eterna	
Mozart	Cassation, K. 99			Eterna	
Mozart	Divertimento, K. 131			Eterna	
Mozart	Galimathias musicum, K. 32			Eterna	
Mozart	Serenade, K. 185			Eterna	
Nielsen	Symphony no. 5			Eterna	

Composer	Work	Orchestra	Soloists	Label	CD	LP	MC
Rachmaninoff	Piano concerto no. 3	Philharmonia	Ousset	EMI	CDC7 49941-2		EL 749941-4
Ravel	Boléro			Eterna			
Ravel	La Valse			Eterna			
Ravel	Ma mère l'oye			Eterna			
Ravel	Pavane pour une infante defunte			Eterna			
Schoenberg	Five pieces for orchestra			Eterna			
Schoenberg	Variations for orchestra			Eterna			
Zimmermann	Sinfonia come un grande lamento			Eterna			

"I remember when I was young and was just getting my career started. I resented the amount of time music took because I loved to travel and I loved to read. Now I just read good murder mysteries on airplanes when I'm going someplace because I just don't have time at home. I love poetry, but I don't get a chance to read it anymore. There were a lot of things that I wanted to do. Somehow this business of being a conductor, of being a musician was so demanding that I actually resented it. I was about thirty-three the first time I conducted the St. Matthew Passion, and when I walked off the stage at the end of the performance, blind and deaf with exhaustion, there was a little voice that said, 'Margaret, when there is music this beautiful in the world, how dare you resent what it asks of you?' Ever since then music has been first in my life."

Margaret Hillis

Margaret Hillis

JW: How did you begin your musical career?

MH: When my mother first started taking me to concerts; when I was a tiny child and still crawling! My formal training of course started later. I did my undergraduate work at Indiana University in composition and graduated there in 1947. At that time there was no chance for a woman at all in the orchestral conducting field. The orchestra was my great love and I'd been the principal double bass in the Indiana University Orchestra all the way through school and before that I'd played in my high school orchestra and my grade school orchestra. When I realized there were no women orchestra conductors on the scene at all I almost had a functional breakdown. I started conducting a chorus because I didn't have the opportunity to conduct an orchestra. I began to realize though, that it was a decent musical instrument. I found that you could phrase, sing in tune, get different colors and so on. When my composition teacher saw me conduct the chorus he advised me to go to Juilliard and study with Bob Shaw. Well, I did go to Juilliard, studied with Bob Shaw, and went right into the choral field. In 1950 I went to Tanglewood and when I got back to the city I started the Tanglewood Alumni Chorus which then evolved into what was later called the New York Concert Choir. We put on a series of concerts in Town Hall, four to six each season for about six years, before we all ran out of money. This was long before the days of the National Endowment for the Arts. I did works generally that the big orchestras had great difficulty doing such as *The St. Matthew Passion, The St. John Passion,* the *B Minor Mass.* Then I also performed a lot of works that no one else did which included a lot of world premieres. I think I did the New York premiere of Stravinsky's *Les Noces.* That piece taught me how to conduct, I'll tell you!

I was also involved with a concert series that featured works for chorus and orchestra in Town Hall. I did a lot of choral preparation for other conductors and did a lot of world premieres there as well. Ned Rorem wrote several pieces for me, as a matter of fact. I also worked very closely with Stravinsky in those New York years. I think I started working with him around 1952 and the association continued throughout his life. There are many recordings that I made with him. So my career just sort of grew!

Gradually I began to get an established reputation. Because of the New York reviews I started getting many out-of-town dates. I also started to guest conduct a little in the orchestral field. I'd already performed *Les Noces* and had recorded it when I was invited by the Pittsburgh Symphony to come and guest conduct a concert with *Les Noces* on the program.

My Chicago affiliation began when Fritz Reiner engaged my concert choir to come and sing with the Chicago Symphony two years in a row. The third year he wanted to do the Verdi Requiem. Now I wasn't about to do that work with the sixty voices that we had brought. The manager called me for a budget and I said, "Look, this is absolutely insane. I refuse even to quote anything." Finally he called again and from the panic in his voice I knew that Reiner had put a good bit of pressure on him. I said, "The bare cost is eighteen thousand and that doesn't even include a fee for me. That's for the pianist, the rehearsal space, the transportation, and sustenance while we're on the road." He sort of gasped and said, "Well, we were thinking more in terms of fourteen thousand." I said, "If you're thinking of fourteen thousand, start your own chorus. Why send this money out of the city of Chicago? It should be used in Chicago for its development." I knew what was going to happen next, so I went to a hotel and got a Chicago telephone directory and started looking in places I knew that singers would be available such as the Harvard Club, all sorts of temples, colleges, universities, and churches. Sure enough, the next morning the phone rang and it was Reiner who asked, "Where do we get the singers and how do we start a chorus?" I said, "First set your date, then announce the date and the repertory (and the Verdi *Requiem* is very attractive!). Go backward from that to your first rehearsals and backward from that to your auditions." I said I would be very happy to work with the manager at that time to show him how to go about doing this. Reiner said, "Yes, but who conducts?" And I said "Well, I would be happy even to come out to Chicago and do a little inquiring around to hear the work of some of the local conductors and maybe recommend one or two or three of them to you." He said, "No, we won't have it unless you conduct." Well that thought had not even crossed my mind! I asked if I could call him back in the morning. Then I looked in my date book and found that I had almost every Monday evening free. Even the week that he was planning to do the Verdi *Requiem* was free. Then I checked with the airlines and found that I could catch a plane out on Sunday night and a midnight flight back on Monday because I had commitments in New York on Tuesday. So I called him back and said, "Yes, I can do it." So, I commuted from New York City for five years. I was much younger and it was before the jet age, too. I remember one flight on an old four-engine propeller Constellation. The stewardess told us, "The head wind is a hundred and fifty miles an hour and it's going to take us six hours to get to Chicago. Fasten your lap straps and westward ho!" Only once in that five years was I not able to make it because of the weather. I was very, very lucky in that respect and was able to meet all the commitments in Chicago plus all of the commitments in New York City.

At that time, the Town Hall Concerts were still continuing and I was also doing a lot of preparation for what was then called the American Opera Society which is no longer in existence. It was a wonderful group. Elisabeth Schwarzkopf and Joan Sutherland made their American debuts there. I also worked with Walter Berry, Eileen Farrell, Maria Callas, and Christa Ludwig. A lot of the big people who had never sung in the United States before made their American debuts with that company. I did all of the choral preparation for them over an eight or nine year period. I must have prepared 120-130 different operas. I also was the choral director and assistant conductor at the New York City Center Opera. So, that period was quite wild, I must say with all the running around. As the assistant conductor I did all the dirty work backstage. I learned how to keep the curtain from coming down from backstage and did a lot of backstage conducting. *Carmen* is terrifying from backstage because you can't tell when (and I got no help from Jean Morel, who was the conductor) to bring in the chorus. I would listen for the recitative on the stage, hoping that there wasn't some chatter going on someplace so that I couldn't hear it. After the performance I always knew I was right because I didn't get screamed at.

It wasn't, however, until I was about forty-two or forty-three years old that I ran across Otto Werner Müller. It was through a summer institute in which choral conductors were put on a podium in front of a professional orchestra. I had been asked by the Union Theological Seminary (which was then right across the street from the Juilliard School) to conduct their small chamber orchestra which was the first real orchestral conducting I'd done in the New York area. Of course, at that time, no women could get a master teacher in orchestral conducting. I already had an established career in the choral field and was going great guns before I really got to a master teacher who made all the difference in the world. So when I was forty-three Otto began to work with me. I went to him you know, sort of behind the scenes. I was the head of the institute but I knew that I wanted to learn from this man and I learned a great deal! We'd use cameras on the kids so I got him to use a camera on me in private sessions; he got my arm working properly. I also finally got my head together on score analysis by working with him. I'd always worked like crazy before, but he showed me an orderly fashion to go about score study. It changed the way I listened and it changed the way I conducted.

I finally stopped commuting from New York and moved to Chicago in 1962 when I got an orchestra up in Kenoshee. I had them for about six years. At that time Kenoshee was entirely American Motors-oriented, which gave it a depression mentality. I just couldn't get it moving. It's changed since American Motors moved out of there. Actually I'm guest conducting there again in just a few weeks. It's a better orchestra now and they have a few professionals in it and a young woman by the name of Elizabeth Schulze is the conductor. She's excellent, I've heard. After I moved to Chicago I started teaching at Northwestern; I gave up Kenoshee and I got the Elgin Orchestra. Elgin was then the kind of orchestra that Kenoshee had been. It was totally amateur; I think they gave three concerts a year to about a quarter-full house.

JW: How old were you at this point?

MH: Well, I was in my mid-forties, I expect. It was very shortly after I'd met Otto. I made certain conditions before going there: that they have a symphony league to help raise money and to help sell tickets; that they have a proper board to go into the community for community relations and fund raising; that they had to expand to four concerts the first season I was there and add children's concerts; that we start exploring a youth orchestra and a children's choir (they already had an adult chorus in the community). When I left it was a totally professional orchestra. They gave a six-concert (in pairs) season, they played three concerts with the local chorus, there was a children's chorus, there was a youth orchestra and a youth string orchestra that plays for the *Nutcracker* and other sorts of things. As a matter of fact, almost a year ago I did a shortened version for children of *Hansel and Gretel* in Orchestra Hall. When they asked me what orchestra I wanted I said, "Elgin." They came and I had one rehearsal with them before we went into the dress rehearsal. They played like dolls; it was wonderful. I felt very proud of the fact that I was the one who had built that orchestra. When I left it was 90 percent professional, now it's 100 percent professional and the community is 200 percent behind it. They have a very active league and a very active board led by the leading businessmen in the community. The community itself is only about 90,000 but they also take their concerts to other areas so that they draw on a community of 300,000 to 400,000. I'm very proud of having done that. I left them because I was beginning to do so much guest conducting that I just couldn't afford the time for them any more.

JW: How long were you there?

MH: Fifteen years.

JW: That's a substantial amount of time.

MH: Well, I've been well over thirty years with the Chicago Symphony Chorus. Actually, at this point, I would say that my musical life is about half choral and half orchestral.

JW: What do you think the major differences are for you between choral conducting and orchestral conducting and which one do you prefer?

MH: Well, that's a very tricky question because I declare no preference. The difference lies in the fact that singers sing words. A cellist from the Chicago

Symphony once asked, "Why does a chorus need so much more rehearsal time than the orchestra?" I said, "Well, my dear, if you had to play your cello in Russian, in Slovakian, in French, Italian, German, and English with a little Russian thrown in wouldn't it take you a little longer?" She said, "It sure would!" It takes longer to rehearse a chorus because of the many languages with which we deal plus the fact that the singers don't have a backlog of repertory the way instrumentalists do because they start their careers later. Singers usually start at twenty or twenty-one. An orchestral player starts at six or seven and comes in for an audition already knowing the exerps for the most difficult things in the repertory. I seldom take a singer younger than twenty-one simply because they haven't yet developed enough of a vocal technique to have the stamina for the work that we do. By twenty to twenty-one an instrumentalist is ready to go out and whip the world!

JW: Hopefully!

MH: Hopefully, yes. Well, he thinks he is! But the singers are a little more tender in that way. By now my Chicago chorus reads very well. I remember, though, the first time, years and years ago, we did the Beethoven Ninth Symphony. We had something like thirty hours of rehearsal! We finally got it. It was clean, the language was good, the dynamics were there, the phrasing, etc. Now, I do one sectional rehearsal with each section and two full rehearsals and that's it for the Ninth. Nine hours and it's ready. At this point this chorus has a large backlog of repertory.

JW: You have been with them thirty years. That must be a wonderful feeling.

MH: Yeah, actually it's been thirty-two. I think this is my thirty-second or thirty-third season. I forget. I started in 1957. But here we do build up a backlog of repertory. We do (for a chorus this is a lot) five or six different sets of repertory in the summer and in the winter there may be as many as ten or twelve sets. For a chorus that's a good bit of repertory.

JW: What about your own musical satisfaction? Is it just as fulfilling to conduct a chorus as an orchestra?

MH: Musically, there's no difference. My two favorite pieces on the face of the earth are the *St. Matthew Passion* and the Bruckner Eighth Symphony. So there you have it; a big choral work and a big orchestral work. Then, if you throw in a few operas I'm in heaven!

JW: Do you think a chorus is harder to work with than an orchestra?

MH: You have to have more patience.

JW: Does it take you the same amount of score study?

MH: In terms of score study there is no difference, no difference whatsoever. I think the split that used to be so apparent between the choral person and the orchestral person is now narrowing. In the past a lot of times the choral director was the choral director because he wasn't good enough to conduct the orchestra. He was usually a singer who sort of vaguely knew what he was doing but couldn't really analyze a score. In my own teaching I insist that a student study the full score with his hands behind his back. My students learn the music and afterwards impose the music on their arms and not their arms on the music. For instance in *Missa Solemnis* the chorus is just another instrument in the orchestra and the conductor's problem is to know what job Beethoven gave to them and he better know the jobs of all the other instruments in the orchestra as well. You need to know, for instance, when the chorus is doubled by the horns or by the flutes and what kind of sound is produced depending on the dynamics. You are always trying to work for what the composer had in his ear. I remember once I was guest conducting the Verdi *Requiem* in Madison, Wisconsin. I couldn't get the right sound from the tenors and I was frustrated by it. During the first orchestra rehearsal I had horns play for the tenors and I said, "Tenors, you hear the horns, that is your color." We played it once again, and the next time, the color was right in the tenor section. You work mainly with their ears. You work with the ears of orchestra players, too, but even more I think with singers. They can't put a finger down to get a pitch.

JW: How do you build the kind of sound that you want with a chorus and with an orchestra? Can you elaborate more on that?

MH: Well, that's a question that's been asked of me many times and you know, I really don't know, I just don't know. I've found in teaching students that I can teach them score analysis and I can teach them how the arm has to work to get certain things to happen. I cannot, however, change their conception of sound and often they don't even have a conception of sound! I scream at them and say, "Before you even lift your arm, you have to have that sound in your ear." You can't teach talent; you can't teach imagination; you can't teach commitment and love for the art. If that isn't there, forget it. Part of a conductor's makeup has to be able to compel the musicians to do well. [Serge] Koussevitsky was awful to follow as a conductor. He was a great musician, though, even if the beat was all over the place. When he stepped on the podium you were under obligation to do it right.

[George] Szell said the first thing a conductor is is a teacher. You have to be able to convey an idea. You have to instill it in people and then get it to grow in them. There is nothing I hate worse than a chorus that sounds as if it's dotted every *i* and crossed every *t* because they were told to. I prepare the

Chicago Symphony Chorus in such a way that by the time they get to the performance all those chains that I've put on them have disciplined them to the point where they're free to make the music. And then there is spontaneous real music making.

JW: So what is your method of score analysis? I'm getting some very interesting answers to this.

MH: Yeah, I bet you are. Of course the score itself tells you how you have to learn it. You have to sit down with it for a while to get to know it well enough for it to teach you how to learn it.

JW: Do you sit down at the piano?

MH: No. I sit down at my study, at my desk. I'll show you a score in a few minutes.

JW: Do you have perfect pitch?

MH: No, thank God. The one thing that does bother me though is that Chicago's A creeps up and up and pretty soon it gets to be above A-440. Then when I go and guest conduct another orchestra and they play an A-440 and I go out of my cotton-pickin' mind. The only perfect pitch I have is for the A. They have to sound it first and then I know whether it's high or low. That I always know. If I had perfect pitch (I call it absolute pitch) and went from orchestra to orchestra where they used different A's, I'd be in the loony bin by now, I think.

JW: So after you've sat with the score for a while what do you do next?

MH: I do a harmonic analysis.

JW: Do you analyze chord by chord?

MH: No. I analyze by the root position of things the first time through. I defy anybody to use a I-IV-V kind of analysis in the sixth movement of the Brahms *Requiem*.

JW: So you just name the chords?

MH: Yeah, you just say C or D or G or G-6 or G-6/5. You can't analyze the sixth movement of the Brahms *Requiem* thinking in terms of a tonic because there is no tonic. The text *"Here we have no continuing place"* goes for 126 bars before you know, "Gee, he's going toward C minor." I do analyze then in terms of the chord function. I decide whether the harmony functions as a tonic or a substitute tonic, subdominant or dominant; whether a Neopolitan 6th is a substitute subdominant or has a dominant function. This helps a great deal, especially in preparing choruses because then you always know where your leading tones are and they always have to be reasonably high.

115

Orchestras do what I call functional intonation. And if I don't know what's going on harmonically, I won't know anything about the functional intonation. So I do the harmonic analysis first and then comes the phrase analysis. I find the large sections first. If you've got a sonata form, I find where the development section begins and where the recapitulation begins. I usually work from the large into the small detail and then back out. I find where the second theme begins, etc. Then I mark in all the phrases. I get out my little ruler and pencil and just mark 'em in. Also, I'm not loath at all to use lots and lots of colored pencils when it comes to materials. I color-code the principal themes.

JW: I'd love to see a score!

MH: Fine. I'll show you one I've studied, I'll show you a couple of them. I'll show you the Bruckner Eighth Symphony and the Mahler Eighth Symphony, which I had to learn in a devil of a hurry. I learned something very valuable from Otto Werner Müller, who said, "When you have to learn something in a hurry, study slowly." I did. My big problem that night, because I had to step in after a day and a half with the score, was to remember to turn pages because I had the second part memorized. I had to keep telling myself, "My God, turn the pages in case you pull a blank!" I hadn't had a chance to test my memory and I wasn't arrogant enough to think I could do it, boom, like that!

JW: You learned the Mahler Eighth in a day and a half! I remember reading about that.

MH: Yeah, well I did have a miniature score in which I had analyzed the root positions of everything as you go through and their functions and so on. But I didn't even bother with that then. Also, I had the work in my ear. The big problem was how quickly these nasty tempo changes come. You know, I didn't even practice it when I came to conduct it. I just knew what the orchestra needed. "Over here they're going to need a clean beat or that eighth note is going to be late. I have to do this here and that there." I didn't try it with my arm.

JW: Had you gone to any of Solti's rehearsals?

MH: Nope. He did, thank God, on Sunday afternoon, ask if I would like to borrow the score. I said, "Yes, I certainly would." I had no idea even where the soloists breathed! My job had been: is the diction clean in the chorus, are they holding the tempo, etc., is the sound right, and are the balances okay? That had been my focus with the chorus. I didn't notice, when it came to the soloists, where they breathed. Well, he went over it with me and said, "My dear, here at this point the soprano needs a deep breath. Take all the sound out and then go on." I thought, "Oh boy, thank God I know that." "Over here this tenor phrase is very long, you have to make an unnoticeable accelerando, or he'll never make it in one breath." Thank God I knew that.

JW: You had no rehearsal? You just jumped into the performance?

MH: Yes, I jumped right into the performance. I had a one hour rehearsal with the chorus, the off-stage brass, and the soloists and the organ on stage at Carnegie Hall on Saturday morning. I didn't see the orchestra until I walked on that night. Thank God I'd conducted several times in Carnegie Hall and I knew what kind of sound I'd get. They tell me the acoustics have changed now; that's heartbreaking because that podium is one of the few in the world where what you get on the podium is exactly what the hall gets. You don't have to set up your false balances and all that nonsense; you *know*. I knew that and trusted the hall so that was a big worry off my head right there. But I did have to learn the score in a hurry. One of the main themes in the score appears in many versions. It appears inverted; it sometimes appears augmented when he wants stress and sometimes appears sped up. I wanted to make sure I always knew where that thematic material was. I took a dark green colored pencil and went through the whole score. When it was right side up, it was the dark green and when it was upside down, it was the light green. It was another color when it was faster or when it was slower. I plotted out that material because that's the thing that holds the whole piece together. I didn't even bother looking into my miniature score. I had a clean full score at home, thank God. I marked it in such a way that a year later when I conducted it at Indiana University I didn't have to put another thing into it. I did do something that I've never done before. I would say things like, "Four bars to allegro, or four bars to vivace." One of the main things that I was worried about was that there might be these nasty three-bar things, which is where conductors can get lost. I hadn't quite finished the bar-line analysis when I got on the plane. I thought, "Oops, better part of valor is go to the end and work backwards." I did and I found a three-bar thing. All I needed was still to be conducting when the orchestra was through!

JW: Did you listen to a recording?

MH: No. I did get a tape of Solti's performance that he had done the previous Thursday night and I started listening to it. I listened for about five minutes and I thought, "This is nonsense."

JW: Yeah, That's dangerous, very dangerous.

MH: Very dangerous because you end up imitating somebody. It becomes absolutely an external performance. I never let my students listen to recordings before they learn a piece. If they want to listen to a recording, fine, *after* you've learned the piece. I often do only after I've learned a work, just to check my ear, especially if it's a composer that I don't know terribly well. But generally I have finished all the work in the score before I'll listen to them. That tape would have been no help at all. At the end of that warmup on Saturday morning I spoke to the chorus and soloists and said, "Now look, the tempi will all be in the same ballpark as Solti's were, but he and I are different musicians; I have to relate to this piece honestly as I *am*. Conceptually, maybe the phrases will turn a little bit differently, maybe the sound will be a little different, just watch. Go with me, because if I try to imitate him, we will have a total disaster on our hands." So I didn't imitate him. You can't because it comes out utterly superficial. To try to learn a piece from a recording is the same imitation and you might make somebody else's mistake. If you've learned the score and then listen to a conductor whom you respect, you can say, "Oh, oh, oh, you missed that!" You can avoid making his mistake.

JW: How long do you live with a score before performing it?

MH: Well, in that case a day and a half. I usually start a year or two ahead though. I do a certain amount of analysis and then lay it aside because there's something else coming up that's pressing. It depends upon when the assignment comes as to when I start it. I've already gotten started on things I'll be doing next spring with the Chicago Symphony. It's still in a very superficial stage but in the next few weeks, I'll get deeper and deeper into it.

•••••

JW: What kind of rehearsal technique do you use?

MH: Well, again, the score teaches me how to learn the score. After I've gotten the score learned, I'll make a chart. I also have charts for the associate and assistant conductor and the chorus. They all get a copy. I call it a homestudy chart. By each section of the work I will put columns where I mark *x*s that rate the difficulty of the section. Sections with relative difficulty have only one *x* and won't need as much rehearsal time, but with a work like [Schoenberg's] *Moses und Aron*, for example, the *x*s will run off of the page! Having a chart of that kind helps me to know where I am in the long line of rehearsals and to know which sections are the most difficult ones and which will need the most concentration. After that has been done I sit down and take a look at the score again. Again, the score tells you how to approach it. I nearly always begin to study without the text, especially in a work that is legato and highly polyphonic. I may even have all of the chorus sing the subject the first time it comes and then put that subject with whoever gets the subject much later. Then, everybody sings the counter-subject and then I put the two counter subjects together before I combine the whole thing. That's one way of rehearsing polyphonic music. It depends upon how difficult the

118

music is to hear. Also, if the choir is not rhythmically clean on the inner parts of a countrapuntal work I have them sing the motives or themes short. Then those who are on whole notes will know what else is going on, for heaven's sake. Those are the only two reasons for ever using short singing. A fair amount of soft singing without text is good for intonation. You don't get good intonation, especially in a vast piece without a certain amount of slow rehearsal and a certain amount of soft rehearsal. The faster the piece is the slower I tend to rehearse.

In slow choruses that are not difficult the problems are usually just a matter of intonation. So if they've had some rehearsal without text I add the text in very soon. The most important thing is for the chorus to hear the total score and not just their individual parts. In some opera choruses, singers learn their part at home and think that they are always singing the main tune. If the chorus thinks that way you will get no balance and no sense out of what's going on musically. So again, it depends entirely on the piece as to how I approach it with the chorus. I try to find the way best to get it into their ears. I work first with their ears, second with their musical feelings, and finally with their voices. In an orchestra, you work first with their ears, second with their musical feelings, and third with their instruments.

I taught for awhile at Northwestern and I've been a visiting professor at Indiana University. In both cases, I insisted that the choral people had to get on the podium in front of an orchestra at least once a year. Many times the poor choral people go out into the field, get a big community chorus that only has the budget for one orchestra rehearsal. With only one rehearsal they'd better know how to bow parts and they'd better know how to mark them! I know Otto's rule always was that the parts have got to be marked in such a way that if the greatest tuba player in the world gets sick and somebody else, not as great, comes in at the last minute they couldn't possibly get lost. The marking of the parts, if properly done, gets five rehearsals out of your way. My rule about bowings is the same as about rehearsal technique; look into the score, find out what the composer says, and bow it with the music, not against it.

JW: Do you do all your own bowings.

MH: Yes. I do all my own bowings and with confidence because first of all I played the double bass and I have picked the brains of every good violinist that I could, people that I knew would bow the music and not bow for the convenience of the violin. I picked their brains enough to be confident about what I do.

JW: You don't work with the concertmaster?

MH: The Chicago Symphony has a long tradition. Now usually to my mind a tradition is the memory of the last bad performance. But they've had this

119

tradition where the concert master always does the bowing and then it's handed to the principal second, and from him to the principal viola and all around. They do their own bowings. Then anything that needs changing is changed; it usually comes out pretty well that way. Now this spring I'm going to be doing Haydn's *Lord Nelson Mass* with the Chicago Symphony. Everybody thinks it is a choral work but it isn't. It's really a concerto for the first and second fiddles. I have bowings of my own that have been used many times, which I know work with the music. So, they're going to have to accept those from me. But they can go ahead and bow the music for the rest of the program themselves if they want to! Rarely in rehearsals with the Chicago Symphony do I have to stop and say, "Look, Sam, could we get rid of that retake?" If I do he says, "Oh sure," and fixes it. Generally, though, I always prefer to do my own bowings. Bowings for Brahms are always a headache because everything is laid down on that page with the markings for a pianist. To play those slurs on a fiddle you'd need either a round bow or one that's sixteen feet long or you'll never make it! That's always a problem.

JW: How do you work with the winds?

MH: Well, I played French horn and a little bit of oboe. I was also a darn good alto saxophone player when I was between the ages of nine and twelve! So I know a lot about problems with reeds and when the clarinets have to change and all that sort of thing. By the way, I could never play the flute without getting dizzy, but I did learn from having tried the flute and having played the oboe a little bit (I didn't want to have to make all those reeds) what the problems are. And I also knew from my own orchestral experience that the oboe and flute are opposites; the flute gets softer the lower it goes and louder the higher it goes and the oboe is just the reverse. I knew those kinds of things from having been a composition major. I was very lucky at Indiana. I had an excellent counterpoint teacher and an excellent composition teacher. I really learned how the instruments sound. I know just enough about the harp to know I wouldn't like to play it. You know the thing that Debussy said about harps? "They spend half their time tuning and the other half playing out of tune." Now everybody says that harpists can't count; well I couldn't count either if I had seven pedals that I had to keep shifting around all the time. So, when I conduct, I'm always with the harpist. Also, I'm always with the timpani, especially if there are any changes of tuning. They might have 75 bars to count and suddenly have to come in fortissimo. I also don't know how anybody has the courage to play cymbals or triangle in an orchestra; they have to count all those bars. In the Bruckner Eighth Symphony they only play in the slow movement. They have to sit there for an hour to play two notes; that's all they play in the whole piece, just two notes! I also know enough about brass playing from having studied the French horn to understand what is difficult for the players and how to help them. I know places in Brahms, for instance, where the horn parts are almost unplayable. Of course you accumulate this knowledge through experience; most of it you accumulate through experience. Unfortunately, this sort of thing usually isn't taught in our universities.

Also, in rehearsal, I'm a real bugbear when it comes to balances, whether in a chorus or orchestra. In the Mahler Eighth there's that wonderful moment, pianissimo, when E flat major comes. Unless everything is balanced through that low E flat, it doesn't come off right because the third sits on top.

JW: So how do you balance it?

MH: I work through their ears. I start from the bottom up. Whether it's a chorus or orchestra, I start with the lowest note and work up through the chord. The next note up from the bottom I have sung or played just a hair less, not so much that you even notice it, a hair less as we go all the way up to the top of the chord. Also, when any instrument or any singer is on the third of the chord I insist that that be the highest and the warmest sound. If you look at the Beethoven Violin Concerto you will find that one of the reasons the second movement is so incredibly warm is that the violin is almost always on the third of the chord. That third gives such warmth. These are the kinds of things I work on. It's so important to get your ensemble to hear them. It doesn't do any good to do it mechanically; they have to do it through their ears and that's where I normally work.

Getting back to rehearsal technique: The score dictates the way you rehearse. Also the level of the ensemble you're working with dictates how you rehearse. If your group is top level you can just play through a work and fix little things after the run-through. All you might need to say, for instance, to the trombones is, "At the marcato would you separate it slightly," or to the strings, "Wherever it's pianissimo it should be *sul tasto.*" Then we try it again. If we run into something that is nasty or if they obviously are not hearing something that's going on you can point out their function to them. For instance, if the bassoons and horns are doubling the cellos they should be aware of it and if the second clarinet is doubling the violas, he should know that he is there to warm up the viola sound and not to play a solo. My function in that respect is to let the orchestra know what kind of job the composer gave to them. Another example is in the second movement of the Brahms *Requiem,* which is scored for two pairs of horns, one in B flat, the other in C (Brahms always used open brass instruments and never the valved instruments, though they were available to him.) Now it is very important to realize that one set of horns is functioning as brass instruments and the other set is functioning as woodwind instruments. As soon as the players know they're woodwinds and not brass, they will play differently. Last year I did the Bruckner Eighth Symphony at Indiana University. Boy, what an orchestra

121

that was! They were just incredible! If we have a minute or two I'll play you part of that tape. Well, after a rehearsal the first trombone player asked if we could have a brass sectional. I said, "Now look, as a trombone player you're sometimes a brass player and you're sometimes a woodwind player. It doesn't make sense to just rehearse the brass. If we can get the woodwinds and the brass together, I don't care whether it's 2:30 in the morning, I'll be there." Well, we scheduled a rehearsal at midnight and we worked from midnight until 3 in the morning. We got all the balances and articulations right!

JW: That's one advantage of an academic situation. Students are willing to put that kind of commitment and time into a performance.

MH: Well, that's obvious when you hear this tape. They play with such commitment that it is hard to believe. Now, the Chicago Symphony also works like tigers in rehearsals and boy do they play and it comes from the heart. However, I have guest conducted other professional orchestras where this commitment doesn't always happen. But the Chicago Symphony has a lot of pride in its playing and it works like demons in rehearsals. You almost are embarassed to correct them for something. You have to be careful how often you raise your eyebrows. The roof may go off! The sound is with your hands all the time and if you move your little finger you will hear a difference. It's an incredible orchestra.

•••••

JW: What's your viewpoint on historical performance practices? Do you believe in taking Beethoven's metronome markings? Would you retouch a score? Some conductors that I've talked to would never retouch Beethoven but do retouch Schumann. What's your opinion?

MH: Well, Schumann was a terrible orchestrator. In his piano concerto, for instance, there are certain crescendos that cry out for a timpani to support them. They simply don't work without the timpani. With Beethoven you have to realize that he was deaf. He never wrote a wrong note, he never made a mistake when it came to structure, but he did make orchestration mistakes. I've worked with enough contemporary composers to see how they change their orchestrations after they hear them to wonder if Beethoven would have done the same had he had the opportunity. So far I haven't retouched the Schumann and Beethoven scores even with all the problems in them. I have touched up Schubert, though. He was also a lousy orchestrator. We lost something when he died so young because he hadn't learned to orchestrate yet. He didn't realize double basses have to have someone, whether it's a second clarinet or cello an octave above them to tie them into the texture. Without that, they sound like a bunch of bumble bees, sawing away down there. There are certain places where Schubert has not doubled them. If the second clarinet is free, I just have him discreetly play those passages with them. You don't really hear the clarinet, but suddenly a focussed sound comes from the double basses. Sometimes I've told an orchestra, "So when these things come along we have to cheat a little bit. I'm going to serve a little bit of kosher ham by adding that second clarinet."

I'm also in doubt about Beethoven's tempo markings simply because there was a lot of correspondence between him and his publishers. He would send a set of tempo markings and they'd lose them. They'd ask for more and when they'd come they would find the old ones, compare them to the new ones and find that they were different. They'd then write and ask which were the correct ones and Beethoven would do a third set which didn't match the first two. I think that partially was because of the deafness. There is that famous place in the Scherzo of the Ninth Symphony where the duplet is marked so that the whole note equals the dotted half. It's almost unplayable. I think either it's a printer's mistake and that it should be the half note that equals the dotted half or Beethoven goofed again. Also, the orchestral recitative in the Ninth should match the vocal version. The metronome markings don't match and I think that Beethoven's sense of structure was stronger than that. I'll go with structure anytime.

Now I do think that the experiments with the earlier instruments are really valid. Once I got a chance to play on a Beethoven piano in Munich and it sounds very similar to our modern harpsichords. You could never ever balance that instrument with one of our contemporary orchestras. No way. Now you need a Hamburg Steinway. So I think there is a virtue in using original instruments. I think there are a great many insights one can get from the music. I've not had the opportunity of hearing any of these authentic performances live yet. I hope I get to. I've talked to many musicians whose ears I trust and they're very excited about it. The tempo thing I do take issue with though. But then, to each his own.

•••••

JW: What are your criteria in programming twentieth-century music?

MH: Well, there are several ways to think about it, depending upon circumstances. On an ideal level, any piece that is a masterpiece sounds as though it were written this morning. Contemporary music has to be part of the flow of the whole musical heritage. There should be no special societies for it. If you're doing several pieces on a program and one is a contemporary piece it shouldn't be stressed. It should fit into a part of our musical lineage. Also, I don't choose something that is going to suffer next to a masterpiece from the past. It has to be a strong piece in its own right.

JW: How do you judge that?

MH: Well, you read the score. It tells you. I've done a lot contemporary music, a lot of world premieres with the Chicago Symphony. The music needs to speak to me. I don't go for any pieces which are what I call, "foundation music," written to get grants and written to please other composers. A piece of music has to communicate and if it doesn't, it ain't for me. I don't care about the style of the music as long as it communicates. For instance, no one remarks anymore whether *Lulu* or *Wozzeck* are twelve-tone pieces. They are now heard as masterpieces. I don't care what the language is as long as the music is there. I just did a work by Marvin Levi based on the Masada. I have done lots of world premieres of his in New York. This particular piece had been performed in Washington after which he completely rewrote it. We performed the rewritten version which is incredibly difficult, but incredibly powerful. The power of a piece is really what I am interested in. I don't care whether it's a lyrical or gentle power or whatever. I'm interested in the strength of a piece.

JW: So you don't care about the compositional method?

MH: As long as it's music and it communicates the composer can stand on his head if he wants to. However, the minimalists don't communicate with me. By the way, have you heard the latest Philip Glass joke?

JW: I think I've heard it, but tell me.

MH: Knock, knock?

JW: Who's there?

MH: Knock, knock?

JW: Who's there?

MH: Knock, knock,

JW: Who's there?

MH: Philip Glass.

JW: Well, they have reached the audience again. They are also making money!

MH: Well, who measures Beethoven by how many millions he earned in his life? That's one of the problems in our contemporary society. You can't write music to earn money. You've got to write music to communicate. If money is foremost in your mind you should forget it.

JW: Well, my point was that they earned money because it did communicate to a lot of people.

MH: Well, maybe it does. If it does, bully for them. I don't get it!

•••••

JW: How should a young conductor go about breaking into the professional conducting world. What is your advice to women conductors?

MH: Now it's not as difficult for women conductors as it once was; I've sort of hoed a row that helped and then the women's movement came along which also helped enormously. Currently there are some excellent women conductors around. I've not seen or heard Catherine Comet yet, but I hear that she's just splendid. Also, there's a young one coming up by the name of Kate Tamarkin who's also *enormously* gifted.

JW: She's the associate conductor in Dallas?

MH: That's right. She is able to communicate nicely with an orchestra. Her face always shows the joy of the music.

JW: Do you think that women have something special to offer the musical world?

MH: Well, C major has no sex, it has no color. When it comes to the making of music I feel that it's human being to human thing.

JW: So you don't think there's anything different about the way a woman would approach it?

MH: I don't think so. I analyze my scores and I find that Bruckner is Bruckner and C major is C major. It's still a little harder for a woman in the field; she has to be a little better than the men, but then that's alright, that's just fine. I think each career is an individual sort of thing. There are, now in America, a few routes that are a little standardized but few conductors make it through them. Most musicians, not just conductors, have to find their own way into a career. There now is the Exxon program which isn't as active as it once was but is still in existence. Being the assistant conductor of an orchestra isn't necessarily a dead end as it used to be. There is also the European model of working for an opera company as a pianist and working your way up through the ranks.

Opera, I think is one of the best routes for conductors. They always need coaches. I tell young conductors to look in the direction of opera houses. You can start out as a coach doing some backstage conducting and then try to get into the position of being an assistant to one of the main conductors. If he gets sick some night you will have to conduct the opera. In Europe that is the route to go. You'd go immediately into the opera house to get your first job. Bruno Walter and many others went this route. Your first job may be as the chorus master. If you really succeeded for a season at that you could move up to be an assistant to one of the main conductors and maybe on the tenth or fifteenth performance would be allowed to conduct; if that went well, the following season you might get to conduct the fourth or the fifth performance; then, if that went very well, the following season you might get to conduct your own opera and you will have entered the roster of the conductors and your career really begins. The United States doesn't have that much of a route set up although I think it is beginning to happen in the opera houses now. The opera teaches you not to play politics and to just play the music though the politics are going around you all of the time. It teaches you how to keep a curtain from coming down. I mean, opera is impossible, absolutely impossible. If you can do opera, you can do anything. So, I think that is one route conductors at least ought to look into. It would take four or five years and a lot of frustration along the line. You'd have to practice keeping your mouth shut when somebody screams at you and they scream a lot in opera houses.

There are also opera schools in opera houses around the country. Now, those can be dead end. I have a pianist who's playing for me now, with the Chicago Symphony and she's looking around for something else to do. She's been a pianist and coach for the Lyric Opera School now for about four years and she has not been taken into the main house. She's good enough to be taken but there just hasn't been an opening. She's looking around on how to get into a main house. She's been doing some conducting, has a fabulous ear and knows her languages thoroughly. A career may very well develop for her. There's also a little bit, well there's a good bit, of luck involved. But the main thing is that you've got to be prepared. It's sort of like what Abe Lincoln said, "I'll make myself prepared and then when the time comes, I'll be ready." That's what I had to do. If you're not ready and you get the chance, you fall on your face.

JW: I would like to know what you feel is your most important personal challenge as a conductor.

MH: To make beautiful music. You know when I stepped in for Solti with the Mahler Eighth my only thought was not to let anyone down. There had been a lot of time and money spent in getting that chorus and orchestra into New York and my only thought was I couldn't let them down. It had to be a beautiful performance and it had to come off. I was just too busy thinking to think of myself! While I was there I stayed with dear friends of mine in New York who brought me the paper the next morning. I discovered that I was on the front page. That was the first moment that I had realized I had made a personal triumph. That had never even entered my head. I didn't even after the performance was over think in terms of personal success until the story came out on the front page of the New York Times. After that my guest conducting took off like crazy and I had the luxury of being able to say "no" often. But, do you know which people were the happiest? My colleagues in the choral conducting field. They said, "IT CAN BE DONE!"

JW: What do you think are your most important qualities?

MH: A sense of humor. I don't think you can survive without it. I also have good stamina. Anyone who goes into conducting has to have that. I have good genes. How old do you think I am? I'll drop a shocker. Two weeks from now I'll be sixty-eight. Now I don't look it, do I? I was just lucky with my genes.

I'll be sixty-eight years old the first of October. Solti doesn't look his seventy-six years of age either. So there has to be stamina; however, a lot of that stamina comes from a love of the work, I'm sure.

JW: And you get more and more energy from doing it.

MH: That's right, you do. Actually I think I've only had to cancel three rehearsals in the forty years of my career for health reasons. I've never canceled a concert.

JW: With such an intense schedule, how does a conductor have a personal life?

MH: It's very difficult, very difficult. So much of your main energies have to be focused on what you do. Your main time has to go there. You have almost no energy or time left over for a personal life. Music in some respects is like a monkey on your back. It bosses you around, tells you what you have to do.

JW: So, have you always had the ability to focus on your work alone without spilling lots of energy into your personal life?

MH: Well, there've been crises in my personal life. Anybody has those, but in a sense it was music that pulled me through them and because of that I feel I owe my life to it. I wouldn't have killed myself or anything, but let's say I owe my sanity to music. It was always there for me and never let me down. I remember when I was young and was just getting my career started. I resented the amount of time music took because I loved to travel and I loved to read. Now I just read good murder mysteries on airplanes when I'm going someplace because I just don't have time at home. I love poetry, but I don't get a chance to read it anymore. There were a lot of things that I wanted to do. Somehow this business of being a conductor, of being a musician was so demanding that I actually resented it. I was about thirty-three the first time I conducted the *St. Matthew Passion,* and when I walked off the stage at the end of the performance, blind and deaf with exhaustion, there was a little voice that said, "Margaret, when there is music this beautiful in the world, how dare you resent what it asks of you?" Ever since then music has been

127

first in my life. Now I try not to work in the month of August if I can possibly arrange it and I travel all over Europe. But music does come first and that's where it sits. A student once came to me and asked, "Do you think I should stay in music?" I answered, "Because you had to ask me that question, the answer is no." I have a singer who had been with me with the Symphony Chorus for about five years when she took a leave of absence for a year. When she came back to sing for me this summer for this fall's season, she said, "You know, I always felt the need to make some money and I went into the business world and got a very good job. I was making a lot more money than I was making as a singer, but, I just can't live without making music." So she's back in it. And you're in it only because you can't live without it. And then you try your darndest not to do anything that will compromise the art.

Biography

Margaret Hillis first captured nationwide attention in the fall of 1977 when she substituted on short notice for the ailing Sir Georg Solti and conducted the Chicago Symphony Orchestra in Mahler's Symphony no. 8 in New York's Carnegie Hall. She made her Chicago Symphony subscription concert debut in 1972 substituting for Rafael Kubelik, and directing the orchestra and chorus in performances of Handel's *Jeptha*. She has in recent seasons led performances of the National, Indianapolis, Milwaukee, Baltimore, Columbus, Seattle, and Oregon symphony orchestras and the New York Choral Society. Ms. Hillis currently holds three posts: director of the Chicago Symphony Chorus, which she founded in 1957 at the request of Fritz Reiner; founder and music director of the American Choral Foundation; and a member of the regular conducting staff of the Civic Orchestra of Chicago.

Margaret Hillis was born October, 1921. She began to study the piano at the age of five and continued with several other instruments including woodwinds and double-bass. She made her conducting debut while still a student, as assistant conductor of her high orchestra. Ms. Hillis then went on to Indiana University, where she received a Bachelor of Music degree in composition and to Juilliard, where she studied choral conducting with Robert Shaw and Julius Herford. Miss Hillis was the music director for many seasons of the Elgin Symphony Orchestra and for the 1982-83 season was appointed director of choral activities for the San Francisco Orchestra. She has also been visiting professor of conducting at her alma mater, Indiana University, and was associated with Northwestern University for a number of years as professor of conducting and the director of choral organizations.

In February 1978, Margaret Hillis added a Grammy Award to her growing list of honors when the RCA Red Seal release of Verdi's *Requiem*, conducted by Sir Georg Solti and featuring the Chicago Symphony Orchestra and Chorus, was named "Best Choral Performance (other than opera)" by the National Academy of Recording Arts and Sciences. Since then, she has won six more Grammys in this category for releases with two conductors on three record labels. Ms. Hillis has also recorded for CBS Masterworks, Epic, Vox, and London/Decca, and has appeared as conductor of both choral and orchestral programs on all three major television networks.

"Maybe [conducting is] similar to the way light is refracted through a prism. The music comes through you, and you have to be available for this to happen. When I go on stage, I have a little ritual that I do that has evolved over the years. I imagine that I am a cylinder, a conduit, open at the top. I can feel the cylinder through my body, from the head through to the fingertips and the toes. I am then available for something to enter. For me, this ritual gives me the moment of tranquility, a time to focus, to allow myself to become receptive to some inexplicable influence. I do it no matter what state of mind I may be in."

Kenneth Kiesler

Kenneth Kiesler

JW: How did you choose your profession as a musician and a conductor?

KK: The decision seems to have made itself. Music's charm and wiles attracted me at an early age. The idea of conducting came much later. My mother had a subscription to hear Toscanini's Carnegie Hall concerts and has always listened to so-called classical music on the radio. It was always present in the house. I remember a set of recordings designed to introduce children to the instruments of the orchestra. I listened to them constantly even before my school years and I was very proud then to be able to identify the instruments by their timbres.

When I entered school I was immediately thrilled by the sound of the elementary school band. I couldn't wait to learn to play one of those instruments and become a member. The Nanuet (New York) public schools sowed the seeds of my music making and nurtured them. I started playing the trumpet there, mostly because my brother Lewis had taken lessons for a brief time and there was a trumpet in the house. My brother David's clarinet didn't appeal to me. Learning to play the trumpet and playing in the school bands, and later orchestra, gave me something which I craved. I loved learning more and more. I loved rehearsing and polishing for the public performances and I looked forward to the day when we would perform for our fellow students and for an admiring audience made up primarily of supportive and enthusiastic parents.

In the third grade I started playing the trumpet and in the fourth grade I began singing in the school chorus. Singing in choruses proved to have a different sort of attraction. I loved the words, the texts, and their influence on the way the music was shaped and colored. I was also attracted to the people who were the music teachers at the schools. They seemed to have such a love for the music and they had a sense of camaraderie because of their common musical joy. I wanted to be a part of their world. Robert Renino and Daniel Rappazzo simply turned me on to music making. Renino was the instrumental conductor and teacher. Rappazzo was the choral person. Renino emphasized good literature and solid ensemble playing. Rappazzo taught us a wide variety of choral music and choral skills which I still use from time to time. Mostly they seemed to live for the music and it rubbed off.

Dan Rappazzo also taught theory and music appreciation. Here, in smaller groups than in band and chorus, it seemed to me that I was being let in on the secrets of music, that I was one of the lucky few who were privileged to be permitted to learn the magician's secret methods.

One particular idea proved to have a significant impact on me. Each week Mr. Rappazzo would play a new work for us on the record player. On Monday he would play it without introduction. Tuesday's playing would be preceded with a few remarks, Wednesday's with a few more and so on. It wasn't until the fifth playing, on Friday, that we would learn the name of the piece and the composer and follow a score. By that time my curiosity was piqued and I had heard the same piece for five consecutive days. As the weeks passed these "Pieces of the Week" formed a kind of aural repertoire. These pieces became friends. The other students and I would begin to make educated guesses as to the period, the composer and the piece and when we figured it out before Friday we had a child's sense of triumph.

I can easily remember the list of pieces we were introduced to that year. It included the Bartók *Concerto for Orchestra*, the Berlioz *Symphonie fantastique*, Stravinsky's *Petrouchka*, Mozart's G minor Symphony, no. 40, Beethoven's Fifth and Seventh and Second, and the Brahms Fourth Symphony. There was also *Don Juan* and *Death and Transfiguration*.

I also had found a new friend in Ronald Thomas, the cellist who now heads the Boston Chamber Music Society. He knew so much more than I did about orchestras and conductors and the repertoire. I wanted to be included and to catch up. He and I went to countless performances together at the Metropolitan Opera and the New York Philharmonic and when he played the first movement of the Dvořák Concerto with the local orchestra after playing it with Philadelphia, I was enraptured.

There were just a few events which conspired to bring conducting to my attention. When I was fifteen Mr. Rappazzo was ill at the time of our Holiday Concert. The administrators were planning to cancel the concert. I was crushed. We had worked so hard to prepare the *Ceremony of Carols* of Benjamin Britten. I almost begged to be allowed to conduct the performance. Ultimately I was given the opportunity. I didn't really know what to do but I had been watching Mr. Rappazzo in the rehearsals and by this time had been playing under Mr. Renino for several years. Somehow I managed to get everyone through the concert. Someone asked me that night if I planned to be a conductor and the idea seemed to light a fire within me.

Shortly after this I sang in the New York All State Chorus. Robert Kingsbury conducted and we performed only two works: *The Lamentations of Jeremiah* by Ginastera and the *Psalms* of Lukas Foss. The sound of that large chorus, the language of the music, and the warm esprit developed by Robert Kingsbury had a lasting effect. I loved every minute.

Kingsbury would give directions and teach, "For those of you who are thinking about being conductors, I would like you to know why I am doing this phrase in this particular way." I would sit up and take notice. I felt something I had also felt with Mr. Renino and Mr. Rappazzo. I felt as though the differences in our age didn't matter as much as our common ground which was the music.

Then there was a blockbuster event for me. It was the occasion of a New York Philharmonic concert conducted by Karl Böhm. The program had only two works. The first half was the Fourth Symphony of Schumann. The second half was the Fourth Symphony of Brahms. Again I was completely overwhelmed. The first set me up and the second knocked me out. It all seems bigger than life to me now. The evening had begun with friends Martha Connolly and Gary Malkin and Ronald Thomas. We sang for the crowd as they entered the building. I can remember we sang the Hallelujah from the Beethoven *Mount of Olives*. We were excited, thrilled. We were in a teenage frenzy when the concert began. When it was over, we were buzzing and the memory lingered – a memory that comes to life when I conduct those two pieces.

The character of my musical work, or maybe the character of my way of living was very much influenced by a summer camp called Medomak Camp. I went there for fourteen years beginning at the age of eight. It wasn't the stereotypical whistle-blowing kind of summer camp. There were extraordinary people there, creative people. Or maybe they were ordinary and found a place in Medomak that encouraged them to take wing and soar.

Oliver Loud wrote and directed plays there. James Kitendaugh sang and entertained and wrote musical comedies, some of which gave me my first excitement of the stage. Harold Krents, the gifted man about whom *Butterflies Are Free* was written, was there. Pulitzer prizewinner Arthur Walworth wrote a book about the first fifty years of Medomak. Some families were represented for several generations at Medomak. The Newton Family had a powerful impact on me. The three sons, Dexter, Jim and Charlie were third generation. Each was and is a strongly etched individual. I learned so much from them about discipline and about thinking and about living in the out of doors. It was there that I learned to be a Maine Guide and began venturing into the wilderness. It was there, too, that I had a long friendship with John Romer. Fifty years my senior, he talked to me of politics, religion, history, literature, and the woods.

Medomak people feel a certain bond. Those people became my extended family.

What was so meaningful was the way in which everyone was encouraged to grow. There was a noncompetitive measure of achievement. No one was in competition with others; we were encouraged, instead, to set personal goals. They had a system called the honor schedule that had thirty-five to forty activities including such diverse things as the 100-yard dash, pull-ups, nature, and astronomy. There were tests that we would take to earn honors and medals were given when a collective number of points were garnered in many disciplines. This encouraged people to set goals in many different areas, not just one. So, generations of boys and later girls grew up with this well-rounded, goal-oriented approach surrounded by peers who communicated that it was O.K. to excel. After earning the points for a coveted Medomak Medal there was one other requirement. Each winner went on a "vigil." We chose a spot in the woods, built a fire, and pondered the meaning of what we had accomplished. We would write answers to questions which were sealed in envelopes to be opened at certain times during the night in a certain order. These questions would stimulate thought and create an atmosphere in which we could recognize both the magnitude of the achievement and the relative insignificance of that achievement in the face of nature. Now, after some concerts I stay up at my desk late into the night – early morning hours – and write. Sometimes I write notes about the repertoire I conducted. I record thoughts which may benefit the next performance. Other times I sit and think. My mind alternately probes in detail and wanders fruitfully but aimlessly. In a sense this is another Medomak vigil. It engenders and is itself engendered by the same feelings. Unfortunately excellence is not always encouraged today. It has become not O.K. to stand out from people around you. Kids who play instruments sometimes don't admit it to their peers. At Medomak we would play and encourage each other. So for me the short term goal was to get one of those Medomak medals and the long-term lesson was to set life goals and to go for them. Also, I learned to respect one's ancestors, heritage, and traditions. This is also very important in music-making. We need to look ahead and to reach for new heights but we also need to look back and have respect for the past in order to carry on our cultural heritage. I often think of Medomak and my experiences with the people there, many of whom are still part of my life. So many of those people are now achieving important things in many different fields. No matter what they are doing they are acting with the sense of humanity and sense of tradition instilled by Medomak.

After those summer experiences I must have felt the need to find something to do with my life that would carry with it the same meaningfulness. Music, with its sense of continuity, direction, heart, and caring, was the path on which I found myself. As a matter of fact, Toscanini said that as performers, as conductors, we don't create, we achieve. So much of what a music director does goes beyond the music. He or she needs to set goals, sometimes musical ones and sometimes extra-musical ones. So for me it is always important to have a goal in front of me. When I reach one often another occurs to me immediately.

JW: What essential elements do you feel you have as a conductor?

KK: Well, if you had asked me or anybody else twenty years ago whether I would be conducting few would have guessed. I was very late in discovering myself and my own talents. Some of the attributes I feel I have must be present to all conductors and some make me who I am. We each have our individual characteristics. For instance, there is the general approach, an attitude. I really don't like the word "performing." It implies putting on an act. We are performers in the sense that like great actors we become something. A great Othello isn't realized by an actor playing Othello but by an actor who *is* Othello. A great conductor *is* the music. I don't mean that he becomes Mahler or Mozart. I mean instead that a great conductor can become the crescendo, he can become the change from minor to major or the colors of the orchestra. I know when this is happening because I am able to feel it. The pulse changes during a performance. It changes because of emotional reactions to the music. I know, for instance, that I can feel a weight either lifted off or placed on my shoulders when the key changes. When I go into sharps I can feel the intensity of the key. When I go into flats I can feel the depth and the darkness, depending on the given context. That is being, breathing and living the piece of music. Conducting opera is not only being the music, but the dramatic character as well. Maybe it's similar to the way light is refracted through a prism. The music comes through you, and you have to be available for this to happen. When I go on stage, I have a little ritual that I do that has evolved over the years. I imagine that I am a cylinder, a conduit, open at the top. I can feel the cylinder through my body, from the head through to the fingertips and the toes. I am then available for something to enter. For me, this ritual gives me the moment of tranquility, a time to focus, to allow myself to become receptive to some inexplicable influence. I do it no matter what state of mind I may be in.

JW: That's a beautiful image. I think of conducting the same way. You have to be a vehicle for the music to pass through. You have to "cleanse the windows of your perception" to let this happen.

KK: That's exactly it. I suspect the great artists must do just that. The other night I was at the opera in St. Louis and I heard Sylvia McNair sing. I've heard her sing dozens of times and I think she has the most extraordinary talent. This time I really sensed that the audience around me was really listening and brought close to her, was attuned to her, watching. Every time she sang it was a gift to the audience and I watched the audience change. With each note, each syllable, the audience changed. There was a difference between Sylvia and everyone else on that stage. They all sang well but I think there was something else going on. *She* was a vessel for the music. It was coming through her from somewhere.

JW: I know what you mean. I've also seen it happen with certain performers. It's very mysterious.

KK: If one possesses that talent one possesses an extraordinary gift. A few years ago I watched Giulini in a conducting class in Siena step up on the podium to demonstrate something. He didn't even take the baton from the conducting student. He just started conducting the orchestra almost casually. That one bar was more magical than anything the conducting student had done in an hour. What happened? When somebody asked him later what there was about him that made the orchestra sound different with only an upbeat he replied, "Nothing. People make that up." He tossed it off. But when Giulini walks into a room, there is a sense that he is different. You see that difference reflected in other people's eyes. You could *see* the effect he was having on that orchestra. I'm sure he was aware of it but he is so modest that he would never claim any personal advantage.

JW: Many of the great artists have such powerful personalities that they affect everyone around them. I think that that is how they change an audience through their performance.

KK: Yes. But it's power that is coming *through* them. People sometimes ask me after a concert if I feel powerful in front of the orchestra. Of course not. No artist in that situation would feel power. How can you feel power when you are faced with the enormous responsibility of performing great music? I'm also interested in how people react to different types of performances. After a performance of *Pines of Rome,* for instance, people will run backstage to share their enthusiasm. When I do the *B Minor Mass* the audience feels a very different thing. Maybe they don't understand the work, maybe it's too long for them or maybe it's too serious. So, it's a much greater challenge to become the prism for the *B Minor Mass* than for the *Pines of Rome.* How many young conductors are doing the *B Minor Mass* or *Missa Solemnis,* or working on the Brahms symphonies? Instead, many want to do *Pictures at an Exhibition, Daphnis and Chloé, The Planets*, and *Firebird.* They often eschew Beethoven, Schumann, Haydn, Mozart, Brahms, or Schubert. A vast repertoire should be learned. The danger is that conductors might want to have standing ovations for all of their concerts at a time when audiences, at least American audiences, are more inclined to be stirred by bombast than by soul searching. Audience response is not always a reliable method of measuring the quality of a performance.

JW: What do you feel is your greatest challenge as a conductor?

KK: To become a better musician and to serve the art in a better way each day. I know that sounds over simplified but when I'm disappointed in myself at the end of a day, I don't sleep well. There can be weeks when I don't sleep well. I sometimes get the equivalent of "writer's block." It's hard to get out of it. Sometimes running, being outdoors, wakes me up again. Other times there are emotional ways of breaking through. And then, what does it mean to become a better musician? Every day it means something different. It depends on the piece I'm working on. Some days I try to hear better in rehearsals. Some days I try to understand a certain piece or some part of a piece a little better, by the end of the day, to go a step farther than I have gone before. I'm not saying that one can do everything in a day, but with the accumulation of days one can grow. So I try to find something new each day. For instance, I've conducted Shostakovich's Fifth many, many times. I thought that I had answered many questions about it. Then I started to study it on the plane coming here. I began to change things and thought, "How could I have conceived of this as I once had?" Suddenly the music meant something different for me. I'm going to need to rework everything! So that's the challenge. Also I try to keep focused on the priorities of being a musician and try not to be distracted by all of the ancillary things I have to do. I have been distracted so often. One begins to learn what those distractions are and then to stay away from them. Sometimes there are also people who try to sabotage you unconsciously. Maybe they see you going into musical places they are afraid to go. I've even heard musicians say, "Oh, you don't need to study that piece. You have done it a hundred times. You know it." Now what does that mean? Why don't they support each other in a way that encourages more depth of knowledge?

JW: What do you feel about the conductor's relationship to the musicians in orchestras and the musicians' relationship with each other? What do you think of the burn-out that tends to occur in major orchestras?

KK: The musicians in the orchestra are colleagues, they are family. Many of us spend more time together than we do even with our personal friends or relatives. The nature, the purpose of our togetherness is unique. We have, dare I say, probably many more meaningful experiences together than with most others. Think of the kinds of emotional connections musicians have with each other. They have to depend on each other. For example, a clarinetist may need to depend on the bassoonist to deliver a phrase in such a way that it can be continued. Musicians need to trust that the conductor will not change something crucial in the performance that has been rehearsed another way. Think of the kind of communication musicians have while performing the Mahler Second together, without a word being spoken. With all its complexities that is a very high level of relating. Conductors need to understand that and need to see musicians as human beings, not as pieces of a puzzle or cogs in a machine. Musicians feel the conductor's attitude and respond to it. With this human approach they will tend to be less jaded and burn-out will be alleviated. The whole process is energized. When the orchestra is energized the conductor can respond better and the cycle is repeated!

I just received two letters from musicians formerly in my orchestra who described the "loving" environment of the Springfield Orchestra. They wrote about the family environment in which everyone cared. That is what keeps a musician from feeling less and smaller than he is. I actually heard a conductor say in a speech yesterday that conductors should know the names of the people in their orchestra! Can you imagine feeling the need to point this out? Is this so remarkable? As if it were something unusual to know the names of the people you work with everyday in such an intimate way. The very nature of the comment points to the depth of the problem.

Of course there will always be differences or disagreements. Not everyone will like you. When I say "like" I don't mean in a personal way. We don't expect to appeal to everybody. But there are people who won't agree with the decisions you make. Also there are people who will want to sabotage you for their own personal reasons. These are the people you need to love the most. As far as the burn-out factor is concerned, I can almost understand it when I know someone has played 200 concerts a year for thirty years. I don't like it and I'd like to see that the conditions under which those musicians work are improved. What I don't understand, though, is when I see a twenty-year-old student who doesn't give a damn about music. Who do they think they are placing their personal interests above the music? They see a paycheck in front of them and nothing else.

JW: Can you describe your relationship with soloists?

KK: There are certain people with whom I have felt very good about performing. There was a real activity in the performance, electrical stuff going back and forth! There have been other times when I felt only like an accompanist and felt almost completely removed from the performance. It's like dancing. You should be able to dance with your partner and move together. However, some soloists dance by themselves and the conductor sits on the sidelines. When that happens it's awful! It is essential to arrive at a joint conception of the work. To compromise is to occasionally sacrifice a point of view. It is better to reexamine the piece together. Having said this, one must recognize the investment of time and study which a soloist has in a particular work. One must respect the artist's insight and experience with a piece.

JW: I'd like to ask some more technical questions if you don't mind. How do you approach a new score for the first time? What is your analysis technique?

KK: It depends on whether the work is by a composer whose works I've done before. If it is I will have an easier time learning the work because I will come to it with the knowledge of the style and will have certain expectations. If it is a work by a new composer I will have to start in a different way. Generally, I start analyzing the structure. I find the phrase lengths, how the small groups come together to form the big groups. I find how the larger groups mark off big sections. I look for basic kinds of repetitions to find what's varied or repeated verbatim in the repetition. Is the key the same, is the orchestration the same, are the dynamics the same? What has been altered? Is the articulation the same and if it's different is it intentional or is it a misprint? If it is intentional then what is the goal which accounts for the difference? Is the composer trying to make the repetition more or less intense? Bigger, smaller, reminiscent or nostalgic? Those are the kinds of questions I ask and try to find answers for.

For instance, Mozart will write an exposition one way and in the recapitulation sometimes bars are inserted or deleted. Why is this the case? Of course these changes usually have to do with the modulations but sometimes they have to do with the fact that by skipping those bars he is speeding up the momentum toward the ultimate goal. Or maybe by adding certain bars a particular moment is more intensified, as if one's ears could be focused on this section the way a painter would have one's eyes focused by using white to highlight sections of a painting.

JW: Do you use a piano when you study or do you study at your desk?

KK: I do my analysis at my desk. I go through the structural analysis and then I do a harmonic analysis.

JW: Do you do a complete harmonic analysis, chord by chord?

KK: Sometimes yes and sometimes no. A chord-by-chord analysis is necessary when a conductor is just beginning. With experience one tends to begin to hear much better and it's not necessary to mark each single chord change after a while. At this point I mark things that are unusual and have some impact, not just every five-one cadence. If there is a move to a flat sixth or Neapolitan sixth, or a pedal tone, I will mark it in the score. Then of course I go down to the nitty-gritty detail of the articulation of every note and the bowings for the strings.

JW: Do you mark all of your own bowings?

KK: Almost all of them. I'm very comfortable doing it after working for years and years with string players, with concertmasters, and with conductors who were string players. I think I have a good feel for it now. It's similar to breathing with some exceptions. When you run out of breath, you run out of bow. If you want an airy sound, you can have an airy sound on the bow. You can have an intense sound by expending less breath and you can have an intense sound by using a more compact bow. Occasionally, though, I'll send a score of parts off to my principal players. Then if I think changes are appropriate we will discuss it. There are certain pieces, though, such as the Mozart *Requiem*, the Bach *Magnificat* or the *B Minor Mass*, that I would not hand over to anyone. I mark my own parts on any piece with a text and when the instrumentalists may not, based on a single orchestral part, understand the ramifications of the text or may not know the choral parts. I know that not every principal player is going to agree with me, but if there has to be a unified approach, then it has to be mine. I think there is no substitute for a conductor doing the bowings, even if they are not used in the performance. The process is enlightening. If the conductor has considered the bowings and has thought about them he will have a much stronger concept of the work. The same is true for the wind parts. It's so important to look at them in terms of articulation, breath, balances. Balance is of crucial importance. Also, it's possible to make an educated guess as to which notes are going to be a problem in terms of intonation. These are the kinds of things I consider when I study the score. I mark the structural matters, the little motives, because they relate to each other. I mark in questions such as, "Should this be different than the last time? Is this a tempo *piu mosso* or *meno mosso*? Is the tempo the same for the second theme?" At first I don't want to get bogged down with all of these things, yet I want to ask questions and allow myself the time to get the best answers.

After this initial process I go to the piano. I'm not a performing pianist, but I play for score study. I will sometimes stay in one place and play with only two notes in a way that focuses my ears and attention. I want to know what those notes might mean in a given context. I then usually end up playing every note in the work. I will discover all sorts of things by doing this. I've discovered many misprints in pitches and rhythms this way. I've learned how certain notes work together and influence the pitch of other notes. I see horizontal relationships that I may have missed the first time through. It's very important for a conductor to know a score vertically and horizontally. One needs to know the harmonic structures vertically and also what a player sees and plays on the horizontal level. Then after all of this work and study, the moment comes when I know that I can conduct the piece. Of course one can also go through all of this work and study and not feel able to conduct it. This is because a greater understanding of the work still needs to take place. I remember, for example, when I was studying the Mozart *Requiem*. I began by looking at the text and studying the choral parts. I tried to imagine Mozart with the blank page before him setting the text. There is a part of the *Requiem* text about "being in the jaws of the lion." I looked at the orchestration and saw that the chorus was in unison and the orchestration was in octaves. Suddenly I realized that visually the score actually looked and sounded like the chorus was in the mouth of the lion. It was illuminating for me to see that. Now that is very different than just knowing, "These are octaves and the chorus is in unison." Now I've heard many people say, "Don't tell the orchestra that this is a sunrise." Well, if the composer intended it to be a sunrise then you better be damn sure the orchestra understands that it's a sunrise! Now if you are only speculating, don't say this sort of thing. But nine times out of ten, it does have an effect on how they play because it does bring about understanding. My occasional teacher, Julius Herford, used to say that rehearsals are not a place to practice. They are a place at which musicians arrive at an understanding of a piece so that they can share that understanding with each other and with the listener. Imagine performing Shostakovich's Symphony No. 14 without knowing the texts. The singers have to share with the orchestra how they feel when they perform that music and what their musical motivation is. The orchestra should want to listen and know what the singers are singing and feeling. Now, many times people tell you not to talk to an orchestra and to conduct the music instead. Well, that's absolutely right to a certain extent when it comes to certain technical matters. But there are some things that need to be said and that can lead to a better understanding. If the orchestra understands what the motivation behind a certain work is it will make a difference in how they play it.

JW: Do you perform by memory and do you think that that is important?

KK: I don't think everything has to be memorized but certain elements should be in the memory. I usually conduct long pieces by memory because I feel that it does benefit the performance. I have a much stronger sense of the structure and architecture of the piece if I am not reading or turning pages. There is some benefit in removing the physical barrier of the music stand. In conducting from memory one is working with the language of music, its aural reality, rather than working with the symbols which represent the music. However, there are some works that I've done over and over in which I still use a score. I don't think that the performance of short pieces improves that much by memory because the overall structure is so condensed.

JW: Do you go over the score in your head practicing your memory?

KK: You bet. Many, many times. After learning a work, to help make the leap from study to performance. It's funny, I have this habit of often standing through a work. I don't wave my arms or anything, I just stand. I close my eyes and "visualize" the sound and play the piece through in my head. If I can't mentally realize the work this way I won't conduct the piece without a score.

JW: Now some conductors say that memory is not that important and that they conduct too much repertoire to put everything to memory. They have to make a choice.

KK: Well, it's true. This past year I did fewer works without a score because at one point I had to conduct eight different programs in a ten-week period.

JW: How do you go about building an orchestra? How do you get the string and wind sound you want?

KK: I don't like the expression the "Kiesler sound" or the "Solti sound." I'm not quite as opposed to something like the "Philadelphia sound" because there is such a thing. Instead of the "Solti sound" we should have a "Bach sound" or a "Beethoven sound," or a "Mozart sound." However, even within a Mozart sound we must seek a hundred different sounds. The strings are capable of more colors than any other section. They are the soul of the orchestra. So the conductor has to not only know what to do with them, but know all the possibilities. The possibilities are really almost limitless. Again, it's like a chorus. It's interesting that we talk about the choir of strings. The strings are like a chorus, they have four-part harmony. In the winds, you only have a few in a section playing different parts. In the strings you have many people playing the same part. They have to play with unanimity or uniformity and still maintain the feeling of being individual artists, each with something to contribute. That's a very difficult task to accomplish. How does a conductor make everyone feel a part of the whole and yet not have them lose their sense of contributing as individuals? I think that it's important to have everybody headed in the same direction with the same goal at the same time. Rather than telling them what *not* to do, such as, "Don't play out, use less bow and so forth," tell them the musical content and very often that is sufficient for them to find the right thing to do. It's very important for a conductor to be able to describe a technical solution to a problem. It's important to be able to say, "Off the string at the frog, on at the tip, off at the middle and in this crescendo start off the string and gradually get more and more on the string." This enables you to achieve the exact sound you are looking for.

Also, the idea of having strong principal players is very important in building an orchestral sound. The principal players in the orchestra, no matter what section, need to be the best players in the section. A principal string player can be a personable leader, can have insightful ideas, can communicate with the section, can relate well to the conductor, but if that person isn't the best player in the section, the house of cards will eventually tumble.

When thinking about the winds one needs to realize that the winds are soloists. Also, the four woodwind principals have most interesting tasks. A clarinetist plays differently when paired with a flute than when paired with an oboe or bassoon. A wind player has to listen to all aspects of harmony. He needs to ask, "Am I on the third of the chord? Is the third major or minor? Am I on the fifth of the chord? Am I on the seventh of the chord? What kind of seventh is it? Does the seventh resolve down or does it hang unresolved?" These considerations will effect the tuning of each note. Also, they need to be thinking about balance. They should be thinking, "Am I playing in thirds? If so should I play stronger or weaker than the other players? If I'm playing fifths or octaves how should I balance my part?" This type of thinking is crucial. They should also be listening to how they fit with the strings. Are they projecting as soloists? Playing a woodwind instrument is a very interesting job. The conductor has to help them with these decisions and also set them free in the music making.

In building an orchestra, it helps to do many pieces by the same composer. With greater understanding the results develop and reach a higher and higher level. When I first started with my orchestra, they had played very little Mozart. I started with the overtures to *The Marriage of Figaro* and *The Magic Flute*. Then we went through more overtures and on to many of the symphonies and concerti. Now when we play Mozart the style and balance are there immediately.

JW: What do you think about the new research in early music performance practices? What do you think about the metronome markings in the Beethoven symphonies?

KK: I think the sound of original instruments can inform a modern performance. Understanding original instruments and performance practice can affect articulation, dynamics, bowing, color, and tempo. Perhaps equally important is to value the overall historical context of a work or body of works. I believe there is merit in the original instrument movement. However, I also believe that performance of this repertoire on modern instruments has its own merit and validity. I think many people toss off the metronome markings too easily, without enough thought. They discard them without enough consideration, serious consideration. Often they will say a marking is too fast because they have never heard it so fast. (Also, perhaps the performance they heard was actually faster than the printed metronome marking.) On the other hand they will argue that a metronome marking is too slow. So, which was it? Was Beethoven's metronome broken in both directions? I can't believe a man of Beethoven's intelligence would make those kinds of mistakes. With or without a metronome he knew that there were 60 beats in a minute. So, it doesn't make any sense that he was as "wrong" as some people say. I had an interesting experience while doing a string master class at a university in Illinois. That year string players were doing an orchestral excerpt from the so-called slow movement of the Beethoven Fifth Symphony. With each variation this student played a different tempo. Finally I asked if he would play just one tempo and not change tempo with each variation. So he tried and couldn't do it; one tempo was too fast and the other was too slow. We worked and worked until we found a tempo that could be used for all the variations. We checked it on the metronome and found it was the exact tempo that Beethoven had marked!

Here was a student who came completely without any prejudice. He hadn't heard Klemperer's or Karajan's or Norrington's recordings.

Now at the same time I can't support the slavish adherence to the exact metronome markings of any composer. Most composers don't sit there with their metronomes going through each note of their composition. They just say, "This is kind of fast, around 120, or this is a little faster, *piu mosso*, 132." I feel that metronome markings are general indications. I remember doing the premeire of Stephen Stucky's Fourth Symphony with the Indianapolis Symphony. He had marked eighth note = 208. We worked at it and worked at it and finally were able to perform it that fast. He came to one of the last rehearsals and said, "Whoa, stop! Why so fast?" "We are following your metronome marks," I replied. He said, "Yeah, I know, but I didn't use a metronome. I just meant it to be really fast, but not *that* fast!"

Then there are other considerations such as the hall and the ability of the orchestra. All in all, though, I think we have to look at a composer's metronome indications seriously and then try and make informed and musical decisions.

JW: Would you consider retouching your scores?

KK: I try to avoid it. I feel guilty when I do it unless I honestly believe that I am clarifying the composer's intentions in doing it. I used to retouch Schumann's Fourth Symphony. I had a score that had been marked by George Szell and saw all of the reorchestrations for which he is famous. I didn't feel good about them. Years later I started with a clean score and worked only with the dynamics. I didn't reorchestrate (I think I added three or four notes to the whole work) and the whole thing suddenly came to life for me. It felt like it was really Schumann. Just the idea of adding trumpets or horns to the melodies feels wrong to me. Wagner and Weingartner did it, so everyone else did it for awhile. It's not necessary to do it now. It changes the entire character of the work. If you do need to balance a melody I think it's better to seek solutions which are sensitive to the sound the composer had in mind. Often the accompaniment can be adjusted in a variety of ways.

JW: Finally, how do you plan repertoire for your own orchestra? Are ticket sales a strong consideration?

KK: Yes and no. I rarely program a piece that I don't feel strongly about. I always want to be an advocate for the composer and when I have done pieces I don't particularly believe in I have felt unclean. I have sworn to myself that I'll never do it again. Unfortunately, I haven't learned that lesson. For the most part I conduct pieces that I feel deeply about. On the other hand, I also feel that the audience needs to hear a great number of works. I am in a situation where I don't have many guest conductors to do the music I don't feel especially attuned to, so I feel the obligation to perform works that I might not program otherwise.

My season has shapes. There are nights when the music brings about a tumultuous audience reaction which can be important, particularly when we are talking about funding. However, there are other nights when the audience can be brought into a different frame of mind. I would not open the season with the *St. Matthew Passion*. But I would certainly do the *St. Matthew Passion* at the appropriate time of year. So a season has a shape and the audience senses that shape. They may not understand it, they may not be able to verbalize it, but they should be able to feel the rhythm, the emotional rhythm of the season. There's some music that doesn't feel right to perform in the summer and there is some music that brings us to a place that is not right for the winter. The season needs to pick up momentum and release that momentum in a certain way at certain times. Also, the individual programs need to fit into the overall shape of the season. For instance, suppose you program the Mahler Second for the second concert of a ten concert series. What would you put on the third, fourth, and fifth concerts after programming the *Resurrection* Symphony so early? How would you conclude the series, where would you put the climax? So you see, the Mahler Second would make more sense programmed at the end of the season. That's an extreme example, but there are more subtle ones within each individual program. For example, I have been criticized both for ending concerts bombastically and for ending them quietly. To imply that a conductor needs to evaluate his choice based on a work's ending does a great disservice to all of us. Board members have actually asked me, "Wouldn't it be better to bring the audience to its feet rather than programming Mahler's Fourth, which ends quietly?" I feel that if the audience comes to their feet at the end of Mahler's Fourth it will be because they were stirred emotionally to do that. Unfortunately, a standing ovation in this country has become the measure of success. People look for it, they watch for it.

JW: What are your considerations in programming twentieth-century pieces? Do you find that the audience reaction to new music is not always very positive and that there is resistance to hearing new works?

KK: One has to keep in mind where the concert is taking place and for what audience. To program the wrong new work for an audience does a disservice instead of a service in promoting new music. So to program the right piece at the right time can help a great deal in enhancing audience reaction to contemporary music. I've very often programmed shorter twentieth-century pieces packaged with standard repertoire. For instance, I programmed Michael Colgrass's *As Quiet As* with *Don Quixote*. Both works paint pictures and fit very nicely together on the same program.

A twentieth-century work has to have the same qualities of greatness that other pieces have of other eras. Does it make sense, does it work musically, is it consistent within its own language? Does the composer understand and use the orchestra well? If a composer specifies an unusual technique, say he or she wants the violinists to tap on the back of their instruments, is the sound an integral part of the piece? Many composers don't understand the relationship of notes and you will find them piled in a way that has no direction. The work has to go somewhere. I don't want to feel the same at the end of the piece as I do at the beginning. Also, quite simply I have to be able to read the piece. I get a large number of scores I can't even read, with wrong transpositions and notes that aren't on the instruments they are scored for!

JW: Do you have help in selecting new works?

KK: Well, when I was the assistant conductor in Indianapolis I was given the assignment of selecting scores for the music director to look at. I didn't like that responsibility because I was selecting scores for *him*. *He* would be the one performing them. So with my own orchestra I try to look through the scores myself even though I have an assistant. I must admit, though, that I am very far behind. Sometimes I will look at one or two scores a day and then other times there will be months when I don't have the time. It's unfortunate. I will often send back a score because I know that I can't perform it. Also, if something comes in that has thirty-five extra players and is ninety-five minutes long I won't be able to consider it. We have certain limitations and parameters. There are certain people like Bill Sisson at Boosey and Hawkes or composers' representatives such as Bette Snapp who are helpful in bringing new works to my attention.

JW: What is your reaction to minimalism?

KK: I don't have a violent reaction to any ism. I try to take a piece based on its own merits. I have done some minimalist music, though. I did a piece by David Stock called *American Accents* at the convention last year in Chicago and I have done some music of John Adams. I think it *can* be wonderful music. Unfortunately, it's become a rage and that rage is tarnishing its image and perhaps affecting the quality of what is being written.

JW: It has brought back an audience for twentieth-century music, though.

KK: Yes, but I've often listened to a few pieces and have become utterly frustrated at the lack of momentum and variety. I say, "Come on, change!" And it doesn't! On the other hand I have listened to other works that were absolutely mesmerizing. They can put one in a state of meditation. Personally, I would rather perform other music because I don't get the same sort of heart and soul satisfaction. John Adams's music can be an exception. There is a certain kind of music that appeals to me, no matter what era it is from. Music that speaks of the human spirit and is ennobling. The Beethoven Violin Concerto has that quality as opposed to a Paganini concerto. The Adagietto from Mahler's Symphony no. 5 has such a human message that is felt and not just heard. I think that unfortunately there is pressure on music directors to perform new music so we can demonstrate a high number of premieres to some government funding agency. Many times music is being performed that shouldn't be performed because of this. On the other hand we need a balance. It's a difficult problem.

JW: In concluding I'd like to know what you think about the ASOL and Exxon conducting programs. As you know it is terribly difficult for conductors to find their way into the conducting profession. Are these organizations helping young American conductors break into the professional conducting world? Do you have other suggestions for young conductors?

KK: Both organizations give certain people breaks and help certain conductors to get started. However, I think there is a danger of using a cookie cutter approach in choosing conductors. I've too often heard things like, "He's so tall. She's so graceful. He's got great publicity pictures." Sometimes I get the feeling that they are trying to find celebrity personalities instead of good musicians. I ran into an Exxon conductor yesterday who did his three years with a major symphony and hasn't been heard of since. Some people went through that program and got good jobs. Some of the conductors were good and some weren't. Yet, this will happen with or without these programs and I think they, and other programs, do much more that is good than not good.

Also, I think that it's an artificial system that doesn't take note of people who have been in the field working, who have grown as musicians, who have studied their scores, and who have given their time to a community. In fact, the more time you give to a community the less likely you are to be on the national scene and the less likely you will be to be rewarded by moving up the ladder. I think this system has to change. There has to be a way of nurturing the many talented people who deserve it. I would suggest young conductors find any available outlet to begin, to be more concerned with the musical experience than with a career.

JW: How would you suggest these organizations find and support talented young conductors?

KK: First of all, to be a professional conductor takes an incredible combination of skills, talent, gifts, insight, and abilities, some of which are musical and some of which aren't. You can almost tell with two equal musicians which one is going to make it into the professional world and which one won't. Also, to be a professional conductor is very different from being a college conductor or a community orchestra conductor. It takes a

149

certain something to get up in front of a different orchestra every few weeks or days and to be constantly giving. Sometimes one might have four rehearsals and sometimes only two or three. That's a very different thing than training a college or community orchestra for six or eight weeks. A conductor must be a leader. Some people are wonderful musicians but are not leaders. A conductor must be able to make the individual musicians in the orchestra feel that they are still artists.

Few of our organizations or educational systems train conductors for the reality of the conducting profession. They don't tell them what to expect in ten years or how to break into the profession. To be a conductor you need to be a self-starter, a self-motivator. You need to be someone who understands yourself and understands the profession in order to know what is needed and how to go about getting it. We need to design conducting programs that reward musical excellence, that reward musical education, that reward musical insight. After that we need to find a method that can direct people into different areas of the field. Some will go into early music, into new music. Someone else will go into college or community work and somebody else will go to conduct the Orchestre de Paris and the Los Angeles Philharmonic and Boston Symphony. Which direction people take will then have to do with personality and leadership abilities. Some will have the abilities to deal with managements, business communities and boards of directors. Others will be better at teaching conductors or working in academic settings. Much has been determined by "charisma," which has come to mean good-looking or flamboyant. As far as I'm concerned, charisma emerges from having authority and the only way to have authority is to have knowledge. Without knowledge a conductor has no business being in front of other musicians. Without knowledge one can't possibly have charisma. Imagine someone getting on the podium trying to be charismatic without knowing anything about music. This is just posturing, just acting, maybe it's even dancing, but it's certainly not being a musician. It's not being what being an artist demands. We have a responsibility for passing on the music of people who have come before us, the great composers, and the responsibility of introducing new music of great, and maybe not-so-great, twentieth-century composers to contemporary audiences. Having charisma, personality, trappings, and 57th Street hype is not going to do the job in the long haul. On the other hand, if somebody is a great musician, then we need to give them the publicity to get them into the public's eye and to sell tickets. Since we need corporate support and ticket sales to support our art we will need to promote them in an appropriate manner. That is a fact of modern life! There is no problem with this as long as we promote real musicians! Leonard Slatkin is a perfect example of this. He is first a musician who also has the ability to inspire an entire organization. Everyone from the management to the stage hands will do the best they can do for him. This happens because he's a good musician first!

I was talking about this yesterday at the ASOL conference. I was on a panel discussing the selection process of music directors. I gave the example of when I received a recent award. The people who gave the award explained to the audience why they had selected me. They mentioned the increase in ticket sales, the increase in attendance, the increase in broadcasts, the out-of-state concerts, the in-state touring. Nobody mentioned the quality of the orchestra or my varied repertoire. Nobody talked about how we had introduced new music to a community that was accustomed to only conservative programming. Nobody mentioned that we performed works by Nielsen, Mahler, Shostakovich, Bartók, and Schoenberg that had never been performed in our community. Afterwards somebody asked the general manager of my orchestra, "You have a great music director. Can he conduct?" How could you even think of calling someone a great music director if they can't conduct? The whole focus for being a music director in this country is on this ancillary stuff. This has to change. The focus has to be on the music. What I mean by this is that the focus has to be on enlightened performance. Many musicians have no idea how one note relates to another note. They are like someone speaking French and not knowing what a subject or verb is. There are some conductors that don't know the function of F-sharp in the key of G, or how it's tuned or that there are several possibilities for tuning. They don't know for instance, that when Bach writes in sharps it feels different than when Bach writes in flats. There are moments in the *St. Matthew Passion* where sharps mean and represent something, where the number of notes in a bar means something.

Conductors should know the details of a work as well as the whole of the piece, when it was written and what it meant to the composer. Music is built on simple building blocks and many musicians have no concept about this at all. I've seen so many conductors conduct only the main entrances of the instruments. Well what happens after the entrance? What is the tone color and what is the meaning of it? Where is the direction or the motion or the shape? So few conductors conduct the direction and the structure. I witnessed a performance recently in which a work had a fantastic dominant pedal in the basses and cellos that gets stronger and stronger. This conductor had his back to them and was only conducting the tune in the violins! A conductor needs to understand the music, to shed light on it, remove the dust and dirt from it, and be able to bring it to life.

We have two separate worlds in the States, the academic and the professional world. The academic world often doesn't trust the professional world and the professional world doesn't respect the academic world. The professional world seems to be saying, "Let's train conductors ourselves, instead of relying on our academic institutions." They seem to be saying, "We

151

are going to provide the Exxon program and the America Conductor's Project. This will help promote and educate our conductors." There should be more cooperation between these two worlds. Admittedly one doesn't simply get a degree and become a conductor! Somebody quoted Blomstedt as saying, "If batons were more expensive there would be fewer conductors."

JW: Now that is someone with a tremendous amount of knowledge!

KK: Yes and musical knowledge takes a long time to acquire. Today we have such difficult musical standards to live up to probably because of Toscanini and all the great conductors that have gone before us. Conductors are expected to be people who sell tickets, have good public relations, a good image, a good appearance, and at the very end of the list they need to be a good musician. Being a good musician means a thousand different things. When someone visits a rehearsal for a choral work, for example, they watch me stop the second violins and tell them to take two downbows because the chorus breathes in a certain place. They watch me explain to the chorus that I want a dental *t* and not an exploded *t*. They learn that a conductor has to know something about history and religion, about percussion, about strings, and also about the tongues in singers' mouths. Conductors must ultimately put this kind of technical know-how to the service of informed, communicative, vital, poetic, and sincere music-making.

JW: The kind of knowledge you are talking about takes a lifetime.

KK: Right. It never stops. What you have to understand is that every person is a work of art in progress. We are all growing and changing. Musicians are like seeds. We need to nurture them and give them many opportunities to grow. Later on we can do some weeding out or provide more light. The health and vitality of this art and profession demand the investment of our diligence, patience, knowledge, and humanity.

Biography

Kenneth Kiesler is one of the most prominent and versatile conductors of his generation. He has recently made debuts conducting the St. Louis Symphony at the Opera Theatre of St. Louis, the San Diego Symphony, the National Symphony at the Kennedy Center—having been honored as one of three conductors selected to participate in the Leonard Bernstein American Conductors Program, and the Chicago Symphony Orchestra in an all-Shostakovich program opening the CSO's '90–'91 subscription series for high school students. He also recently returned to the Jerusalem Symphony where he led a program including the Nielsen Symphony No. 4. He led the Illinois Chamber Orchestra in its 1987 New York debut at Lincoln Center's Alice Tully Hall featuring the Fourteenth Symphony of Shostakovich, and in its 1990 debut at Carnegie Hall featuring the premiere of Gunther Schuller's Concerto for Two Pianos-Three Hands.

Kenneth Kiesler's conducting appearances have also included the Detroit Symphony, the Osaka Philharmonic, the Indianapolis Symphony, Long Island Philharmonic, Virginia Symphony, Albany Symphony, Puerto Rico Symphony, the Omaha and Texas Chamber Orchestras and the Festivals of Meadowbrook, Skaneateles, Sewanee, and Aspen.

His upcoming engagements include debuts with the Ohio Chamber Orchestra in Cleveland, the Haifa Symphony in Israel, a production of *Madama Butterfly* at the Chattanooga Opera and two all-Shostakovich programs with the St. Cecilia Orchestra including a live National Public Radio broadcast on the renowned "Morning Pro Musica with Robert J. Lurtsema" and concerts in Symphony Hall in Boston, Veterans Memorial Auditorium in Providence and Town Hall in New York City.

During his eleven seasons as Music Director of the Springfield Symphony Orchestra he has inspired dramatic artistic growth and achievement including the establishment of the Illinois Chamber Orchestra and the Springfield Symphony Chorus, the launching of a six-concert series at Illinois State University, a five-fold expansion in the number of concerts, two "Illinois Orchestra of the Year" awards, tour and run-out concerts, national and international broadcasts, televised concerts and several premieres.

Kenneth Kiesler was the recipient of the 1988 Helen M. Thompson Award which is presented every two years to the outstanding American Music Director under the age of 35 by the American Symphony Orchestra League. He was a finalist and winner of the second prize at the 1986 Leopold Stokowski Conducting Competition at Avery Fisher Hall. He has held the posts of Music Director of the South Bend Symphony and the Congress of Strings.

Born in New York City in the summer of 1953 and raised in Nanuet, New York, Kenneth Kiesler received the Bachelor of Music in Music History and Performance from the University of New Hampshire, and the Master of Music in Orchestral Conducting from the Peabody Conservatory of the Johns Hopkins University where he held assistantships in orchestra, chorus and opera. He received a Fellowship in Orchestral Conducting and was later a member of the faculty at the Aspen Music School. He has also studied at the Accademia Musicale Chigiana in Siena, Italy, and at Indiana University where, at the age of 23, he became the youngest conductor of a full production *(Così fan Tutte)* in the history of the Indiana University Opera Theatre. His teachers have included John Nelson, Fiora Contino, Julius Herford and James Wimer, and he has participated in courses led by Erich Leinsdorf and Carlo Maria Giulini. He was one of four American conductors to receive a special invitation to work with Pierre Boulez and his Ensemble InterContemporain during the festivities celebrating the Centenary of Carnegie Hall.

August 1991

"With the combination of technical perfection and beauty, you can discover much more about the music. My orchestra and I, of course, after seventeen years together know each other very well. They know exactly how I want the music to sound. They know what I want if I move my hand, head, or eyes in a certain way. I can work on the surface or in depth."

_____ Kurt Masur

Kurt Masur

JW: When did you decide to become a conductor and what is your musical background?

KM: I had a normal childhood. I grew up in a small city with a population of 40,000 in the eastern part of Germany that is now Poland. My name, Masur, is Polish, which means there must be somebody in my background who was of that nationality. Both my sisters and I were naturally musical. When my sisters learned to play the piano I was only five. I used to listen and learn what they were taught. Finally I received my own private piano lessons at the age of ten. I enjoyed music more and more, but I was also interested in being a technician. My father was an engineer so I learned to be an electrical technician which is something I still do well. I had the choice of being either a musician or an engineer. At the age of sixteen I heard my first symphony concert. The orchestra played Beethoven's Ninth! I was so affected by it that I walked around as though I were deaf for three days. When I woke up I decided that the only thing I could do was to become a conductor. When I first told this to my family they couldn't believe their ears because I was a very shy young man. However, I had decided that I needed to go all the way into music. It was very clear. I learned to play the piano and organ but couldn't make a professional career of them because of a disease in my right hand. I could conduct, though! My father begged me to do a "real" profession that was safe, but I couldn't.

The end of the war came and we had to move because the section we were living in was now Poland. I discovered at this time that they were beginning to give lessons again at the conservatory in Leipzig. I traveled there by train and got the permission to enroll and started to study in February of 1946. I studied conducting, piano, cello, singing, and composition. The students formed a band to earn money so we wouldn't be hungry. We had to go on with life after the war and actually we had a wonderful time. For me this was the very beginning of my career. In 1948 I got a job as an opera coach in the Opera House in Halle. I worked there for six months as a piano coach and got my first opportunity to conduct the *Christmas Tale* for children in a Christmas play. The orchestra liked me and I was given my first opportunity to conduct opera at the age of twenty-one.

JW: That was very soon!

KM: Yes, that was very soon because, you know, a lot of men died in the war. We were needed. A lot of very young guys like me got their first opportunities that way. It was wonderful for me. I could do nearly anything I wanted in the theater. I sang *Fidelio,* I played the piano, I played the organ, I was the ballet coach, I played in the orchestra's percussion section the first half of a concert and the second half I was conducting. It was wonderful! This type of varied musical experience and training was normal in our country. For three years I ran from theater to theater.

I came to Leipzig very soon after I was conducting in Halle and became the opera conductor from the years 1953 to 1955. Then a former teacher invited me to Dresden to become the second conductor of the Dresden Philharmonic. I had three wonderful years learning the symphonic repertoire and the main opera repertoire. After those years I went to Schwerin and became the music director at the age of thirty. So you see I had quite a steady career. Until then I had worked very hard to get better and better but found that I had to work harder still and needed to go into greater depth in my score study. I had conducted a lot of different operas (more than sixty) and a lot of symphonic pieces. Most of them, of course, I had learned very fast because it was necessary. If I had said "no" to the opportunities I would never have been invited again. So, I said "yes" to everything that came along.

After that I came to Walter Felsenstein, who had seen me conduct in Berlin. He wanted me to work with him. Felsenstein was a great stage director and finally I had the opportunity to work very hard and in depth on different opera performances. We started with [Verdi's] *Otello* and then did a work of Benjamin Britten. We rehearsed for six months before the production came out! I really learned at this point how to study in depth. I had the time to go into details. I went to the libraries to study the original scores so I could bring my knowledge and interpretation of what the composer really wanted into the rehearsals. I think it was at this time, when I was thirty-five or thirty-six, that I had the opportunity to settle down and to make sure I had quality and not only quantity of knowledge and routine.

After this I did a lot of guest conducting of both the operatic and symphonic repertoire. I still always try to do both. In 1967, I was asked to take over the principal conductor position with the Dresden Philharmonic. It was a wonderful feeling to come to an orchestra which liked me very much and which I liked also. We had a wonderful connection and we grew up together. After three years I was also asked to take over the principal conductor position with the Gewandhaus Orchestra and for two years I conducted both orchestras together. After that the arrangement didn't work any more. It was just too much work. So, in 1972 I decided to stay only in Leipzig with the Gewandhaus.

This was the beginning of my international career though I had started to give concerts outside my country in 1957 when I was thirty. I am very grateful that from the beginning I was not pushed into a career. I had the time to let myself grow naturally. I had enough time to be a human being with a wife and children. I had the time to have a life outside of my career. After 1972 I quickly became better known and was in demand with orchestras in Europe and the United States. This gave me a lot of experience with the styles, imagination, and mentality of other orchestras and countries besides my own. I had the opportunity to learn the nationalistic styles of different orchestras which gave me a better understanding of composers.

JW: What are the stylistic differences between the orchestras in the States and those in Europe?

KM: Well, within the States you have very different types of orchestras. You can't really define what an American orchestra is. However, there is one point which for us is a little bit negative. In the States the orchestras ask first for technical perfection. They ask for beauty, meaning, and truth of expression second. In Europe it's the other way around. This is a major difference between European and American orchestras. I always make the joke, "If my orchestra plays a lot of wrong notes, at least they play them beautifully." So it's just another way to view musical performance. However, if you are an experienced conductor it's wonderful to do both. With the combination of technical perfection and beauty, you can discover much more about the music. My orchestra and I, of course, after seventeen years together know each other very well. They know exactly how I want the music to sound. They know what I want if I move my hand, head, or eyes in a certain way. I can work on the surface or in depth.

You have different traditions in your orchestras also. The most flexible orchestra might still be the Boston Symphony, which is very American but also has the ability to feel the German and European tradition very strongly. The Cleveland Orchestra is a very delicate ensemble. I love them. They are wonderful. So, with them it's also a joy to work. They are a very serious orchestra. I always say that I'm jealous that Szell is still alive. He is still living in the orchestra. However, it is wonderful that his time has not gone away. The San Francisco Symphony is a reflection of the wonderful, beautiful city and of the freshness of California. It's a young, ambitious orchestra that can do nearly everything. They will go step by step to the highest level. I do not worry about the San Francisco Symphony! They will come up because they are surrounded by wonderful opportunities to work and to live beautifully. The East Coast orchestras like Philadelphia have a wonderful sound in all romantic pieces. What Riccardo Muti added to Philadelphia is the lightness of the Italian style and of the classical pieces. They have a remarkable and beautiful sound. The New York Philharmonic I like because it has New

York's character. They have a nervous expression combined with outstanding virtuosity which sometimes has the character of impatience. So, if you compare all of them you will find that they are really quite different.

In Europe there are many different styles. The Berlin Philharmonic, for example, is a master orchestra, a very selected group of personalities. I think it has the highest level possible for an orchestra. They come closest in style to my orchestra because they very often had the same conductors. Artur Nikisch, Bruno Walter, and Wilhelm Furtwängler were in both orchestras. We still have in our sound and imagination the feeling of what Berlin does.

Italian orchestras have a difficult time. Their whole economy is shaky, they're not paid very well, and they need two or three jobs in order to make a family living. So, it's a very hard world. However, they play perfectly the easy-going style of Verdi or Rossini, which is difficult for us Germans to do because we have a heavier sound. English orchestras sound a little cool to us, but they are very polished and have a beautiful sound. And then there is the wonderful French style. French orchestras are somewhat in a state of anarchy, but on the other hand they play beautifully and with a lot of fantasy. What I've just described might be known as the main stream European orchestras. The Russian orchestras play their own repertoire very convincingly and are very powerful.

JW: What can young conductors do to gain the type of experience necessary for an international career?

KM: I must tell you one thing. I'm very sad in the moment. I can only tell young conductors idealistic things which are not realistic. If I tell you what I did and what I tried to do for some young American conductors you would find that it's basically a sad story because I was able to help only a few. The opportunity to get a job is very hard and limited. More and more limited all the time. What can I tell the young conductors? There are some of them trying to make a career at the very beginning of their studies. That was never my way. It was not even in my imagination to have an international career. I was astonished as my own career began. I wanted to be an honest musician and a good musician. But the possibility of having an international career was something I never even thought about. If I give this advice to young conductors here in the States they will think that this old-fashioned guy is stupid because with such an attitude they will never succeed. Now they could go to Europe if they have the opportunity and could grow silently. If they are hired as conductors coming from Europe back to the States they will be accepted. But I don't know even a handful of American conductors who are being steadily supported by American orchestras. Cleveland does support assistant conductors and they have very good results. I remember Jahja Ling who came first to San Francisco. Now this wonderful man is in Cleveland and has grown up and developed very well musically. But I know a lot of other talented people here who have had the great opportunity to go to Tanglewood and to be selected as Fellow conductors in Tanglewood. They study for two months and are given a fantastic opportunity. However, after this nothing normally happens. All of these conductors are too dependent on money. I would say in this moment to these young conductors to please continue to work. Continue so that you are ready to be a very good conductor if you are called. But on the other hand young conductors are losing their self-confidence. If they are not conducting, they become more and more shy and begin to fear the orchestras after a while. If the orchestras are not supportive, they get lost. I've seen highly talented conductors get lost. So, in our country we try to support young conductors very clearly. If we find a talented man we help him.

JW: And you don't think that's true in the States?

KM: Really, it's very difficult here, very difficult. I know that Exxon did a lot for young conductors but they stopped because of the money. This is very sad. I cannot say anything against Exxon. Surely they had to decide that. Surely they are not happy about that but what can you do? So, again my advice to young conductors is that they should study the scores as though they were to conduct them tomorrow. It's not good to conduct difficult works too soon. It takes time to learn them well. So, a young conductor cannot be too prepared! I studied the most difficult pieces as long as I could before I conducted them. When I did conduct them it was much easier than if I had been pushed to have to conduct them tomorrow. I was forced though, to learn *Otello* in an afternoon. It was an opportunity but it was also a shock!

The other thing young conductors should do is to learn other languages. This is very important. If you can talk to an orchestra in their own language you have a much easier understanding with them. If you must use a translator, music-making becomes very difficult. Also, young conductors are not given very much rehearsal time. So it's better that they learn to feel how an orchestra wants to play a piece before they try to change it. An orchestra has a certain character, experience and ways of feeling the music which the young conductor should not try to immediately change. I gain the greatest respect if I meet an orchestra and don't try to change them rapidly in a certain direction or course. I have my concept of a piece, of a sound and I try to get it. However, I have to be attentive to what and how the orchestra plays and to combine that with my ideas. This is the best way to make a cooperative effort. You cannot change the Vienna Philharmonic and you would be stupid to tell them how to play a Vienna Waltz. A young conductor coming to the Berlin Philharmonic, of course, should be happy if the orchestra follows him at all! The Berlin orchestra has such a high standard that you should respect what they are doing first and only then ask for the things you want to add or change.

161

JW: How do you learn a score? What process do you go through? Do you have a certain method?

KM: I read a score like a book. A conductor of my age has the experience to read an ordinary score or contemporary score and has the imagination to hear the sound.

JW: Do you analyze the score while you are reading it?

KM: Yes, I do an analysis if you can do an analysis. At first I want to discover if I'm attracted to a work or not. Then I make the decision to conduct it or not. If I have decided to conduct the piece I will already know what lines are convincing to me and what the weak points of the work are. Then of course, I always try to find out if the composer's alive or not and if I can ask him certain questions that I have. If not, I try to find out why he chose, for instance, a form other than an ordinary classical symphonic form. "Why did he change this or that, why did he break this phrase, or why did he use this particular orchestral color?"

Twenty years ago analysis was thought of as a kind of non-musical field. It was felt that the music must speak for itself. You shouldn't add things, you shouldn't talk about the musical connections with poetry. I think this is strange because if a musician plays without meaning the result is dead music. Every note [Alfred] Brendel plays, for instance, is filled with meaning.

JW: How would you teach a student to learn a score? Would you suggest a certain method for analysis?

KM: My students are already doing analysis with other teachers. They can learn form and harmonic analysis from them. However, as you know, some modern pieces don't have traditional forms. In that case I ask my students to be flexible enough to discover the new things. I ask my pupils, "What do you feel? What is the composer's main idea? Why did he compose the work? What does it say to an audience?"

JW: Could you be specific. For example, how would you teach a student the Eroica?

KM: I would have them find out what Beethoven's main idea for the *Eroica* was. They would need to know that Beethoven's main philosophy at the time was the French revolution. He was influenced by the *egalité, fraternité, liberté* ideals. Humanism was the basic philosophy of his life. The student would need to know that Beethoven first dedicated the piece to Napoleon until he discovered that Napoleon intended to become emperor. He was so furious that he destroyed the first page. Now this means that Beethoven's idea was not dependent on one person though it was still dependent on the ideas of the French revolution. He had the same basic humanistic ideas in *Fidelio*.

"Good people should be victorious!" This morality goes throughout his whole life. He had an idealistic vision of the brotherhood of man. He also had an idealistic picture of women. He thought they were angels. He could never have had a relationship with a woman that was real. The grave mistake that people often make is to identify the concept of heroism with Beethoven the man. Beethoven didn't want to be a hero. He wanted to write in the musical language of humanity, humanism. And you can follow this concept throughout the whole score.

So, I would explain all of this to my students and then ask them to look in the score and to find out what it means. "What does the first movement of the *Eroica* mean?" I would also ask them to follow Beethoven's use of themes. For example the first theme is used as a contradance in the *Eroica Variations* for piano. Then very importantly Beethoven took the *Prometheus* theme and used it as the final theme of the *Eroica*. It's very necessary to study these relationships. The second movement is supposed to be a funeral march. However, it's not a funeral march to bury someone. (Unfortunately it's used very often to bury someone!) This movement has the sound of the dead coming to life! It's so complex in it's meaning. The music sometimes goes right into heaven. It's not meant to be sad, not sad at all! So the *Eroica* is Beethoven's first symphony in which he tried to bring his philosophic ideas into the symphonic repertory. This is really outstanding. It was a huge jump from his Second Symphony. Also, I find it somehow very touching to discover the inner connections between themes. Like discovering in the Introduction of the Second Symphony the main theme of the first movement of the Ninth Symphony. You must see what was inside this man and what was inside his compositions at the same time. This is just too complex to talk about now. I mentioned it to give you an example of how I work with my pupils. If they start to conduct and make a *ritardando* where it was not written, I always say, "You can do it but tell me why? Why do you need it now? What do you want to do?" And then I can tell them what impressions I have of what they are doing. I've learned a lot from my pupils this way. I've discovered many things about myself through them.

JW: How do you conceive or arrive at the right tempo or tempo relationships in Beethoven's works? What is your viewpoint on Beethoven's metronome markings? Do you observe them or ignore them?

KM: Beethoven's metronome markings are still a question mark. For me they are not so much an enigma because I have my own opinions and will write about them in 1990. We are bringing out a new Peters edition of the old scores of all nine Beethoven symphonies. I will be recording this edition with my orchestra. I'll write my viewpoint on them then. So it's better not to talk about it now.

JW: I can't wait for the recordings to come out!

KM: I'm already doing what I found out. There are so many contradictory things being written about them. However, one thing is absolutely clear. Most metronome markings in the symphonies from the First Symphony to the Eighth Symphony are too fast! If an orchestra of our time that is clearly technically superior than the orchestras of Beethoven's time is unable to play those tempos, the markings must be absolutely wrong! I have my own explanation, which I'll tell you in two years.

JW: Could you comment on the tempos in the trios? For example, the trios of the Third Symphony and the Fifth Symphony are usually taken a little bit slower than the scherzo sections. However, there is no tempo indication for this change.

KM: It is mainly a tradition. But it is not always a tradition to take the trios slower because, as you might know, in Handel's time they made the B part of an aria faster than the original tempo!

JW: However, Beethoven did mark some of the trios meno presto, *for example, the trio in the Seventh Symphony. Why didn't he mark the other trios with a slower tempo if he intended them to be slower?*

KM: Beethoven marked that trio *meno presto* and of course you have to do it that way. However, don't do it too slowly! The *meno presto* of the Seventh Symphony is really an Italian song. It is simply a southern Italian song with a southern rhythm. You can find a lot of those songs in Naples. Now usually I don't make a tempo change in the Second Symphony. I think Beethoven's idea in this case was really to make a scherzo. This was a new form for him and he didn't play games with it. So, I don't change the tempos of the trios in the First or Second Symphonies. I begin to change them in the Third Symphony. You have to because of the horn motive in the trio. It needs a different character. The Fourth Symphony is quite clear. It is all *poco meno* and has a Viennese style. In the Fifth Symphony the tempo goes straight through and should be stormy and wild.

•••••

JW: How do you plan your repertoire for the Gewandhaus and for your guest conducting engagements?

KM: The programming for my orchestra, unfortunately, has to be quite practical because we tour two or three times a year. We often travel to the same countries and are asked for main repertory, traditional repertory. Nobody wants to hear French impressionistic music though we can do it very well. If we are going abroad we play repertory people know, repertory that our orchestra specializes in. I'm conducting fourteen or fifteen different concerts and here I'm doing around twelve or thirteen different programs. I chose only one program myself! Usually the programs depend on the next tour or on the next recordings we are doing and so on. This means that we do the main repertory of the Gewandhaus. We do all the Beethoven symphonies, all the Brahms symphonies, all the Bruckner, Mahler, Tchaikovsky, Mendelssohn, and Schumann symphonies.

JW: What type of contemporary music do you do and what are your criteria in selecting a contemporary work? Also, do you perform mostly German or East German contemporary works with the Gewandhaus?

KM: No. But we feel the duty and we are doing it steadily, to give two or three of our composers a commissioned work each year. The criterion for us and for me is that it must have a meaning. It must have meaning even if it's a work by a young composer who is doing crazy experiments. That's something I actually like! It must be outstanding in any style. I never perform what I hate or what I think is mediocre. I don't compromise even if the composer is seventy years old and I should be more gentle and give him a chance. I find that I must be gentle with my audience first and I feel responsible for what they hear. They must know and trust that the new work has quality and is outstanding. The other criteria is that I feel responsibility for the composer. I must be personally touched by the piece. If I'm reading a score which I think is good but which doesn't go to my feelings, if my brain can't sense the meaning of the work, I won't do it. I might ask other conductors to do it. So that's one of my main criteria. Also, it must bring out the major points of my orchestra. The sound of our orchestra is very special and if I commission a piece with a composer, he must know the sound of our orchestra so that he can write for us. We have had a lot of beautiful new compositions in the last years and I must say I believe the composers in our country have a very good life. We have eighty-eight orchestras, not all of them high quality, that can play. Each of them commissions around two new symphonic works a year. So, a composer has opportunities to hear 150-160 new performances each year.

I also like to work with composers on their concept of the piece. If they tell me that they want to do a piece for children or for the schools we exchange ideas. We work together and usually it comes out very good. We also do many compositions from other countries because I'm a member of the Academy of Arts in Berlin and I know a lot of composers from all over Europe. We connect and I ask them what they could compose for us, what they have at the moment, or what they think is their best work. So I select from a wide range and we give a lot of opportunities. I never could play in the States a piece we did two years ago. It was the first performance of the *Michelangelo Symphony* by a young Leipzig composer. The work lasts ninety-five minutes! The chorus had to rehearse for three months, the children's chorus rehearsed for three months, and we needed twelve orchestra rehearsals. My orchestra always comes prepared but this was an extremely difficult work! Nobody would pay for that many rehearsals anywhere else. So, this is a wonderful thing to be able to give an opportunity to a talented guy. He asked me, "Would you be interested? I have a fantastic idea, a little bit too great perhaps, but I want to bring out the spirit of Michelangelo." He did it and you must respect him for it. What he composed was outstanding and also outstandingly difficult. In the normal world where every dollar counts, nobody would have paid for it, nobody.

JW: What is your view of performance and how do you prepare for performance?

KM: I must tell you that I always try to prepare for a good performance starting with the first rehearsal. It's the best way to have a good concert. The major fault and what I sometimes see young and unexperienced conductors doing, is to try to show the orchestra what a good conductor you are. If you have that attitude you will have no results. An orchestra is only interested if you can do a piece well. An orchestra wants a conductor to help them play as well as they can. Don't tie the orchestra in a spiritual way. Don't talk about things they should have understood already. It's very difficult to talk about music. A lot of music has such a complex meaning. How can you describe a theme by Mozart! "Is it sad, still in heaven, or happy?" There's such a different meaning to every theme. Take the first theme of Mozart's A Major Piano Sonata. Try to describe what it is. You can't because it has everything in it. Therefore, I don't talk much but listen instead to the orchestra. I try to show them how I want to have the work played. I will talk only if I discover that we have a misunderstanding. I expect the orchestra to know the piece not only technically but also in the general feeling they have for the piece. If I feel their feeling for the piece is contrary to my own feelings then I talk. This helps a lot to keep the freshness of the piece alive.

Biography

Kurt Masur, music director of the Gewandhaus Orchestra of Leipzig, will become music director of the New York Philharmonic beginning with the 1992-93 season.

Kurt Masur's debut in the United States was with the Cleveland Orchestra in 1974, the same year he first toured America with the Gewandhaus Orchestra. Since then, Mr. Masur and the Gewandhaus Orchestra have appeared regularly in North America and have been featured in New York with a Beethoven cycle at Carnegie Hall in 1984 and a Brahms cycle at Avery Fisher Hall in 1986. Their U.S. tour during the spring of 1987 included appearances at the Ann Arbor May Festival, Carnegie Hall, Pasadena, and San Francisco, and continued on to the Far East. In the spring of 1989, Mr. Masur and the Gewandhaus were featured in New York for five concerts with André Watts performing all of the Beethoven piano concertos, and also appeared in Boston, Toronto, Montreal, and Ottawa, and at the Ann Arbor May Festival, where they have been invited to return during their tour of the United States during the spring of 1991.

Since his American Debut, Mr. Masur has appeared with the Toronto Symphony, the Dallas Symphony, the Boston Symphony, the San Francisco Symphony, and the Philadelphia Orchestra. He has also conducted such prestigious international ensembles as the Berlin, Vienna, Czech, Leningrad, Stockholm, Munich, and Royal Philharmonic orchestras, the Dresden Staatskapelle, the Orchestre de Paris, the Philharmonia, and the Israel Philharmonic, both in Israel and on tour in the United States at major festivals.

Born July 18, 1927 in Silesia, Germany, Mr. Masur's first musical training was at the piano, which he studied, along with conducting, at the Music College of Leipzig. Upon graduation, he served as orchestra coach at the Halle County Theater, and later as Kapellmeister of the Erfurt and Leipzig Opera theaters. He became a conductor of the Dresden Philharmonic in 1955 and in 1958 he returned to opera as general director of music of the Mecklenburg State Theater of Schwerin. From 1960 to 1964 he was senior director of music at Berlin's Komische Oper, collaborating with Professor Walter Felsenstein, one of German opera's most influential directors. The Komische Oper's world tours were instrumental in building Kurt Masur's international reputation, which grew quickly with numerous guest conducting appearances in Europe. In 1967 Mr. Masur was appointed chief conductor of the Dresden Philharmonic, a post he held until 1972, concurrently with his position with the Gewandhaus Orchestra, where he became music director in 1970. In 1975 he became a professor at the Leipzig Academy of Music.

He has recorded nearly one hundred albums; those with the Gewandhaus Orchestra include the complete symphonies of Beethoven, Brahms, Mendelssohn, Bruckner, and Schumann, Dvořák's *Slavonic Dances*, Mendelssohn's *Paulus,* Schubert's *Rosamunde,* the *Four Last Songs* of Richard Strauss with soprano Jessye Norman, and an album of Strauss songs with tenor Siegfried Jerusalem.

Kurt Masur Discography

Composer	Work	Orchestra	Soloists	Label	CD	LP	MC
Bach	Violin concerto in a	Leipzig Gewandhaus	Suske	Ars Vivendi		017	
Bach	Violin concerto in D	Leipzig Gewandhaus	Suske	Ars Vivendi		017	
Beethoven	Concerto for violin, cello, and piano	Czech Philharmonic	Suk, Chuchro, Panenka	Supraphon		2SUP-0017	
Beethoven	Concerto for violin, cello, and piano	Leipzig Gewandhaus	Hoelscher, Schiff, Zacharias	Angel	CDC-47427		
Beethoven	Fidelio	Leipzig Gewandhaus	Adam, Nimsgern, Jerusalem, Altmeyer	Eurodisc	GD 69030		GK 69030
Beethoven	Symphonies (9)	Leipzig Gewandhaus	Tomowa-Sintow, Burmeister, Schreier, Adam	Philips	416 274-2		
Beethoven	Symphony no. 8	Dresden Philharmonic		Pilz	442060		
Beethoven	Violin romance in F	Leipzig Gewandhaus	Hoelscher	Angel	CDC-47427		
Beethoven	Violin romance in G	Leipzig Gewandhaus	Hoelscher	Angel	CDC-47427		
Brahms	Concerto for violin and cello	Leipzig Gewandhaus	R. Ricci, G. Ricci	Vox			CT-4593
Brahms	Concerto for violin and cello	New Philharmonia	R. Ricci, G. Ricci	Vox			CT-4593
Brahms	Hungarian Dances (21)	Leipzig Gewandhaus		Philips	411 426-2		
Brahms	Piano concerto no. 2	Leipzig Gewandhaus	Ousset	Accord	CD 201152		
Brahms	Variations on a Theme of Paganini	Leipzig Gewandhaus		Accord	CD 201152		
Bruch	Swedish Dances	Leipzig Gewandhaus		Philips	420 932-2		
Bruch	Symphony no. 1	Leipzig Gewandhaus		Philips	420 932-2		
Bruch	Symphony no. 2	Leipzig Gewandhaus		Philips	420 932-2		
Bruch	Symphony no. 3	Leipzig Gewandhaus		Philips	420 932-2		
Bruckner	Symphonies (9)	Leipzig Gewandhaus		Eurodisc	GD 69227		
Busoni	Flute divertimento	Leipzig Gewandhaus	Nicolet	Philips	412 728-2		

Composer	Work	Orchestra	Soloists	Label	CD	LP	MC
Chabrier	Larghetto for horn	Leipzig Gewandhaus	Baumann	Philips	416 380-2		
Dukas	Villanelle for horn	Leipzig Gewandhaus	Baumann	Philips	416 380-2		
Dvořák	Slavonic Dances	Leipzig Gewandhaus		Philips	416 623-2		
Dvořák	Slavonic Dances	Leipzig Gewandhaus		Philips	416 624-2		
Dvořák	Slavonic Rhapsodies (3)	Leipzig Gewandhaus		Philips	416 624-2		
Gershwin	Rhapsody in Blue	Leipzig Gewandhaus	Stöckigt	DG	413 258-2		413 258-4
Glière	Horn concerto	Leipzig Gewandhaus	Baumann	Philips	416 380-2		
Grieg	Peer Gynt	Leipzig Gewandhaus	Wiens, Vogel, Denner. Markert	Philips	422 343-2		422 343-4
Liszt	Faust Symphony	Leipzig Gewandhaus	König	Seraphim			4XG-60442
Liszt	Hungarian Rhapsodies	Leipzig Gewandhaus		Philips	412 724-2		
Liszt	Les Préludes	Leipzig Gewandhaus		Angel	CDM-69022		4AM-34745
Liszt	Mazeppa	Leipzig Gewandhaus		Angel	CDM-69022		4AM-34745
Liszt	Orpheus	Leipzig Gewandhaus		Angel	CDM-69022		4AM-34745
Liszt	Piano concerto no. 1	Dresden Philharmonic	Ringeisen	Pilz	442060		
Liszt	Tasso	Leipzig Gewandhaus		Angel	CDM-69022		4AM-34745
Mendelssohn	St. Paul	Leipzig Gewandhaus	Janowitz, Lang, Blochwitz, Adam	Philips	420 212-2		
Mendelssohn	Symphony no. 1	Leipzig Gewandhaus		Eurodisc	GD 69237		
Mendelssohn	Symphony no. 1	Leipzig Gewandhaus		Teldec	244 933-2		
Mendelssohn	Symphony no. 2	Leipzig Gewandhaus		Eurodisc	GD 69237		
Mendelssohn	Symphony no. 2	Leipzig Gewandhaus	Casapietra, Schreier, Stolte Bonney, Wiens, Schreier	Teldec	422 178-2	422 178-1	422 178-4
Mendelssohn	Symphony no. 3	Leipzig Gewandhaus		Eurodisc	GD 69237		
Mendelssohn	Symphony no. 4	Leipzig Gewandhaus		Eurodisc	GD 69237		
Mendelssohn	Symphony no. 5	Leipzig Gewandhaus		Eurodisc	GD 69237		
Mendelssohn	Symphony no. 5	Leipzig Gewandhaus		Teldec	244 933-2		
Nielsen	Flute concerto	Leipzig Gewandhaus	Nicolet	Philips	412 728-2		
Prokofiev	Piano concerto no. 1	Leipzig Gewandhaus	Beroff	Angel			4AM-34762
Prokofiev	Piano concerto no. 2	Leipzig Gewandhaus	Beroff	Angel			4AM-34705

Composer	Work	Orchestra	Soloists	Label	CD	LP	MC
Prokofiev	Piano concerto no. 3	Leipzig Gewandhaus	Beroff	Angel			4AM-34705
Prokofiev	Piano concerto no. 4	Leipzig Gewandhaus	Beroff	Angel			4AM-34762
Prokofiev	Piano concerto no. 5	Leipzig Gewandhaus	Beroff	Angel			4AM-34762
Reinecke	Flute concerto in D	Leipzig Gewandhaus	Nicolet	Philips	412 728-2		
Saint-Saëns	Morceau de concert for horn	Leipzig Gewandhaus	Baumann	Philips	416 380-2		
Schubert	Rosamunde (complete incidental music)	Leipzig Gewandhaus	Ameling	Philips	412 432-2		
Schubert	Rosamunde Overture	Dresden Philharmonic		Pilz	442060		
Schumann	Symphony no. 1	London Philharmonic		Teldec	2292 46445-2		2292 46445-4
Schumann	Symphony no. 2	London Philharmonic		Teldec	2292 46445-2		2292 46445-4
Schumann	Violin fantasy in C	Leipzig Gewandhaus	R. Ricci	Vox			CT-4593
Strauss, R.	Ariadne auf Naxos	Leipzig Gewandhaus	Norman, Varady, Gruberova, Frey, Bär, Fischer-Dieskau	Philips	422 084-4		
Strauss, R.	Cäcilie	Leipzig Gewandhaus	Norman	Philips	411 052-2		411 052-4
Strauss, R.	Four Last Songs	Leipzig Gewandhaus	Norman	Philips	411 052-2		411 052-4
Strauss, R.	Horn concerto no. 1	Leipzig Gewandhaus	Baumann	Philips	412 237-2		
Strauss, R.	Horn concerto no. 2	Leipzig Gewandhaus	Baumann	Philips	412 237-2		
Strauss, R.	Meinem Kinde	Leipzig Gewandhaus	Norman	Philips	411 052-2		411 052-4
Strauss, R.	Morgen	Leipzig Gewandhaus	Norman	Philips	411 052-2		411 052-4
Strauss, R.	Ruhe, meine Seele	Leipzig Gewandhaus	Norman	Philips	411 052-2		411 052-4
Strauss, R.	Wiegenlied	Leipzig Gewandhaus	Norman	Philips	411 052-2		411 052-4
Strauss, R.	Zueignung	Leipzig Gewandhaus	Norman	Philips	411 052-2		411 052-4
Tchaikovsky	Francesca da Rimini	Leipzig Gewandhaus		Teldec	44939		
Tchaikovsky	Symphony no. 1	Leipzig Gewandhaus		Teldec	244 939-2		
Tchaikovsky	Symphony no. 2	Leipzig Gewandhaus		Teldec	244 939-2		
Tchaikovsky	Romeo and Juliet	Leipzig Gewandhaus		Teldec	2292 44943-2		2292 44943-4
Weber	Horn concertino	Leipzig Gewandhaus	Baumann	Philips	412 237-2		

"I think of the score as the genuine creation of an individual's mind, reflecting, in a way, human frailties eventually reaching for heaven, revealing poetic summits of beauty or even ugliness, but always human, always the patent result of an intelligent earthly mind sharing a poetic essence in sounds with us. So, I prefer, and try, to be well within the composer's mind when I attempt an interpretation."

Eduardo Mata

Eduardo Mata

JW: The Dallas Symphony has such a wonderful sound. What have you done to develop it?

EM: The basic sound of the winds was here before I came. Virtually none of the players, except for the first horn, coprincipal trumpet, and piccolo (which I brought in) have changed since I was appointed music director. I needed to work with them on phrasing, balance, and style. My real problem was the strings! The orchestra had only been revived for two years after it went under in 1974, when I was appointed music director. The string family was drastically decimated. It has taken me eight years to get the right concertmaster and most of the principals I wanted. I really had to work hard at this before achieving any tangible results.

JW: How did you work with them to achieve the type of sound you wanted?

EM: For starters, my present concertmaster and I have a very good *rapport*. We work in advance on the bowings. He understands my ideas very well. We also incorporate the other principals into this process and try to arrive at the rehearsals with clear ideas on how things are going to be approached. We work not only on bowings, but on strokes and fingerings. Doing this ahead of time, rehearsals can be very concentrated. We also have sectionals from time to time. Further than that, it was a matter of unifying sound concepts according to the different styles and epochs.

JW: Do you conduct the sectionals?

EM: I supervise the sectionals and personally conduct them sometimes. It is an accumulative work, week after week, trying always to go in the same direction. I tell them the same things that many conductors say all the time: "What is the direction of the phrases?" "Where do we want to go?" For me, the semantics of music are of the greatest importance. I ask myself and my musicians: "What is the music trying to say?" "What is the real meaning of melodies, intervals, modulations?" I always share my thoughts with the orchestra so that we can go in the same direction. One thing I can say is that the Dallas Symphony is a very happy orchestra. For a major American symphonic ensemble, we are rather exceptional. One finds a lot of bitter and

173

frustrated people among musicians in American orchestras. They have played the standard repertoire for years and they are not looking forward to playing it anymore. I am sure there are a few players in Dallas who feel that way also, but fortunately they are in the minority.

JW: Why do you think you were able to create this happy situation?

EM: I really don't know. I do know that we have the type of musical discipline I care about, and somehow the orchestra takes pride in doing things well. We don't waste time. Technical problems are largely solved by the musicians themselves so that we can concentrate all the available rehearsal time on musical problems and balance. I guess the musicians appreciate an efficient utilization of time, granted the artistic results are plausible.

The type of rehearsal where we can address only problems of color, meaning, balance, etc., is my greatest joy. We don't pretend to have a distinct sound in the sense that the Philadelphia Orchestra or the Chicago Symphony have it. We want the flexibility to adapt ourselves to the sounds required by each composer and/or style. In that respect, we have a long way to go with music of the classical period. Our old Fair Park Music Hall was not conducive to music-making that required intimacy and warmth. Smaller ensembles were always at a disadvantage there. It has been easier to build the lush and romantic sound that a Tchaikovsky or Rachmaninoff symphony require, than the type of sound and approach needed for Bach, Mozart, or Haydn.

JW: What are your views of the research being done on historically informed performance?

EM: I don't have many illusions about trying to reproduce what is supposed to be the authentic late eighteenth century sound for a variety of reasons. Our *A* is different. It is generally higher than theirs was. Our wind instruments are very different; we progressed in their design so as to get more sound out of them, but by doing this, we have changed the basic color and sound projection potential. This altogether modifies the orchestral sound palette and the balance perspective. So it is not realistic to try to achieve the eighteenth century sound with modern instruments. What concerns me more than "authentic" sound is articulation, phrasing, transparency, character, and, of course, tempi. Polyphonic textures represent the biggest challenge in terms of articulation.

JW: How would you achieve this type of polyphonic clarity?

EM: Through articulation and phrasing, I follow the principle of the natural decay of sound as opposed to the *sostenuto* concept so typical of the nineteenth century. Mapping out the phrasing and articulation with the "sound decay" concept in mind, one creates the natural voids or "valleys" for "other" things to be heard. In pursuing these ideas, one has to take into account oral traditions still alive in vocal and instrumental music of a vernacular origin.

JW: Would you ever retouch the orchestration of a work?

EM: Well, we have to be as faithful as possible to the original intentions of the composer. But we still have to make personal choices, and that is a very dangerous area. For instance, many conductors retouch the trumpets in the beginning of the fourth movement of Beethoven's Ninth Symphony. They rewrite the part so that the trumpets play the complete descending arpeggio with the violins. That is not in the original of course. In the original, the trumpets play only the tonic and dominant in that great monstrosity of a chord. This creates a sense of struggle that is inherent to the texture of that wonderful beginning. Beethoven obviously had that harmonic conflict and sense of struggle in mind. Conductors from earlier in our century would be prone to "clarify" places like this. They wanted to hear clearly the melodic design, but by rewriting the trumpet line, the struggle no longer existed. The conflict was eliminated, destroying Beethoven's original intent! That's a classic example. There are many others like this one. Of course the argument can be made by the other side, alleging that we are really realizing the original intentions of the composer if one is convinced that what Beethoven wanted was the clarity of the melodic line rather than the stupendous struggle that leads into the *recitativo*.

JW: Where do you draw the line?

EM: The whole thing becomes a matter of conscience and sense of responsibility on the part of the interpreter. One would expect from him or her first-class information and experience to make the final decisions.

In Mexico, I conduct an experimental group (about twelve players). We are deeply immersed in performance practices of the baroque period. We have just recorded the *Brandenburg Concertos*, we are working on the Bach *Suites*, Mozart, and Pergolesi. We use gut strings, baroque bows, a lower A, and a small portative organ and/or harpsichord in the continuo. However, we are going for things other than just trying to duplicate the original sound of the instruments. Our experiments have to do with phrasing, articulation, *tempi*, and, overall, character. We look deeply into the semantics of music. For us, the realization of a *basso continuo* is more important than the instrument on which it is played.

JW: What is your approach to score study?

EM: I studied with Carlos Chávez, who taught us the possibility of analyzing scores exhaustively. He seldom used the traditional form analysis techniques which he thought were just child's play. "Anybody can see where the exposition ends and the development begins!" He used anatomical and morphological analysis related to the density and importance of the material utilized; the "motivical" analysis was fascinating since it provided the awareness of all the rhythmical, intervalic, and harmonic transformations and utilizations of the smallest cell of recognizable musical material: the motive. Needless to say, harmonic dissections in Chávez's analyses were total, including of course, the psychological connotation of chords, sequences. and modulations. Rules did not have a value, a priori, but always a posteriori, once we knew where the composer wanted to go, or more simply, what was really his language or idiosyncracies. In essence, what we did in this type of analysis is go through the same mechanical processes as the composers in giving shape and form to their music. Of course this was oriented toward a composition career. Soon I realized that there is no better way to learn scores. Being able to stand as an interpreter from within the score, rather than in front of it, made all the difference in the world.

Of course this type of score study through analysis takes a long time. By the time I finish working on the analysis of a piece of music, I have almost memorized it.

Sergiu Celibidache, the famous Romanian conductor presently music director of the Munich Philharmonic, works with a fantastic attention to detail, to orchestral balance, and to intonation. In many respects, he is a role model. However, he has the idea that all music, great music, "exists" even before the composer captured it from his mind and put it on a piece of paper. Therefore, as an interpreter, he seems to claim the privilege of knowing what the music demands in terms of interpretation or realization in time, sometimes in open contradiction to the specific instructions in the score as written by the composer, as if the latter were only a "translator" or "medium" who relates those sounds to us. In other words, Celibidache seems to respond to the inner laws of a given score, deducting tempi, balance, phrasing, etc., from the character of the music. The premise obviously stimulates the imagination and the authority of the performer, taking for granted a great culture, a great experience, a formidable inner ear and a first-class musical intuition. That sounds like God, doesn't it? Although I respect Celibidache's approach, I think of the score as the genuine creation of an individual's mind, reflecting, in a way, human frailties eventually reaching for heaven, revealing poetic summits of beauty or even ugliness, but always human, always the patent result of an intelligent, earthly, mind sharing a poetic essence in sounds with us. So, I prefer, and try, to be well within the composer's mind when I attempt an interpretation.

JW: This type of detailed study takes a long time! What do you think of conductors who learn scores overnight?

EM: There is no mystery about reading and learning a score overnight in a purely mechanical sense. The real problem is assuming the score as your own, knowing not only its morphology and exterior features, but its most recondit secrets and overall meaning. Sometimes to perform a piece, one should wait, even if it takes years, and it does take years! I am always working on new scores, but I am more concerned with the ones I think I already know.

JW: Do you study at the piano?

EM: Mostly yes, unless I am studying a piece that has been in my inner ear for many years, such as a Brahms symphony. Sometimes it can be a very good exercise to listen to as many interpretations (live or recorded) of a piece as you may have access to, including those by people you admire and those by people you don't care for. It is very illuminating to see how differently people have approached certain problems. After I have listened to many different interpretations, my mind clears up and focuses on my own conceptions. You cannot ignore that there are many wonderful musicians out there who have agonized over the same musical problems as you. In those instances, it's good to hear what others have done. It is dangerous though, particularly for an inexperienced person, to try to learn through recordings only. The subconscious plays tricks. The idiosyncracies of a particular performance will tend to stay in the subconscious, making it very difficult for the person to discern what is genuine intuition, and what is subconscious background.

JW: Can you speak a little more about your rehearsal technique?

EM: My rehearsals are quiet and businesslike. In the first rehearsal, I try to run through the piece. I conduct large sections to give the orchestra a sense of the direction of the work. They have to know what the important material is. This is practical, especially in scores that are complicated from the standpoint of orchestral texture. It is important for the orchestra to know what should be heard. Once that process is completed, we work on the details. It is at this point that the musicians already know what the music is about and can work on it from a much higher plateau. I have to share the knowledge and the images with the orchestra. Sometimes we pull everything apart and then, if everything else has failed, we do sectionals. We might spend fifty minutes rehearsing two measures! We will rehearse until everyone understands why the shape of phrases needs to be realized in a certain way, where the climax of a phrase or sentence is, and what is the right amount of instrumental color needed for a plausible orchestral mixture.

JW: This must be why there is such clarity and depth in your performances! Do you rehearse with this kind of thoroughness when you guest conduct?

EM: Of course if I can. More and more I limit my guest conducting to the type of orchestra where this approach is possible. However, I do not always have the luxury of rehearsal time that I have in Dallas; that forces my rehearsal technique into other directions.

JW: How many rehearsals do you have in Dallas per concert?

EM: It varies with the type of program. For a difficult one, we may get six or seven rehearsals. For a typical nineteenth-century repertoire program, more like three or four. With the St. Paul Chamber Orchestra, for instance, I can rehearse with the same concentration, the same kind of attention to detail, the same sense of purpose as I can in Dallas. I love that orchestra. They have a wonderful cohesiveness and consensus of approach. I will be conducting them again in March of 1990.

JW: I'll be there! What are your criteria in programming and performing twentieth-century works?

EM: That's a very difficult question. I think that the guiding factor for me in judging a new score is to decide to what degree a composer is offering something "new" to me, the orchestra and the audience. When I say "new," I don't necessarily mean new in absolute terms, but new in the sense that the language is arranged in new ways to suggest specific feelings and emotions. It is the same in poetry. The important thing is how the poet mixes the same words to give poetic images in different ways. In music, I look for the language in which a composer speaks. "What are the semantics or meaning of his style?" When you are talking about words, it is very clear what semantics mean. In music, however, semantics are what I would call the inner meaning of intervals, phrases, rhythms, or harmonic pulses. So, when I talk of "new," it does not necessarily have to be innovative from a technical aspect. If it is innovative on top of everything else, fine! But I still consider the possibility of a new work which says something new even if is written in 4/4 time, with tonal harmony and traditional form. Now you ask me, "Can you judge a piece of contemporary music?" Probably not. I can judge the practicality of an idea and the feasibility of the medium for which it has been written. I can judge the professionalism of the composer to express himself in understandable and practical terms. I say that because notation realization is extremely important. Sometimes the worst obstacle for a composer is writing down in a clear and understandable form what he has heard in his mind. The composer has to be skilled in writing down everything in the clearest possible way for the interpreters. But, judging the quality of a piece of music in an innovative language is another matter that takes time, the only way to have

178

perspective. There have been instances, however, in which I saw scores that I recognized immediately as masterpieces! More often than not, though, particularly when you see young composers' works, you don't have a clear perception of the quality of the piece. You have to realize as accurately as possible what is in the score and hope that the piece will carry on by its own merits.

One of the big problems of our age is that a lot of works only get one performance – the premiere – and that's it! The National Endowment for the Arts is after American orchestras all the time to get them to play as many works by American composers as possible. They don't seem to care if they are performed well. The NEA slashed a substantial amount from the grant they gave us last year because we didn't play a sufficient number of contemporary American works. If we didn't play enough different pieces, it is precisely because of my commitment to contemporary music! What we did play, though, was well rehearsed and well performed. A lot of other orchestras that get substantial NEA grants don't "perform" contemporary scores, they "read" them. My argument is that of course it is important to play contemporary music, as long as you are honest about the quality of the performance. We schedule more rehearsal time for contemporary works than the majority of major orchestras in the U.S. I can give you examples in which we have had to postpone performances because of insufficient rehearsal time. I can remember programming *Music for the "Magic Theatre"* by George Rochberg. The writing of this piece is so complex that we couldn't do with the rehearsal time allotted the year before we knew the piece. I took the score home and even rewrote a couple of things to simplify the realization. The second time around, we had sufficient time, we performed the work very well, and I was proud of the result. We have done similar things for other composers.

JW: You are also a composer. Do you feel a conflict between your composing and conducting careers?

EM: Not so far. I've been very happy conducting these years. I like being in the middle of the interpretative problems, but I am planning to return to composing. I think that I can take advantage of my experience as a conductor and put that experience to work for my own benefit. Actually I am ready to do it. After 1992 I am planning to take some time to compose.

JW: Why did you come to the United States and would you accept another Mexican post?

EM: The reason I am in the United States is simply that as a conductor/interpreter, I have the possibility of building the kind of instrument of my dreams. There is a crisis of morale in American symphony orchestras, and with few exceptions, one finds a feeling of frustration and disenchantment among musicians. I would hope I can contribute to change this pattern and to be able to build an instrument that we will all be proud of. I don't think I will accept another post in Mexico in the near future, particularly a full-time one. As it is now, I have my hands full with some responsibilities down there. I am a life-time member of the Colegio Nacional for which I lecture on a regular basis. I am an advisor to the National Autonomous University of Mexico in musical affairs, and I also conduct my chamber group called "Solistas de Mexico." I advise the National Council for Culture and the Arts on matters relating to the national system of youth orchestras, and I am on the boards of other promotional and artistic organizations.

JW: Do you feel this disenchantment in American orchestras is pretty widespread?

EM: Unfortunately, yes. A lot of it has to do with the system. We are locked into a very unhealthy habit of playing different programs every week and forcing ourselves to play these concerts with only three or four rehearsals. This system is not conducive to the best music-making or to the constant exploration of new repertoire. The reason we do this, of course, is to make the orchestras financially feasible. I think we have to use our imagination to look for other ways to solve the financial problem. I feel that redistributing rehearsal time is one of the ways in which we can try to overcome this problem. We need to give the musicians the opportunity to be deep and profound about something! Further than that, it is a matter of exercising one's imagination in programming, packaging, and marketing our product, always with the subliminal intention of widening the horizons of our audiences. More and more I feel the players themselves have to be involved with chamber music activities within the orchestras' programs. They also have to be utilized as soloists, and they should be able to give artistic input on the activities they are directly involved with.

JW: I think that you've been able to achieve some of that here in Dallas. The concerts I've heard you conduct have been deep from many levels and the musicians seem to have an unusual amount of commitment!

EM: I am glad it gives that impression, but we are still far from the goals I have described before. The most important thing is to restore, among the young, the plausibility of our profession, the kind of "messianic" commitment to music-making that drives the great soloists to be what they are. I see that new idealism resurging in certain places in Europe, particularly in West Germany and northern Europe. The Vienna Philharmonic, the Berlin Philharmonic, and the Concertgebouw Orchestra are still three of the greatest orchestras in the world. Although the last two have had their share of imported musicians mainly from Japan, the bulk of the new personnel from those three orchestras comes from their respective countries of origin. Pride and honor to be a member of one of those orchestras is still the most powerful drive behind musicians there. Of course this brings about status and great musical satisfaction. Less and less do I see this happening in the United States. Cynicism and a money-making single mindedness seem to be the rule among musicians in American orchestras, with some honorable exceptions, of course.

JW: You don't see the possibility for this kind of motivation happening in Mexico?

EM: Not yet unfortunately. We do have all the natural ingredients to be a potent musical force. We have talent and musical inclination among the basic stratus of the population. We have audiences! As a matter of fact, the demand is much greater than the offer. What we do not have is a viable educational system to take advantage of the abundant musical talent found there. We don't have, either, a clear sense of what we are or want to be, and therefore what the policies and directives are that need to be implemented to take us in the right direction. The study plans of our various conservatories and musical academies are modeled after the French schools of the turn of the century. Government (state and federal) funds arts organizations, but ignores the cracking foundations of our educational system. It is really a tragedy! Mexico has been an important world force in literature and the visual arts, and it could have been also a musical force if all the pioneering efforts of Carlos Chávez in the thirties, forties, and fifties had caught on in a more mature political establishment, thus able to guarantee continuity. I really feel very frustrated about everything that could, but doesn't happen in Mexico.

JW: Well, I think that is very understandable. I think that you really are contributing to the cultural situation in Mexico by being here. You are programming a lot of Latin American works and are doing special radio broadcasts of Latin American music in Dallas for national broadcast. That contributes a lot!

EM: Well, Mexico doesn't see it that way, but that's beside the point.

JW: You have programmed so many early twentieth-century Mexican works. Why aren't you programming more recent Mexican music?

EM: I belong to a generation of composers who felt the impact of the emerging European schools and trends coming to this side of the Atlantic in the late fifties and early sixties. My personal frustration took me away from composing. For a time, I felt it was important to establish in the audiences outside of Mexico the identity of a Mexican music that is distinct, powerful, original. It is like trying to build a plateau to build upon.

I am closely related to the music of Chávez and **Revueltas**, the greatest Mexican composers, because besides quality and appeal, they have something which I find missing with few honorable exceptions in the music being composed today in Mexico: identity. This has nothing to do with the quality of some of the works coming out of the pens of very important composers of the generation that now is between forty and sixty years of age. I just find that the impact of the music of the previous generation (not only Mexican composers, but Latin Americans in general) is greater to the ears of an international public looking for a distinct and original language. My leanings also have to do with my personal frustrations in exploring the serialist and post-serialist idioms. The total absence of tonality and conventional rhythmic patterns took us, as it did with many others, away form some of the most natural and idiosyncratic tendencies closer to our environment and immediate influences. Nevertheless, I have played contemporary Mexican works on specific occasions although not as frequently as I have played Chávez and Revueltas. Now is the time to perform works from the most recent generation of composers like Mario Lavista.

JW: Do you program more twentieth-century Latin American music than other types of twentieth-century music?

EM: No, I try to achieve a balance. I personally believe that, in a sense, Latin American music is at an early stage of development. Our visual arts and literature are more powerful and developed than our musical expressions. Up to the twentieth century, the best music of our countries and the most important influence on our composers have been our regional folklore. It was in the thirties and forties that concert music started to have a distinct personality down there.

JW: Are there any particular trends or schools in the music from Latin America?

EM: I don't think local national trends or schools in Latin American are as relevant as the immense amount of similarities we share in our common culture south of the Rio Grande. Our largely common heritage, advanced native civilizations and the Hispanic influence, along with the geography, made us very similar. This is particularly clear in literature. The literary movement called the Latin American boom is recognized throughout the world as one of the most vital, innovative and forceful. The great literary figures like Rulfo, Vargas Llosa, and Garcia Marquez have much more in common, as languages go, than the relatively small differences stemming from their diverse nationalities. The concept of "magic realism" closely associated to our literature is prevalent throughout the Americas. "Magic realism" is more than a literary fashion; it is our way to see the world; it is the glorified expression of our daily co-existence with the paranormal, the parapsychological, and the close relation of man to his environment full of unexplainable happenings. In the predominantly Anglo-Saxon world, "Magic Realism" may only have a value as fiction, and there one may find the huge gap of understanding between our basically different worlds. Any popular raconteur we may find in a small village in Mexico, in Peru, or in the mountains of Bolivia is a potential troubadour of saga of the underworld, as if they were – because they are – facts of our daily life.

JW: I've always been fascinated with this subject! In fact I wrote my doctoral thesis for Stanford University on this subject. I tried by the technical analysis of works by three twentieth-century Mexican composers (Mario Lavista, Alicia Urreta, and Manuel Enriquez) to find musical reasons for what I perceived was magical perception of reality in their music. Of course, analysis fails when you talk of these things.

EM: That's the supreme mystery of art. You can't put it into words. You will hear it in a Candelario Huizar's Symphony, in the works of Villa-Lobos, and of course you still hear it in the vast folkloric tradition of Ibero America.

JW: How does it feel to live in the United States where most of the people have very little perception of this reality?

EM: If the gap exists with the majority of the Anglo-Saxon population, it does not exist with the native Indian American, with a good part of the black population, or with any other group that has not given its back to nature, tradition, and popular wisdom. The closest we've come in the United States to this world is through the works of Carlos Castaneda. Do you know him?

JW: Of course, I've read all of his books.

EM: People think of these works as very original, perhaps for the wrong reasons. They wonder if it is the work of a serious anthropologist or simply the product of a great fiction writer. I think the explanation is obvious.

JW: I think the Western equivalent of this world is found in some types of psychoanalysis such as Jungian analysis. I think this is the Western parallel.

EM: You may be right, but Jung is something that we approach in a scholarly and/or intellectual way, whereas in Latin America, the cohabitation with magic and the perception of the subconscious reality is in everyday life. Fiction and reality are inexorably intertwined, and as such, they come out from the writer or the poet.

JW: Don't you think that the North American, European, and Nordic cultures are becoming more attracted to alternative world views such as "magical realism"? If that is the case, Latin America has a lot to offer us!

EM: Art is essentially man's invention. How our natural environment, our world, pre-conditions us to express beauty is relevant to our originality. We're just discovering that we descended from civilizations that knew more about the world and man's mission on the planet than we do now. They didn't have technology as we know it today, but they had a superior wisdom. A few years ago, I went with my wife to Cancún (Mexico) after a long European concert tour. We rented a car and went to see Cobá which is one of the largest Mayan settlements yet discovered, although most of it is still under the jungle. The city has overpasses and sophisticated water systems. When I stood there on top of one of the pyramids, I had this strange feeling: "I am in the center of the world." These people knew what the world was about and why man was on this planet. This ancient city didn't have the feeling of decay at all. It felt so alive, so pulsating, so vital and transcendental! Looking at the details of the architecture, one realizes that everything is in close relation to nature and in exquisite harmony with the cosmos. This is a vital component of our heritage.

The fusion of the Spanish with the Indian forged and nurtured a different kind of perception of the world which is what makes our culture different and original. One can be aware of this, for instance, listening to the natives of the Mesoamerican jungles play and sing their folk music. At the bottom of it, you may detect a Gregorian hymn. It is syncretism *par excellence!* In that sense, Latin America has a lot to offer to the world. Probably our best concert music is still in the future. But the creation of that music will happen only if we are aware of the need to be unified, once we identify and assume that wonderful community of heritage we have, and recognize the solid plateau already built by our fathers and forefathers: Villa-Lobos, Chávez, Revueltas, Estévez, Ginastera, Orbón, and many more.

Biography

Eduardo Mata has been music director of the Dallas Symphony Orchestra since 1977. He served as principal conductor and musical advisor of the Phoenix Symphony Orchestra from 1974 through the 1977-78 season. Since 1978 he has also been active on a regular basis with the London Symphony Orchestra, conducting both concerts and recordings.

Mr. Mata was born in Mexico City in 1942. He began to conduct professionally at the age of fifteen, and studied composition at the National Conservatory of Music with Carlos Chávez and Julián Orbon. In 1964 he was in residence at Tanglewood (the Berkshire Music Center). His first conducting post was that of music director of the Guadalajara Symphony Orchestra, which he assumed at the age of twenty-two. From 1966 to 1975 he was music director and conductor of the Orquestra Filarmonica of the National University of Mexico City. The activities of that ensemble were the impetus for a vastly increased interest in music in Mexico. He also served as artistic director of one of Mexico's major festivals, "Puebla Ciudad Musical," artistic director of the National Symphony in Mexico City in 1975, and technical director and principal conductor of the Casals Festival in Mexico in 1976. In 1975 he served as artistic director of the San Salvador Festival. From 1983 through 1985 he served as artistic advisor of the National Opera in Mexico City.

Mr. Mata has guest-conducted extensively in Europe, the United States, and Latin America. He has worked with most major London orchestras and conducted many British regional orchestras. His continental appearances have included the Rotterdam Philharmonic and orchestras in Stuttgart, Hamburg, Frankfurt, and Baden-Baden. In Italy he has led engagements at La Scala in Milan, in Florence, and in Venice. In the U.S., Mr. Mata has conducted the Chicago, Philadelphia, Boston, Detroit, Denver, Atlanta, and Pittsburgh symphonies, the Cleveland Orchestra, and the St. Paul Chamber Orchestra, among other orchestras.

Mr. Mata's records for the RCA, Angel, and ProArte labels with the Dallas Symphony, the London Symphony, the Philadelphia Orchestra, and the National Arts Centre Orchestra. Two of his recordings have received Grammy nominations.

Mr. Mata is also a composer whose works include symphonic music, chamber works, ballets, vocal music, and works created directly for tape. In 1974 the Mexican Union of Musicians honored him with the Golden Lyre Award. In 1975 the Mexican government gave Mr. Mata the Elias Sourasky Prize in Arts, an honor presented only biannually and the highest award of its kind given in that country. In August of 1984 he received life membership in the prestigious Colegio Nacional (the National College), where he lectures on a yearly basis.

Eduardo Mata Discography

Composer	Work	Orchestra	Soloists	Label	CD	LP	MC
Beethoven	Consecration of the House Overture	Dallas Symphony		Pro Arte	479		
Bizet	Symphony in C	Dallas Symphony		RCA	RCD1-4689		
Chávez	Symphony India	London Symphony		MMG	10002		
Chávez	Symphony no. 2	London Symphony		MMG	10002		
Chávez	Symphony no. 3	London Symphony		MMG	10002		
Copland	Appalachian Spring	Dallas Symphony		RCA			ARK1-2862
Copland	Rodeo	Dallas Symphony		RCA			ARK1-2862
Copland	El Salon México	Dallas Symphony		Angel	CDC-47606	DS-37365	4DS-37365
Copland	Symphony no. 3	Dallas Symphony		Angel	CDC-47606	DS-37365	4DS-37365
Copland	Danzón Cubano	Dallas Symphony		Angel	CDC-47606	DS-37365	4DS-37365
Kodály	Háry János Suite	Dallas Symphony		Pro Arte	CDD-403		
Mahler	Symphony no. 2	Dallas Symphony	McNair, Van Nes	Pro Arte	479		
Mozart	Flute and harp concerto	London Symphony	Galway, Robles	RCA	6723-2 RG	AGL1-5442	AGK1-5442
Mozart	Flute Concerto in G	London Symphony	Galway	RCA		AGL1-5442	AGK1-5442
Mozart	Divertimento 11	Dallas Symphony		RCA	RCD1-4689		
Orff	Carmina Burana	London Symphony	Hendricks, Aler, Hagegard	RCA	RCD1-4550		
Prokofiev	Lt. Kijé Suite	Dallas Symphony		Pro Arte	CDD-403		
Ravel	Boléro	Dallas Symphony		RCA	VD 60485		VK 60485
Ravel	La Valse	Dallas Symphony		RCA	VD 60485		VK 60485
Rodrigo	Concerto pastoral	Philharmonia	Galway	RCA			AGK1-5446
Rodrigo	Fantasia para un gentilhombre	Philharmonia	Galway	RCA			AGK1-5446
Strauss, R.	Le bourgeois gentilhomme, suite	Canadian National Arts Centre		RCA	RCD1-5362		
Strauss, R.	Till Eulenspiegel	Dallas Symphony		Pro Arte	CDD-403		
Stravinsky	Firebird; Fireworks	Dallas Symphony		Pro Arte	443		
Wirén	Serenade	Canadian National Arts Centre		RCA	RCD1-5362		

"When I sang under Klemperer, one of the great conducting giants, I thought that that was the way the music had to go. Beethoven's slow movements had to sound painful or they weren't 'Beethoven.' Now don't forget that those performances are an orthodoxy.

"You see, I think that only true believers in a faith are not worried about orthodoxy. If you really believe in something, you don't need a hierarchy. You don't need a pope. You have a personal relationship with God, like Beethoven had. Beethoven didn't go to church, though he thought God was terrific. If you love music and it gets to you and you go with it, you won't be worried about adhering to a specific orthodoxy."

— Roger Norrington

Roger Norrington

JW: When did you first become interested in conducting?

RN: When I was at college in Westminster, London. I had my first experience conducting when I was eighteen years old and was put in charge of the House choir. At Cambridge I sang and played the violin a lot and was always in several groups either as a violinist or a singer. Sometimes these groups needed a conductor and I would give it a try. I actually put on my first concert at Cambridge. It was a very elegant affair, an evening of Bach and Handel. Of course, at this stage, I was an amateur in all three things, playing, singing and conducting. I was getting a degree in literature not in music. But I had always had my eye on conductors and watched them a lot. Actually, I learned more from the bad conductors than from the good ones! It's hard to see exactly what the good conductors are doing. They make the art of conducting seem like conjuring or something. With the bad ones, you can see exactly what to avoid!

JW: When did you decide to go professional?

RN: Around ten years after college when I was twenty-eight years old. Actually it might be good for young conductors to know that one can start a conducting career later in life. Also, I don't even have Grade One on any musical instrument! I only went to the Royal Conservatory *after* I had been a professional musician for a year. In this sense, I am about the least qualified musician in the world! But I was incredibly *experienced* from years and years of performing music. When I finished Cambridge I became a book publisher for four or five years and did music on the side until I was twenty-eight. Music was a terrific hobby for me, a very serious hobby. You know that in London there is an entire world of extremely talented amateurs, violinists, singers, and even conductors. So I was really in the musical field for all those years though I made my living as a publisher.

I finally left publishing and decided that I just had to do music full time. It hadn't struck me before because I had only thought of myself as an amateur. I hadn't seriously studied, but I was a (trained) tenor and it wasn't difficult to start getting professional work as a singer. I had been studying singing for ten years and had been singing in choirs, in consorts, in oratorios, and in operas where I had several lyric tenor roles. So I was very employable. I was also a very good amateur violinist and I started getting asked to perform a few dates.

Going about a career this way has one great advantage. You never think of music as a job. It is something you do because you want to. That's a kind of secret weapon. Because I enjoy it so much I still expect other musicians to enjoy it. As a conductor I hope that the orchestra is enjoying what they are doing (though maybe that is not always the case). So, before I became professional, I was an amateur who loved music. All that time I did it only because I loved to do it. Before I left publishing I had been playing only in the evenings and on weekends. I was booked almost every weekend and holiday and after working all day in my company I would pursue my musical interests at night. I would sing in the choir on Monday, play in my quartet on Tuesday, sing in a different choir on Wednesday, and play in the orchestra on Thursday. Then on Friday and weekends there were often concerts. Eventually I got ill trying to do so much. So it was actually a relief when I decided to go professional. I could practice during the day time instead of working. I began taking a lot of auditions and began working as a singer almost immediately. I eventually gave up the violin which I had played since I was ten because I couldn't do everything; and I waited to see about conducting. I only conducted a choir occasionally, and I made my living for three years mostly from singing. Gradually my conducting career grew and I gave up singing to follow that. My living was never half teaching and half conducting. It was half singing and half conducting.

JW: It was wonderful that you were able to make a living in music immediately after leaving your publishing business.

RN: Yes, it worked straight away, the first year. Then I went back to college at twenty-nine! I entered the Royal College of Music and they were very kind to me. They said that I didn't need to take any exams and to just come and study anything I wished. It was very good for me at that time. I learned a lot.

JW: What kind of courses did you take?

RN: I took conducting from Adrian Boult, I studied composition, music history, and keyboard. I played violin and percussion in the orchestra. Now Boult was quite interesting. I had only conducted by instinct before. He gave me time to think about what I was doing. I didn't become a very Boult kind of conductor. He was so grand and gentlemanly and I was a bit wild and gutsy. But I learned a lot from him. It was a very good time, because I was earning a living in music as well. I began to see how the profession worked and began to live down the reputation of amateur.

JW: When did you first become interested in early music practices?

RN: While I was at college. We used to sing a lot of madrigals and masses, things by William Byrd and Palestrina. At home in Oxford, I was living in a cultured community, a community in which we played quartets, sang madrigals, and sang in choirs. While I was at Cambridge I was a choral scholar and we sang a lot of early choral music. The music of composers like Palestrina and Victoria became common ground to us. But the idea of using early instruments began much later.

When I left publishing and decided to go professional, one of my main activities was to start a Schütz Choir that specialized in seventeenth-century music. You know my career has always been based on *projects*. Of course, I did other things as well, but basically I always had a project, things that I thought *needed to be done*. One of my first projects was the Schütz Choir, an amateur group. I wanted to perform this particular music which was hardly ever sung. Conducting this choir gradually led me to the question of original instruments. When I looked at the scores and saw things like cornetto, regals, and organ, I began to think of what a performance would sound like with those instruments. At the same time other people also began to experiment with early instruments. David Munrow was around with his medieval stuff, and Chris Hogwood was just beginning. In fact, one of my early records with the Schütz Choir was with David Munrow *and* Chris Hogwood.

JW: Chris Hogwood has a very similar background to you.

RN: Well, I think he studied music more formally.

JW: He didn't start out in music. He started out in the classics, I believe.

RN: That's interesting. I didn't know that. Well, he was sometimes a continuo player in our group and at that time (1964) we were all jamming together and learning from each other's concerts. It was wonderful! We made quite a lot of records, some with early instruments as they became available, and some with modern instruments. We didn't have a "policy" like we do now. Our interest for early instruments grew out of some sort of need to hear what a seventeenth-century sound was like. We didn't know. Nobody knew. When we first gave the Monteverdi *Vespers* we used modern trumpets because we didn't have good cornetti. Gradually though, the word got out and we encouraged musicians to learn to play them. We would say motivating things like, "In two years time we want to do the *Vespers* with original instruments, so be ready! Next year we will be doing the *Symphonie fantastique,* so be ready." Ever since then it's been like that. Now it's Brahms. In September we are going to record the Symphony no. 1 of Brahms.

So you see from the beginning we have been the frontiersmen. Actually the Schütz Choir and the London Classical Players were always more advanced than the other groups. It happened to be our thing to always be on the forefront. We did the first original instrument version of *Vespers* in Britain, the first Handel's *Messiah,* the first *Creation,* the first *St. John's Passion.* We did around three concerts a year but we were always ahead. We wanted to hear what these works sounded like. Now it's Brahms's First Symphony instead of Beethoven.

JW: Are you going to do all the Brahms symphonies?

RN: Maybe not, but we might do the first two. So you see, the Schütz Choir naturally led to this. We needed an orchestra of the most excellent players to accompany us, so we formed the London Baroque Players. We remained, however, a basically choir-oriented project. From 1962-72 we did mostly a cappella singing. We performed a lot of Monteverdi, Purcell, Schütz, Steffani, and lots of other seventeenth-century works. We created incredibly obscure programs like the Church Music of Bologna from 1670-90, early French, Germany, Italian, and English music. We did whole programs of Schütz. People flocked to this stuff. Five hundred people would fill a church. Finally in 1972 we dropped the amateur choir and I stayed with a professional choir.

During 1972-82, my second project was reconstructions of seventeenth- and eighteenth-century works with a professional choir of soloists and with original instruments. The size of the professional choir was more historical. The amateur choir was always a bit big. Sometimes now we would do works with only six people. We did the *Vespers* with twelve singers. These were the original size of the early groups anyway. When we did the [Bach] *St. John's Passion* it was with a professional choir of men and boys all whom sang the solos. That was the idea. So during 1972-82 I did reconstructions of the great masterpieces we thought we knew: the [Monteverdi] *Vespers,* [Handel] *Messiah,* [Haydn] *Creation,* and *Requiem* by Mozart. After that period of musical history, you get into an area where there isn't as much singing. You enter the world of the symphony. The symphony suddenly becomes extremely important. So after having worked my way through the sixteenth and seventeenth centuries of choral music, I decided to put the choir on hold and to bring the orchestra forward. We began to do the Haydn symphonies and then the Beethoven. When we got to Beethoven a lot more people began to notice us.

JW: Weren't you also involved with the Kent Opera during this same period?

RN: Yes. My main work at this time was as musical director of the Kent Opera. For fifteen years I did over four hundred performances of thirty different operas. Now the Schütz Choir and the Beethoven symphonies were projects, but the Kent Opera was a job. We only performed three months a year, but the position certainly was like being a music director of an American orchestra. It was a big job! It lasted most of the year and occupied most of my time. That was one reason The London Classical Players weren't as well known until we started doing the Beethoven symphonies. I did one or two of my symphony projects a year and we did a few performances of things like the *Messiah,* but I was so busy doing opera that I didn't record. I wasn't minding the shop, so to speak. After I would do the first performance of Handel's *Messiah,* Chris [Hogwood] would come along and record it six months later with the same players. While they were recording, I was busy running off and doing operas with Kent. When I left Kent I started wondering what to do. At that point we were starting the Beethoven symphonies and people were really beginning to be interested. Suddenly everybody sat up and realized that this was a hell of a good orchestra. The record companies came to us, we didn't have to ask. Maybe it was good that this recognition didn't come any earlier because we were really getting good by the time they came along.

So, that's roughly how the original instruments came into my performances. They also came into the Kent Opera performances. We did quite a lot of early music performances, including all the Monteverdi operas. We gave the first performance of *L'incoronazione di Poppea* in modern times using the original pitches for the singers, original instruments, and orchestration. These were really pioneering performances. We did *Orfeo* with a cast of sixteen. We also did operas by Handel and Purcell with the original instruments. We didn't do Mozart operas that way though. That's one of reasons that I left Kent Opera. The artistic director didn't want to do Mozart operas with original instruments. It seems incredible now! Only ten years ago and people still thought that original instruments couldn't play in tune. You know, all the usual complaints. But, all in all Kent Opera was a fruitful area. We were always pushing musicians into things they weren't quite sure of. We just plunged into projects without really knowing how to do them. It was terrifying sometimes, but very creative.

My concert master Holloway and I were always pushing each other. It's still that way. It so happened that the premiere of *Poppea* was going to take place in Lisbon. The musicians wanted to take both types of instruments, the old and the new, along on tour. I said, "No, we take only the old. That way we have to *make* it work. You can't go home and get your fiddle. We have to make it work." That is one of the subtexts of the whole operation. You have to make it work. Take the risk.

JW: All of this research has certainly cast a new light on standard traditional performances.

RN: Yes, because we were determined to find out what music might have sounded like. When we did [Berlioz's] *Symphonie fantastique* we were committed to perform and record that piece before we even knew we could play it. It forces you to think. Under that type of pressure you don't fool around, you really go for it. It's very dangerous but kind of exciting as well. When we did the Berlioz we suddenly realized that the piece really did need those older instruments. Now maybe in another ten years everybody will be playing on original instruments, or maybe it's just a fad and will all have disappeared! Either way, it is still incredible what we have learned by having to think anew.

JW: Well, I think your recording of Symphonie fantastique *is extraordinary. I heard a lot of things I had never heard before in other recordings.*

RN: That recording happened the same way as the Beethoven recordings. I didn't particularly like the way a lot of other people did them. I would ask: "Couldn't it sound like this? Couldn't there be some phrasing and do we *have* to have those slow tempi?" I wanted to get in there in the same way I had with Mozart, Haydn, and Beethoven. But when it came to Berlioz I thought, "This is ridiculous. We don't even know whether these instruments will work and anyway Abbado just made an incredible recording with Chicago." I thought, "We can't play like that. We might sound like the kitchen sink." We went ahead anyway because we wanted to know what it sounded like on those instruments. You have to be prepared to fall flat on your face in this early music business. You have to be prepared to make terrible mistakes. Each project I thought would be the end of the road. But by now we have actually worked our way, one project at a time, from the sixteenth century to 1870. We have done Schubert, Schumann, and even Wagner. With the Schubert Ninth, which I think is one of our best recordings, you hear very different sonorities and phrasing than those you usually hear.

JW: How do you feel about guest conducting modern orchestras after all of your experiences with your own group with original instruments?

RN: It feels absolutely normal to me. You see I was a *modern* violinist. I never played the baroque fiddle and I never gave up vibrato. I've only converted in my mind. If I play with my kids, they say, "What is all that vibrato, Dad?" I still can only play like that. I have this sort of rictus of the left hand! So, in one sense I'm perfectly used to modern orchestras. I've been playing in them and conducting them since my early twenties. I'm not like those people who began as lute players, harpsichordists, or recorder players. The modern orchestra is not a strange animal to me.

JW: Are there any advantages in working with a modern orchestra?

RN: I conduct exactly half the year with modern orchestras. In one sense it does become more and more of a challenge to conduct them because of all the other sounds that I have in my head. But it seems to be important for me to do this. I think that I would also become a little bit frustrated only working with original instruments because I've been conducting modern instruments all along in my career. In the Kent Opera we were doing Verdi and Mozart and Britten and Tchaikovsky with modern instruments. But maybe I want to change modern orchestras in some respects. That is the next project.

JW: That's interesting. Many people are saying that orchestras are only museums of eighteenth- and nineteenth-century music. Do you think the orchestra has a future? How would you like to change it?

RN: Well, I can't tell the future but I would like to change some aspects of it. For a start if we are going to live in a museum, I want to live in an interesting museum. Since 1950 the penny has dropped. The early music thing really only got under way after World War II. By 1950 most of the programs we liked were by dead composers. Before that people listened to living composers such as Brahms, Liszt, Mahler, and Stravinsky.

JW: Don't you think this situation will change? Don't you think that people will want to hear the music of living composers once again?

RN: I do hope this will change. I hope that people will stop writing such hostile new music. You have to admit that a lot of modern music is incredibly hostile. Either we will get used to hostility (it's like getting used to concrete buildings), or the composers will change. I think the orchestra has a future playing new pieces. Smaller orchestras also have a future, or larger orchestras might break up into different groups. A large orchestra might be four orchestras in one.

On the historical side we will go on playing earlier music. What happened in 1950 was important. It led to the current reevaluation. There was a need to look for a change in how to play Handel and Bach. There was a need to reevaluate the way we played. If we are to live in a museum we have to paint it. We have to show people around. We have to make sure we are looking at an Egyptian piece of statuary we understand something about, and not just label it an ancient piece of statuary. We have to stop saying we don't know how Bach was played.

Actually museums themselves have undergone a great change since 1950. They are wonderful places packed with information. You can go around with headphones and be told what things are. Museums are not boring old places where antiquarians live. They are very exciting ways of traveling to the past. And the past is not as far away as you think. There are whole masses of information that make it very exciting. The past is filled with this exciting information and it is only a reach away.

So, I think that's what happened to me. I stopped thinking that you can't really know how they played Bach. It's a more complete journey now. And if you want to find out about Eskimos you head north and not to the Caribbean! I hope that the museum culture of the twenty-first century will be an intelligent, aware, culture which will enjoy the past, not at arms length, but by trying to get as close to it as possible. There will also be new music.

So, I believe there is indeed a place for the orchestra. The orchestra has to change, though. I don't know exactly how; I go on instinct. When I do projects I only realize the direction in which I headed afterwards. I don't always plan the direction in advance. I do what needs doing now; and there are certain things around that need doing. One of those things is opera and the way it could be staged historically. Currently I'm doing nineteenth-century orchestra music. So, at least we are making a stab at sorting things out.

But what shall we do about these modern symphony orchestras? Are we going to go on playing as if we don't know how Mozart was played? Are we going to accept that our inherited approaches are just fine? Are we going to accept that they are right and that the new way is wrong? What are we going to do? There is such a dichotomy between the way the London Classical Players play a Mozart symphony and the way big symphony orchestras play them. One of them ought to be right or maybe the truth lies somewhere in the middle. If that is true then they both need to head toward that middle. I just want to offer any symphony orchestra that can stand it the opportunity for this type of appraisal and the chance to change. It's a challenge to perform Mozart or Beethoven symphonies with modern instruments. It's a challenge to make the musicians change a bit – to make them play in a way that will suit them and yet also make the music recognizable to me.

JW: One of the main criticisms about early music performance practices by conductors that conduct in the traditional manner is that they are afraid there will be a trend to perform this music only one way. It's not that they don't respect the research, they just want the freedom to still do the [Bach] St. Matthew Passion, for instance, their own way.

RN: No one is looking for "authentic" performances. There is no such thing. There is also no one way of doing a piece. I think that you can already tell enormous differences in the early music performances of, for instance, Beethoven's *Eroica*. There are currently five performances recorded on early instruments, yet they are very different from each other. Following historical principles doesn't result in only one performance. It just means that you are getting in the ball park in terms of performing the music the way the composer would recognize it. It isn't even the notes or the dots. It's the subtext, the aesthetic of that period of time. You try to get a bit nearer to it. However, if people want to hear the *St. Matthew Passion* played in a nineteenth-century manner they should be able to hear it. Early music fans will not want to go. They wouldn't recognize the piece! But there can be a choice.

JW: Another argument is that great music transcends the performance practices.

RN: Yes, it does, but I think what will happen is that gradually some performance practices will be questioned. One of the reasons we revved up the early music movement was because of the crescendo of late romanticism. Performances were getting slower and slower and grander and grander – performances that we can safely say were under the "Karajan influence," now that he's dead. I sang under Klemperer; I think I know what he was doing and it was very impressive. But I found myself looking for something different. Currently David and Goliath are butted up against each other. What I imagine will happen is that David will become more street-wise and will develop a business sense and become a corporation. And Goliath will take off his armor and go on a diet of macrobiotic food. In five years there might be less difference between the two.

JW: Well, I discovered that most conductors won't retouch scores anymore, though it was a common practice a few years ago. A few even perform with Beethoven's metronome markings, David Zinman and Edo de Waart, for instance.

RN: Edo is reducing the size of orchestras as well.

JW: Dohnányi won't retouch scores either and he's certainly from the old school of European maestros.

RN: Well, he's quite interested in our recordings but he and his orchestra won't go that way. They are quite resistant to any change. People will get used to the new way. People will be get nearer to Bach. They will let it dance more. There is room for all of this. But you *don't* want to invent an orthodoxy that won't allow you to do it any other way.

JW: That was Dutoit's fear. That early music performances would become a kind of religion.

RN: Yes, it might become too "trendy." But he's quite interested in my work; I'm going to his orchestra in December. And I've got a lot to learn from him, and other conductors too. I've got a lot to learn from watching them work. We need to learn from each other. It's super. I don't seek an orthodoxy. I just want to recognize a composer in a performance that I'm doing. When I'm doing the *St. Matthew Passion* every movement has to dance. It's not a ballet but it is about dance music. That's where the music comes from. I've sat through performances and played in performances where the conductors take these terribly slow tempos. It's really quite interesting when I go back far enough to remember all these types of performances. When I sang under Klemperer, one of the great conducting giants, I thought that that was the way the music had to go. Beethoven's slow movements had to sound painful or they weren't "Beethoven." Now don't forget that those performances are an orthodoxy.

You see, I think that only true believers in a faith are not worried about orthodoxy. If you really believe in something, you don't need a hierarchy. You don't need a pope. You have a personal relationship with God, like Beethoven had. Beethoven didn't go to church, though he thought God was terrific. If you love music and it gets to you and you go with it, you won't be worried about adhering to a specific orthodoxy. It's only worrying when kids are taught there is only one way to do a thing, whether it's my way or Klemperer's. They should find out for themselves. People shouldn't need an orthodoxy.

JW: Well, after watching and listening to your rehearsals and concerts, I found that it didn't matter whether one agreed with you or not. One thing I found so gripping about your performances was your belief in what you are doing. And you communicate that belief in the moment.

RN: Yeah, it's a local call. I try and make it feel like a local call to the composer!

JW: No one can resist that type of conviction.

RN: I've also found out why I want to do it like that. I remember the Beethoven Eighth Symphony being taught in class. Boult told me it had to be conducted in three because Beethoven's metronome was faulty. Well, forget about the metronome marking! If you conduct it in three the music becomes incredibly tedious. So I would go to orchestras and tell them I was conducting in one and would never be invited back again. I went through that sort of stuff. Eventually, after my Beethoven recordings, I came back armed to the teeth with information and experience with using those tempos and early instruments. I knew how they really sounded. Some orchestras still get upset about some of these tempos but a lot of them love it! I have arrived at this stuff by myself. I don't belong to an orthodoxy of early music. I created my own. I had to invent my performances of Haydn and Mozart, Beethoven, Berlioz, Schumann, and Brahms.

JW: Your approach reminds me of what Joseph Campbell said about his favorite hero, Parsifal. He said that Parsifal was one of the greatest Medieval heros because he went against the established religion of his time and found his own inner path.

RN: Ah, the perfect fool. The pure fool.

JW: That is one of the things I find is so wonderful about your approach. You definitely have found your own way. Many people only follow the established way of doing things and are threatened when someone does it differently.

RN: The audiences usually like it a lot, but some musicians and critics can get threatened. That's the difficult thing about conducting modern orchestras. Some of the musicians think, "I've got a thirty-year commitment playing this music in a certain manner. Now, he's implying I'm wrong." But generous musicians say, "This is fun," and a few even say, "I've always wanted to play it like this anyway." One of the violinists here in San Francisco told me he had been waiting forty years to end the *Pastoral* Symphony like we did it. There are usually two or three people who come up and say things like that. So you always have some people who are ready to change but then you have others who are committed to performing a certain way. It's a minefield. You are dealing with issues of self esteem.

JW: It's difficult to change.

RN: Yes, but somehow it needs to be done. And remember, we do have *facts* behind our performances. It's not just some sort of zany notion about early music practices. It's rather well informed. You can read about how they did this stuff. Sometimes I get a bit annoyed because people are constantly challenging you with, "Why do you have to do it differently." Well, why do *they* have to do it demonstrably contrary to what the composer says? I try to do what the composer asked for. Sometimes, David should be given a little leeway. Ask Goliath what is he wearing all that funny armor for. But of course it may take a while for people to accept this turnabout.

JW: Then someone else will come and shake them up again.

RN: Well, maybe.

JW: I see you at the forefront of this movement now. You are really shaking up the modern orchestra.

RN: It's kind of frightening. But it is great when orchestras accept what you are doing and don't think that it is just mad. The performance of the *Pastoral* went really well here [San Francisco]. When an orchestra gets that close to what I want I feel very happy. It's fantastic! Now St. Luke's in New York, where I'm music director, will go all the way with me, because they are crazy people. And I'm not trying to turn them into an early music orchestra. I only want to see how far we can go with a modern one. That is what interests me.

I have been asking orchestras for ten years now to do classical bowing, baroque bowing and phrasing, and new tempi. What I haven't changed yet is *vibrato*. I haven't dealt with that question or the gut string question. Those considerations are enormous question marks. But isn't that what a modern orchestra should be doing part of the time? Shouldn't we tackle vibrato? Or is it just too near the knuckle? Then there is the question of playing on the string instead of always playing spiccato. Spiccato playing is almost totally unhistorical up to Brahms. Orchestras played on the string until then. But if you ask the players to bow without spiccato they get very, very nervous. It's possible that in ten years time you may hear a symphony orchestra go onto gut strings and lighter bows for three months of the year. Then the timpani and percussion could change to classical styles. The winds might also use earlier instruments as well as their modern ones. The symphony orchestra might take this in their stride. They will have their repertoire back again. They won't stop playing Bach; they will leap at it instead. You will have a section of the orchestra that will be particularly interested in the Baroque and then all of them will understand the classical and romantic literature and some will do modern music as well.

That's how I see a future orchestra: an orchestra with lots of chamber groups working inside of it and a tremendous understanding of historical style. In one concert they could do a piece by Bach, a piece by Xenakis, and a piece by Mendelssohn. Each would sound incredibly different. Today everything sounds like Mahler! Currently there is a danger that all music will be subsumed into the sound of the symphony orchestra in 1950. It hasn't changed since then. Mozart, Bach, and Monteverdi all sound like Mahler being played in 1950. That's a frightening prospect; it doesn't allow the composers any individuality.

JW: Would you consider doing modern music? Do you enjoy it?

RN: I have done a *lot* of modern music. I've done fifty to sixty premieres. I enjoy it if it's good. My criterion is if it gets to me. I've done a lot of Britten, a lot of the English school: Michael Tippett, Nicolas Maw, Roger Smalley, and Robert Simpson. That's another way in which I'm atypical for an early music conductor. I have always done modern music as well. I take this stuff in my stride. I sing madrigals, I play modern violins, and I conduct avant-garde music. There is really no period of music I'm uncomfortable with. I'm not saying that I'm so great, I've just been particularly lucky because I've had a very diverse experience. But I want to do it like it was meant to be done. I don't want it to be like homogenized Kraft cheese. I want Cheddar, Gruyère, or Brie. I want all the different cheeses and I want a particular cheese, not a processed one. It's great being Bach in the morning, Mozart in the afternoon, Dittersdorf in the evening, and the next day, Elliott Carter. There is a huge disparity. Let's not homogenize music. That's the danger of orthodoxies. I want to be free. I'm a free actor. I want to be able to do comedies, tragedies, or whatever. I want to find what it is about. Orchestras should be like that. They should be free to do any kind of performance they want to. A *St. Matthew Passion* that's huge and grand or one that's very small. I don't even think size is important. It isn't size, it's the gesture that is important, it's the dance.

JW: What are your score study techniques?

RN: I study in lots of different ways. If I don't know a piece I'll listen to a recording. If it's a premiere I'll try and talk to the composer about it. But if it's a Liszt symphony, for instance, I'll listen to it. I'd listen to it a lot.

JW: Would you use different recordings?

RN: No, any recording would do. I'd listen just to get the sound of the score in my head. I'd probably listen to it while driving. I'd just get used to it subconsciously. It may not be the first thing I'd do but it would be one of the things. So if I'm driving it's good because I can't look at the score. I have to listen to what's happening. Then of course I look at the structure in the score. One of the very first things I do is to go through and mark the bar structure, the periodicity, and the form. It's very important to me. I have to know the periodicity. That's number one. I learn the short-term grammar and then the long-term grammar – what the music is doing and where it's going. I find what the big blocks are. I realized one day how important this was because of a ballet I was working on. Every phrase is the phrase of the dance. If the choreographer sets something across one of those lines it's not correct. The structure is really related to the dance shape.

Every classical symphony is related to the dance. There is no music from the baroque or classical era that is not related to the dance. Everything can be seen in those terms. The audience in 1800-1900 all danced. They might not have all played musical instruments, but they all danced. They listened to music through their feet. They understood this music because they danced it. Perhaps they didn't hear the harmonic structure but they did hear the dance. I always conduct scherzos in 3 or in 4 groups of bars, never in one. When the phrase structure is irregular you can really hear it.

Finally I'll make the harmonic structure analysis. Other people might do it the other way around because they do it at the keyboard, which I don't. I like to listen a lot. I'm a violinist rather than a pianist, and when I grew up we didn't even have a piano in the house. I never learned how to play piano well.

JW: How much detail do you go into?

RN: Oh, a whole lot of detail. I might not label every chord but I know what it's doing and where it's going. Then I go through the score with a more inventive mind, forgetting about structure. I ask, "What's *really* happening?" I don't mean the story line but I ask whether the music is funny or serious, whether a particular gesture is tragic or comic? I ask what the flavour is. "Is this music a fanfare? Is the composer showing off or is he celebrating?" The dramatic subtext of the music is very important to me. It's what a director has

201

to decide about in an opera. In a symphony there is usually no "action," but the feeling should be there that this music could suddenly burst into a painting or a novel or a play. There is always that dramatic poetic potential.

JW: I noticed when you were rehearsing that you used a lot of dramatic metaphors? I think they worked!

RN: I use them to focus the mind. Of course when there are words you *do* know what the music means. I'm used to opera, so I'm used to the orchestra painting those words. You know exactly what they mean. Symphonies are not *so* different than that. They came out of operas. They are parallel to operas in many ways. Imagine, Beethoven's nine operas! I'm not saying that you have to write a story but then again you may write six stories or you might not write any. I wrote about twelve stories for Beethoven's Ninth. I wrote my own as well as read other's stories. I read Berlioz's story and Hoffmann's story. *Every* critic thought a symphony was "about" something at that time.

JW: So you obviously do a lot of background study on your scores!

RN: Yes. I want to know what people thought about a work when it first came out. Take Beethoven's Ninth: I found what they *didn't* mention was the chorus. It *wasn't* strange to have a chorus in a symphony. Now people always mention the chorus but at the time people took that for granted, partly because of the influence of opera, partly because every concert had singing in it. In fact there were no concerts without singing at that time. In the first performance of the Ninth, Beethoven programmed the overture for *The Consecration of the House,* three movements of the *Missa Solemnis* with singing, and the Ninth Symphony with the singing at the end. It was completely normal to have singing in concerts. It makes one have quite a different attitude about it. Also if you realize that all the critics thought that there were too many woodwinds in Symphonies 1 and 2, you realize that the woodwind parts are really very important. Don't hide them. Bring them out. So, know the background of a work. It's the emotional information about a symphony. It's very important.

JW: This is an enormous amount of preparation. How long do you live with a work before performing it?

RN: Minimum six months. Hopefully a year.

JW: Do you ever learn anything over night and perform it?

RN: I have, and I can do it, but I don't now. It just doesn't interest me and so I refuse to do it at this point in my career. I start a year in advance and get a preliminary view and then work on the score whenever I can. I also like to conduct by memory, but don't make a fetish of it. I like to do certain pieces by memory and I'd like to know any piece well enough to be able to do it. I don't tend to do operas by memory or masses. Too dangerous. It worries singers a lot and it just seems to be an enormous job to do it. You don't have to own a mass as much as a symphony. Or maybe I'm just too lazy! I do the pieces by memory that I feel completely comfortable doing. I don't have that incredible a memory. I couldn't write a piece out. I don't know them that well. If I can conduct better without a score I do it. If not, I don't. I don't have a photographic memory. There is something special about doing something by memory though. You are freer. You can watch the orchestra, which is especially important if you don't know them. You can think about what's coming next. It's very exciting. You can compose the piece when you conduct by memory. With the score you are following some one else's piece.

JW: Do you have perfect pitch?

RN: No.

JW: Do you have a rehearsal technique?

RN: No. I rehearse the music.

Biography

Roger Norrington was born in 1934 in Oxford. He sang and played the violin from an early age, studied English Literature at Cambridge University, and conducting at the Royal College of Music in London. He worked as a professional tenor and violinist and in 1962 he formed the Schütz Choir, with which he gave numerous innovative concerts and made many recordings. He became musical director of Kent Opera at its founding in 1969 until 1984. From 1985 to 1988 he was principal conductor and artistic advisor of the Bournemouth Sinfonietta and principal guest conductor of the Jerusalem Symphony.

He has an exclusive contract with EMI Classics for whom he has recorded the complete Beethoven symphonies and piano concertos, as well as works by composers such as Mozart, Berlioz, Schubert, Schumann, Weber, and Wagner. Several of these recordings have won important prizes, including the Gramophone Award for Period Performance in 1987 for the Beethoven Symphonies nos. 2 and 8, the Grand Prix Caecilia of Belgium in 1989 for the Beethoven Symphonies nos. 1 and 6, the Ovation Award in the U.S. for Berlioz's *Symphonie fantastique,* and the Deutsche Schallplattenpreis in 1990 for the complete Beethoven symphonies.

These recordings have been made with the London Classical Players, the orchestra he founded in 1978 with the specific aim of exploring historical performance practice. Norrington and the London Classical Players perform regularly at the South Bank. They also appear in the BBC's Promenade

Concert Series and at major European festivals and concert halls in cities such as Amsterdam, Salzburg, Paris, Vienna, Frankfurt, and Brussels. They tour the U.S. giving concerts at Lincoln Center, New York, and in Boston, San Francisco, Los Angeles, and Chicago. They have also made numerous television programs, including the complete Beethoven symphonies for the BBC.

Roger Norrington has worked with most of the leading symphony orchestras in the UK, and in London with the Philharmonia, the London Philharmonic, the London Symphony, the BBC Symphony, the English Chamber Orchestra, and the Chamber Orchestra of Europe. In North America he is music director of the Orchestra of St. Luke's in New York and appears each season with the Boston and San Francisco symphonies as well as the Los Angeles Philharmonic and the Montreal, Toronto, Ottowa, Minnesota, and Baltimore symphonies, the Cleveland Orchestra, and the St. Paul Chamber Orchestra. In Europe he appears with the Hamburg Staatsorchester, Frankfurt Museums-Gesellschaft, Stockholm Philharmonic, and Swedish Radio orchestras.

At the Royal Opera House, Covent Garden, he conducted Handel's *Samson* in 1986, Britten's *Albert Herring* during 1988-89, and *Peter Grimes* during 1989-90. Other operatic appearances include the English National Opera, La Scala Milan, La Fenice Venice, and the Teatro Comunale Florence. During his musical directorship of Kent Opera he conducted over 400 performances of forty different works covering a wide ranging repertoire from Monteverdi to Tippett.

Although Norrington's interest in historical performance is best known through his activities with the London Classical Players, he also appears with other organizations using period instruments, including the Orchestra of the 18th Century, the Boston Early Music Festival, and the Netherlands Bach Society. He is codirector with Kay Lawrence of Historic Arts, which administrates not only the London Classical Players but also the Early Opera Project, the Early Dance Project, the Schüutz Choir, and Norrington's acclaimed "Experience" weekends.

Roger Norrington was made an OBE in 1979, Cavaliere (Italy) in 1980, and a CBE in 1990.

Roger Norrington Discography

Composer	Work	Orchestra	Soloists	Label	CD	LP	MC
Beethoven	Choral Fantasy	London Classical Players	Tan	Angel	CDC-49509		4DS-49509
Beethoven	Piano concerto no. 1	London Classical Players	Tan	Angel	CDC-49509		4DS-49509
Beethoven	Piano concerto no. 2	London Classical Players	Tan	Angel	CDC-49509		4DS-49509
Beethoven	Prometheus Overture	London Classical Players		Angel	CDC-49101		4DS-49101
Beethoven	Symphonies (9)	London Classical Players	Kenny, Walker, Power, Salomaa	Angel	CDS 7 49852 2		
Beethoven	Symphony no. 1	London Classical Players		Angel			
Beethoven	Symphony no. 2	London Classical Players		Angel	CDC-47698	DS-47698	4DS-47698
Beethoven	Symphony no. 3	London Classical Players		Angel	CDC-49101		4DS-49101
Beethoven	Symphony no. 4	London Classical Players		Angel			
Beethoven	Symphony no. 5	London Classical Players		Angel			
Beethoven	Symphony no. 6	London Classical Players		Angel			
Beethoven	Symphony no. 7	London Classical Players		Angel			
Beethoven	Symphony no. 8	London Classical Players		Angel	CDC-47698	DS-47698	4DS-47698
Beethoven	Symphony no. 9	London Classical Players	Kenny, Walker, Power, Salomaa	Angel	CDC-49221	DS-49221	4DS-49221

Composer	Work	Orchestra	Soloists	Label	CD	LP	MC
Berlioz	Symphonie Fantastique	London Classical Players		Angel	CDC-49541		4DS-49541
Brahms	Symphony no. 1	London Classical Players		Angel			
Fauré	Caligula	Monte-Carlo Opera		PG		7466	
Fauré	Prométhée	Monte-Carlo Opera	Galland	PG		7466	
Liszt	Hungarian fantasia for piano	Hague Residentie	Clidat	PG	PCD-7464	7464	
Liszt	Piano concerto no. 1	Hague Residentie	Clidat	PG		7375	
Liszt	Piano concerto no. 2	Hague Residentie	Clidat	PG		7375	
Mendelssohn	Symphony no. 3	London Classical Players		Angel	CDC 7 54000 2		
Mendelssohn	Symphony no. 4	London Classical Players		Angel	CDC 7 54000 2		EL 754000-4
Schubert	Symphony no. 5	London Classical Players		Angel	CDC 7 499682		
Schubert	Symphony no. 8	London Classical Players		Angel	CDC 7 499682		
Schumann	Symphony no. 3	London Classical Players		Angel	CDC 7 54025 2		
Schumann	Symphony no. 4	London Classical Players		Angel	CDC 7 54025 2		
Wagner	Der Fliegende Holländer: Dutchman Overture	London Classical Players		Angel			

"The wonderful thing about the conducting profession is that no matter how many times you perform a piece, it is always a premiere. Something different will happen each time, and you will have found something new. I don't care if it's one new bar. That one bar will make the piece a brand new experience. That's why I think that people in our profession (to a large enough extent to make the generality possible) are never bored. We can be bored with the periphery of conducting. God knows, you get bored with airports and boards of governors and ladies luncheons and all that stuff, but the actual music-making is never boring because something is always brand new in the piece. You can run full tilt after the repertoire for your entire life and may find only near the end of your life that you will have caught up a little bit. That's wonderful!"

——————————————————————————— André Previn

André Previn

JW: I was shocked to read in Time *magazine that you were leaving the Los Angeles Philharmonic. What happened?*

AP: Well, when I first came here one of the principals, a great player, said to me, "You haven't been in this country for the last twenty years. I had better explain something to you. The Philadelphia Orchestra is famous for strings; the Chicago Symphony is famous for brass; the Cleveland Orchestra is famous for clarity; the Boston Symphony is famous for elegance, and the Los Angeles Philharmonic is famous for its manager." Ernst Fleishmann is a man of great knowledge but he cannot let go of any part of any kind of authority. He really wants to make every decision himself, whether it is musical or managerial. When he saw that he couldn't do that with me things just got out of hand.

JW: Did he try to make musical decisions for Carlo Maria Giulini as well?

AP: I can't answer that because I don't know. Giulini left the Los Angeles Philharmonic because his wife was ill. I've seen Giulini since, though, and he said to me, "You are going to have a time when you are going to ask, 'Who is the music director here?'" People were hired without letting me know, repertoire was made without letting me know, soloists were engaged without letting me know. It was just insane. I finally called the bluff and said, "This won't do." It was very sad.

JW: Are you going to be here next year?

AP: I'm coming back but not for as long a period of time. I really love the orchestra so I'll also be coming back for quite a few weeks the following two years as well. I want to come back without a title, take the orchestra on tour, and make some records. That means the management can run the operation and I can just conduct, which is all I care about anyway.

JW: So are you going back to London?

AP: No. The house in England is for sale because living there is no longer practical. I have just bought a house in Bedford, New York, which is on the border of Connecticut. It's very beautiful there and is only an hour and a half to the Kennedy Airport. So while I guest conduct in Europe I'll stay in hotels and keep my main house in upstate New York.

JW: Are you away from your family a lot now or do they travel with you?

AP: At this point in my life the only time that I ever leave my little boy [Lukas, who is six years old] at home is when I have to do too much skipping around. That's too hard on him. But he has gone on Japanese tours and European tours and is the official mascot of the Vienna Philharmonic. He's been everywhere. I never leave him. I still think that to go around the world with your father is better than any amount of Kindergarten lessons in one city. This is going to come to a halt pretty soon but by then he will be old enough to cope with it. By now he also knows that when I do go away for a week or two that I'll be back soon. He never has to ask, "When is he coming back?" He knows. And when I'm away I call him and my wife every day. Also, I have started having holidays. I had not had a holiday in my adult life until four years ago! My wife and I decided that this was ridiculous and began organizing them. One year we went skiing for two weeks and last year we went to Hawaii. It was wonderful. It just rejuvenates everything. You have to be ruthless, though. You have to say "No" even if someone calls up and says this is the only time you can record the Mahler Fifth with the Concertgebouw.

My wife has also been wonderfully understanding about all of the performance pressures. Though she loves and needs music, she had never been a performer so she had to learn a lot about the performing world. Once she asked me in my dressing room before a concert, "Do you have so-and-so's phone number?" I answered, "That will be fine." She realized I hadn't heard a word. Now she looks at her watch and says jokingly, "Yes, that'll be fine" and leaves. She knows that when it's getting close to the concert I am in another world and have already started working. Once though, I remember Itzhak Perlman waiting with me back stage to do the Beethoven Violin Concerto with the Chicago Symphony. After a few minutes, Itzhak said to me, "O.K., what's this?" He played something on the violin and I said, "That's the theme for *My Three Sons*" and he said, "Good, give me one." I whistled something and he said, "Oh please, that's *Andy Griffith.*" Then he played something else on the violin and I said, "I don't know." He said, "Come on, you've heard it," and I said, "Yeah, but I don't know what it is." By this time the guys have the stage door open and I said, "Itzhak, I haven't got time now, what is it?" He said, *"Leave It to Beaver.* Don't you ever see those reruns?" Then we were off. When we came back Shirley Fleming, the editor of *High Fidelity* magazine, couldn't believe what she had heard before we went out. She said, "I'm going to pretend I didn't hear this. It's blown my concept of classical music completely. You two clowns were backstage worrying about the theme of *Leave It to Beaver* ten seconds before you walked out to perform. Itzhak said those little games were what kept him from getting terribly nervous.

•••••

JW: Do you have a system of score analysis? How do you approach a new score?

AP: When you say new score do you mean something that was written last Wednesday?

JW: I mean a score that is not in your repertoire. Do you have a technique for learning and analyzing it?

AP: A score such as Dvořák's Symphony no. 1 (I don't even know if it's in print) perhaps? Well, first of all, if it's not a contemporary piece it will very likely be by a composer whose other works I have played or conducted. So, let's stick to the Dvořák example. Out of his nine symphonies, I think I have done five. Because I have already done five of his symphonies, I will know stylistically how to solve most of the problems. The first thing I would do after looking through the score would be to take it to the piano and play through it. Then I try to do some kind of structural, motivic, and harmonic analysis. After that I'd start marking the score. I have a tendency to mark my scores up wildly with all kinds of colors and things which have no meaning to anybody else. They tend to be full of reminders. After I've learned the score I can be given a blank one and it won't matter anymore. All my marks simply help me to learn the piece. So, I play the score at the piano, do a structural, motivic, and harmonic analysis, mark it up, and by that time I usually know the piece. When I was younger, at the beginning of my career, I used to memorize absolutely every note I'd conduct, but at this point in my life I'm not a big memorizing freak.

JW: Did you have a technique for that or was memory the result of your score study?

AP: By the time I finished studying I usually had the piece memorized. I have a good sense of retention. Part of my ability, I say with some apology, is visual. In other words, if I had been studying a score I was soon able to see the page numbers and where the notes lay on the page. But if I used another edition where the page turns were different I had to start over. It really threw me. Isn't that terrible?

JW: Do you have perfect pitch?

AP: Yes, but that doesn't really help you.

JW: It must help in harmonic analysis.

AP: Well, yes, I suppose. But what really helps me are the many years I spent orchestrating for a living. I can now look at a page and hear it. If it's a piece by a standard composer (like the Dvořák example) that I haven't done before, the chances of the work being very alien to me are slim.

Personal taste also plays a role in learning scores. There are pieces that I don't do because I hate them. If I hate them I have a hell of a time learning them. For instance, I have never done the Saint-Saëns *Organ Symphony* because I really find it ghastly. You see, I've learned at my age, if at all possible, to only conduct works that I have a strong feeling for. I like to think that by now I have enough technique to conduct anything so that's not the issue. How I feel about the music is the issue. So, if there's an important piece that is programmed in the season that I basically don't like, I'll bring in a conductor who has an affinity for the piece to perform it. He'll bring much more to it than technique. Of course, that goes for any music, not only contemporary scores. I do have a closed mind though with certain contemporary music. I once said as a joke that if the explanatory footnotes to a piece were longer than the piece, I didn't want to know it. I don't want to learn scores that say, "This symbol means to hit the cello with a Coke bottle." I'm too busy for that sort of thing.

There are works though, when you finally get your own orchestra with a huge season, that you are forced to learn. Sometimes you have to learn pieces in two or three days. It can be done very easily if you have the technique to do it with, but the failing comes after the performance because you forget the piece as easily as you learned it. The next week you may have no idea how it goes. And of course, this is not a very laudable way to learn scores. But on the other hand, if you have to cover an enormous repertoire every year, you haven't got time to spend six months learning the Seventh Symphony of Benjamin Frankel. You just can't spend that kind of time. You have to learn it fast and get it over with.

Learning contemporary scores quickly can be more difficult because they tend to be hard to beat (you have to figure out how to conduct it) and it is not always apparent from the score how the piece will sound. I'm a great fan of people who orchestrate so that what's on the page is exactly what you hear. That doesn't mean the music has to be simplistic either! John Harbison (who won the Pulitzer Prize a couple years ago) and Steve Stucky were composers-in-residence here in L.A. Though they both wrote difficult music, their music was beautifully written in the sense that what was on the page was how the piece sounded. You see, I am too big a dummy, for instance, to be able to know what Elliott Carter's pieces sound like. When I first look at his scores I think that this is the most superbly logical music I've ever seen, but after I make the first downbeat I get lost. I don't hear what's on the page.

JW: What is your programming philosophy as a music director?

AP: As a music director you have to keep certain things in mind such as your responsibility to the community. You really have to see to it that your audience hears a good spectrum of the world's music. If you don't particularly want to do all of it yourself, you can invite the right people to guest conduct. In Los Angeles, for example, Chris Hogwood and Boulez come and do the repertoire that I don't do. While personally I don't particularly want to do their repertoire, I also know that it should be heard. As for myself, I will load the season with things that I love. My programs also depend on where I am. I'm taking the Vienna Philharmonic on tour to Japan the year after next with programs of only Mozart. Now I wouldn't do that with let's say, the Chicago Symphony, because it wouldn't make any sense. But that type of programming makes infinite sense with the Vienna Philharmonic. I don't think repertoire selection is very mysterious. I think simply that the conductor should do what he knows he can do the best and what he feels the strongest about.

Programming concertos is another story. Once a student at Tanglewood asked me, "Do you tell soloists what you want them to play?" I said, "No. They usually have a list of what they are offering that year and you get to choose from their list." He said, "Well suppose Isaac Stern says that he wants to play the Bruch and you would really like him to play the Hindemith. Could you talk him into it?" I said, "No, I'll leave it up to you to try. I want the right to listen in on that call, though. You may wind up playing the Hindemith, but it won't be with him and it won't be in that city." This is a hard lesson to learn when you are young. When you are young you think that you are the representative of St. Cecilia and that you have the right to tell soloists what to play. However, remember that people like Perlman and Stern have paid their dues. If they want to play X, Y, or Z, chances are that you will have to go along with it. You'll have a terrific time and you'll get a terrific performance.

Sometimes there are exceptions. After Manny [Emanuel] Ax, a great pianist, and I had recorded the five Beethoven concertos, and played the Brahms concertos and endless Mozart concertos together, he came up to me and said he would like to play something more unusual. I gave him two recommendations: the Tippett Piano Concerto and the Schoenberg Piano Concerto (I don't really like the Schoenberg concerto, but I find it's an amazing piece nevertheless). By God, Manny learned them and did the Tippett with me here in Los Angeles and the Schoenberg with me in London. He did not get the audience reaction that he would have received if he had played [Beethoven's] *Emperor,* but he didn't care, which was really extraordinary of him. I also did a world premiere of Peter Maxwell Davies's Violin Concerto with Isaac Stern. So you will find people of enormous reputation who are willing to learn new concertos, but then very likely, they won't want to do them with a young conductor. So there the young conductor is up against it again. If they are going to play a chancy piece the soloists will probably opt for an experienced conductor. So, it's difficult. I don't know of a harder profession in which to gain a comfortable foothold.

JW: What are your criteria in programming contemporary music?

AP: I think one of the great problems of programming new music is that the audience is recalcitrant. According to Leonard Bernstein, an alienation between the composer and audience took place roughly at the end of World War I. People don't really want to come and hear new music now. A normal concert audience is not immediately receptive to something brand new. You just don't hear people saying, "Oh boy, I hear Olivier Messiaen has just written a new piece." Also, to add to this problem, a great many performers and conductors don't really want to perform or conduct new music and orchestras don't like to play it. Generally speaking, if you put a new piece in front of an orchestra, the first reaction will be a kind of sullen, "Why do we have to do this?"

Your major concern, however, is not with your performers or orchestra. It is how to get an audience to attend concerts in which you have programmed new music. My advice is this (and I don't want to sound cynical): if you are going to do a premiere or a relatively unknown new piece, put it with a piece of standard repertoire with a famous soloist or you won't get an audience. For example, I did a long forty-five-minute piece of John Harbison's (who is a dear friend of mine) last season. A contemporary piece that lasts 45 minutes is a considerable undertaking for both the orchestra and the audience. In order to get an audience, I programmed it with Itzhak Perlman playing the Tchaikovsky Violin Concerto. I called John and said, "Listen, I am going to have to put Perlman in this program playing the Tchaikovsky otherwise no one's going to come." He said, "I understand perfectly." With Perlman playing the Tchaikovsky it didn't matter what else was on the concert!

JW: Don't you think, though, that the minimalists have brought audience interest back to contemporary music? A lot of audiences love this type of music.

AP: Yes. They have helped a little. But do you really like the stuff? I watched Simon Rattle do a piece here by John Adams, whom I respect a lot. It was a very long piece and the orchestra said that Rattle got terribly lost. Well, I didn't blame him. If a piece repeats an F major chord for thirty minutes anyone could get lost! But, like in any other style, there are good and bad pieces being written. I think Philip Glass, for instance, is close to being a fraud! On the other hand, Steve Reich writes very nice things. John Adams, the best in my opinion, has an extraordinary orchestral imagination. A lot of his music sounds really beautiful. I think that he's a composer who is about to bid that style farewell.

Personally, in spite of all the programming problems, I've done a lot of new music, though I don't tend to do terribly off-the-wall avant-garde pieces. Last year, to name a few, I did a Roger Sessions symphony, a new piece by Steve Stucky, a big Messiaen evening, and Harold Shapero's *Symphony*. That performance is a story in itself!

JW: Tell me.

AP: You know that Harold is the man who runs the music department at Brandeis University. Well, I happened to re-read a book of Copland's called *Our New Music*, which was written in the late forties. Copland says in the book that the best of all the young American composers and the one with the biggest future was Harold Shapero. I did a little research and found that he had a symphony. The publisher was defunct but my librarian, who was wonderful, traced it down and got a ridiculously battered copy of the score which was the size of *Die Meistersinger*. When I looked through the score I was really excited. I thought, "This is truly a great piece! By any yard stick, this is a great piece!" Though the symphony is almost an hour long, I decided to program it on my next season. When Harold Shapero, who's an angel (I met him later on), was told by his publisher that André Previn was going to conduct four performances of his symphony, he asked incredulously, "My symphony? Call ASCAP and see if there is another Harold Shapero who has written a symphony because they can't be doing mine." The publishers called ASCAP and confirmed, "No they are doing yours!" The symphony had been played once in New York in 1948 and had never been played again. This is probably because it's very long and is technically very difficult. It also is not the last word in *whistles* and *plunks* which was so in vogue in academic circles. Instead of being avant-garde, the symphony is written in a very mainstream language and is absolutely beautiful. We did it here and it was an enormous hit. Then I took it to New York where it also got a lot of good press.

JW: What were the parts like?

AP: Absolutely impossible! We had to have whole stretches of it recopied at our expense because we couldn't read it. But I programmed it again for the following season with another four performances and then recorded it. Harold was so happy. He's a man in his seventies and for the first time in over twenty-five years is writing music again.

JW: That is incredibly touching.

AP: Oh it's wonderful. If you hear that piece you will hear a monumental symphony. I said to him, "Harold, how could this symphony get lost?" He

215

said, "It was too long and too hard. That's why I had a hard time believing that forty years later someone had found the score and was willing to do four performances of it!" What's interesting to me is that the one performance by the New York City Center Orchestra had been conducted by Leonard Bernstein who was a kid then. There was a performance tape issued by Columbia Records for about six months and then it was withdrawn. Harold had it and wanted to know whether I wanted it. I said at the time, "Not now, wait until after our performance." So, after our concert we played Leonard's early version. It was very inaccurate! The orchestra wasn't up to it. There are rhythmic things in the score which are absolutely hair-raising.

JW: What kind of style is it written in? How would you describe the piece?

AP: It's very American, though you can feel Stravinsky's influence. One reason I love it is that I think it has the finest slow movement anybody's ever written in America. It's got a real adagio, a Beethoven-like adagio, that lasts for about twenty minutes. It's just heart-breakingly beautiful.

•••••

JW: How do you feel about early music research and the current emphasis on authentic performance practice?

AP: I think early music played by consort groups and orchestras that specialize in it is interesting. I think that some of these gentlemen who conduct these groups are very admirable musicians. I can also see that from a scholarly point of view this research is very interesting. One finds in the pursuit of such scholarship that there are always offshoots which can be very valuable in normal work. Things can come to life about manuscripts and about performing practices which are very good to know and to apply.

On the other hand, I don't think that early music performance practices work with "normal" orchestras. Conductors that specialize in this music sometimes get disastrous results from trying to get an original instrument interpretation from a modern orchestra. Once I saw a guest conductor in Boston convince (let's say charitably) a quarter of the strings to play it his way. Well, the remaining strings didn't go along with him and the performance was a shambles.

Personally, I don't want to do this type of repertoire (I let other people do it) though I think the research is important. Once Chris Hogwood, a very personable and nice man, asked me with much amusement, "You don't really like this stuff do you?" I said, "No, I don't and I'll tell you what bothers me. You come to a 'normal' orchestra and then have to go overtime in order to make sure that everybody plays out of tune. I don't quite understand the point of that." He laughed but was furious.

JW: How do you feel about retouching scores? Would you ever do it?

AP: I don't personally retouch scores. However, I know many wonderful people who do.

JW: You wouldn't consider doubling the woodwinds, for instance, in Beethoven symphonies?

AP: No, I wouldn't. I don't double the woodwinds and I don't add trumpets or horns. I believe Beethoven knew what he wanted and I'm faithful to his wishes. I have done certain tiny revisions in the Schumann symphonies and occasionally in certain other repertoire I'll ask the basses to play an octave down because that's possible now. I never really reorchestrate, retouch, or double, though. I remember hearing the Beethoven *Triple Concerto* at the Festival Hall in London with my friend the pianist, [Vladimir] Ashkenazy. When I saw triple woodwinds and a full string section walk out on stage, I turned to him and asked, "Aren't we going to hear the Beethoven *Triple?*" He said, "I thought we were but they must have changed the program." Unfortunately, they performed the *Triple* using the gigantic orchestra with everybody doubling and tripling. It didn't help anything. But that's just my opinion and you'll get different answers from everybody. For instance, I know that [Claudio] Abbado whom I admire boundlessly, does endless retouching in everything. He retouches Beethoven, Brahms, and Schumann and would be able to give you really expert and logical reasons for doing it. From my own insular point of view, I fail to see why. I think the music is very good without doing all of those things to it.

JW: What about metronome markings? Do you follow Beethoven's metronome markings in his symphonies?

AP: Do you remember William Steinberg? He has the prize possession of a photostat copy of a letter (in some archive in Germany) from Beethoven to the company from which he had bought his metronome. In the letter Beethoven wrote that he was returning the metronome because it was completely off. Steinberg's position then was to use your own tempos because nobody has figured out when Beethoven's metronome was off and what markings are off because of it. Another argument is that composers change their mind about tempos all the time. For instance, I compose a lot myself (though I have no delusions about my compositions) and my pieces get performed a lot. When I put down metronome marks I often find that they are wrong later on. So if it happens to a duffer like me it must have happened to everybody. You have to try and represent what the composer wants realizing that metronome marks are not always that accurate.

Tempos are difficult to find with or without metronome marks. It's very difficult to decide the tempo when Brahms writes *allegro non troppo*. What does that mean anyway? Or to find the right tempo in Mozart symphonies. That is very, very difficult. My favorite tempo indications are Bartók's. He puts musical paragraphs at the end of his pieces which say things like, "approximately (I love the word approximately) two minutes and forty-seven seconds." If your performance is somewhere near that you know that's what he wanted. I think you have to come to the conclusion that you will try and represent the wishes of the composer as much as possible. But there is a paradox in this, because in order to represent the composer you have to also be convinced personally, even if only for a moment, that the way you are going to do it is the way it should go. If you can't cope with the metronome markings in a Beethoven symphony, don't do them. If you are convinced by them by all means do them because without any question you will change your mind later on anyway.

I think that absolute adherence to any musical law is unnecessary. Once I was helping out at the Royal Academy in London by giving some classes in orchestration. A young woman asked me how Stravinsky got a certain string effect in *Rossignol* that she had heard the night before. I said, "Good question," and proceeded to go to the blackboard and draw the orchestration out the best that I could. It was really extraordinary. The violas were scored on top of the violins and the cellos were scored partially on top of them, creating a very strange effect. The young woman, who was a good musician, said, "But I was told never to do that." I asked by whom and she replied by a professor there at the academy. I replied, "Then you must never do it." There was a shocked pause and then everyone laughed. I'm sure that Stravinsky's professors also told him never to orchestrate like that.

•••••

JW: After so many years in the business, what are the aspects of conducting that you enjoy the most?

AP: The wonderful thing about the conducting profession is that no matter how many times you perform a piece, it is always a premiere. Something different will happen each time, and you will have found something new. I don't care if it's one new bar. That one bar will make the piece a brand new experience. That's why I think that people in our profession (to a large enough extent to make the generality possible) are never bored. We can be bored with the periphery of conducting. God knows, you get bored with airports and boards of governors and ladies luncheons and all that stuff, but the actual music-making is never boring because something is always brand new in the piece. You can run full tilt after the repertoire for your entire life and may find only near the end of your life that you will have caught up a little bit. That's wonderful!

One aspect of this profession that I find shocking, though, is how much your own performances change throughout the years. When I emptied my house in England where I had been living for twenty-three years, I found some early tapes of mine which were, for the main part, really deeply embarrassing. I mean they just weren't any good. At the time I had thought they were terrific. That's the thing that's difficult to come to grips with. When you are a relative beginner you go out and do your *Eroica* and Brahms's Fourth Symphony and think you are wonderful. Then you hear it a quarter of a century later and if you are lucky realize that you didn't have any idea what you were doing. The same thing happened when I did a lesser played Beethoven symphony which I hadn't touched in about eight years. When I got my score out and saw my old markings from years ago I had to go and buy a new score because I couldn't stand looking at them. They were almost the antithesis of what I want out of an orchestra now. People outside this profession have a difficult time understanding this. But, the point is that I'm always very pleased when I have a completely different view of a piece than I did even five years ago. If I had the same viewpoint I would know that there was something desperately wrong. That's why in my opinion it is perfectly valid to re-record something after many years. The earlier performance is an entirely different one from what you might do now. I've made if anything too many records. As a conductor, I'm well over the 200 mark, which is really a terrific amount of recordings. But when people say, "Why don't you remake the *Pastoral,* or the *New World,* or the Prokofiev Fifth, I really look forward to it. It will be a completely different piece!

This profession also means constantly experiencing new things. You never know what will happen next. A wonderful thing that happened recently illustrates this point. We have a school here in Los Angeles called Crossroads. I had heard that they had a very remarkable student orchestra, with orchestra members between the ages of twelve to seventeen. They are taught very well by our [Los Angeles Philharmonic] principal violist, Mr. Ohyama. I went and heard them and was completely floored. I made arrangements to do a concert and rehearsed them for a couple of weeks. I probably learned more during those rehearsal periods than they did. We did an all Mozart repertoire because I wanted the program to be difficult and transparent. I wanted them to get used to my articulations and note lengths. They just played like dreams. There was a kind of thrilling newness to that concert that you don't get if you step up in front of the Boston Symphony or the Vienna Philharmonic. That sense of newness is impossible with a professional orchestra because they have played the pieces too often. This concert with the kids was absolutely mind-blowing. Wonderful!

JW: What types of articulations and note lengths did you want?

AP: I tend to have a German conception of this music. There is a kind of geographical generality in how Mozart is performed. In England, orchestras tend to play notes very short with lots of stuff off the string. If there is a dot over the note it is also usually played very short. In Vienna and in Germany, note lengths tend to be longer and that is the sound I have in my ear. I like full value notes. That's not everybody's thing, but I enjoy that American orchestras play according to the tastes of their music director. They are phenomenally adaptable.

JW: How would you compare English, European, and American orchestras?

AP: Well, like I said, American orchestras reflect the tastes and styles of whomever their current music director is. They are not only adaptable but also have enough money to be able to rehearse things a lot more than they do in England. In England, the orchestras have probably the greatest sight readers I've ever encountered. That is because it's a sink or swim situation. They usually get a piece, play it through once, have one more rehearsal on it, and perform it. The sad thing about that situation is that English orchestras don't have the wherewithal to do a lot of new music because that predicates a lot of rehearsal time and there is no money for it.

On the other hand, orchestras in the States usually spend a lot of time on new music and tend to put the standard repertoire together rather quickly. Actually, the standard repertoire tends to be neglected here! I found that in the years I've been a music director in the States (in Pittsburgh and Los Angeles), I have liked to spend a lot of rehearsal time on the pieces that are generally overplayed. If we were going to do, let's say Tchaikovsky's Fourth Symphony or Beethoven's *Pastoral,* I would use a lot of rehearsal time so as not to get last week's performance.

Another big difference between European and American orchestras is the working conditions. The orchestras in England and in Europe usually have much harder schedules than the orchestras in the States. I really noticed it when I first came here. After having worked in England for twenty-two years before coming here, it used to make me laugh when people in an American orchestra would say that they were on a killing schedule! I'd look at them and think that they weren't doing even half of what any English orchestra does and the English make far less money as well.

In Vienna, the orchestra musicians make a good living, much better than the musicians in English orchestras. But they have an incredibly hard schedule. Apart from their normal concert season and recordings, they play three hundred operas a year! Of course they have enough people so that they trade personnel off a lot. But I remember once when I had a double rehearsal in Vienna of the Mahler Fifth Symphony. At the end of six hours of rehearsing, around five o'clock, I turned to the first cellist, Franz, who is my best friend there and asked him if he wanted to have dinner somewhere. He said he couldn't because he had to play an opera. I said, "Now? What's on tonight?" thinking that at least it might be a relatively small opera. He replied, *"Parsifal"!* I couldn't believe it. Nobody rehearses the Mahler Fifth for six hours, has a supper break, plays *Parsifal* and then comes to a rehearsal again the next morning. They do it though! Whatever they are paid is not enough as far as I'm concerned.

JW: That is eleven hours of playing.

AP: Yes, it's horrible. I said, "Franz, I wouldn't even be able to come and hear *Parsifal.*" He then made a very salient remark. He said, "After a double rehearsal it would be much harder to sit and listen to *Parsifal* than it would be to play it." He's got a point. At least you are busy if you are playing it.

Another thing that I find remarkable about the Vienna Philharmonic is their desire to work hard in spite of that killing schedule. I remember some years ago after I had done a lot of work with them (after I had taken them on tours and had made many records with them), the chairman of the orchestra, who is a terribly nice man, a cellist, came to me and said, "Can I offer, not a criticism, but a request?" I said, "Of course," and he said, "Could you be a little bit more dissatisfied?" I said, "Uhhh yes. But not when it doesn't warrant it." He said, "Oh, come on, Maestro, something always warrants it. We would like it if you were a little rougher about getting what you want." Well, personally I think it's very difficult to say, "No, no, no, no" to the Vienna Philharmonic in the middle of a Mozart symphony. You feel like lightning will come through the ceiling.

I've actually found, though, that most orchestras (European and American) are receptive to criticism. They like to keep working on something. I've seen youngsters harangue at them for no reason and that turns an orchestra off quicker than anything in the world. Youngsters talk so much. They always have anecdotes about Beethoven. That's not what the orchestra wants to hear. Everybody wants to go home. Quitting early is a very popular thing to do if it can be done. If not, though, it really shouldn't be done. I've quit early many times because there genuinely wasn't anything left to do, but no orchestra minds going right up to the minute if they know that they are accomplishing some good work. But if the two and a half hours of rehearsal time is taken up with as much talking as it is with playing, the orchestra will be fed up. I have an old personal maxim: if an orchestra is tired they can cope, if an orchestra hates a piece they can cope, if the orchestra hates you they can cope, but what they can't cope with is boredom! If an orchestra is bored you might as well go home because nothing is going to sink in.

JW: Do you prefer to conduct here or in Europe?

AP: There is no preference. I tend to conduct the same orchestras by now. In the States I conduct in Los Angeles, New York, Chicago, Philadelphia, Boston, and Cleveland; in Europe I conduct in Berlin, Vienna, and Amsterdam. I don't add additional orchestras to that list. Those are the great orchestras and a great orchestra is a great orchestra. They may dress differently, they may play indigenous music that is different, but the actual work process with them is not so different as to be able to be defined. What's very different is the structure of the working conditions of each orchestra. That would be a whole separate book for you!

•••••

JW: How does a young conductor in the States break into the professional conducting world? Do you have any suggestions?

AP: In answering this I am going to take for granted that the conductor already has the technical knowledge needed for a career in conducting. He should know how to beat something in 17/16, if necessary; be able to read all the transpositions, the clefs; know a certain amount of repertoire. Conductors can get that knowledge privately or at a conservatory somewhere. After a solid musical training, a young conductor can enter a program like the Exxon Conducting Program, which is good (though it has gigantic flaws), and summer programs such as Tanglewood and Aspen. These programs can be extremely valuable. They give students the opportunity to meet their peers and to compete with them on a friendly and non-cutthroat basis. They can find out from the visiting teachers what is going on around the country. Some people still advise conductors to go to Europe and work your way up through the opera companies. I don't think that route is easier and it certainly doesn't guarantee success. The world is so small now that anybody that is oriented to success (and by success I mean a career that includes records, tours, and all of that) is no longer willing to hide for ten years in an opera company.

The next important thing for a young conductor is to get some practical experience which is often hard to come by. I taught at Tanglewood for seven or eight years and one of the great sadnesses was to have to tell the conducting students that it was difficult to find groups to practice with. Instrumentalists and singers can go home and practice, but if conductors don't have a group they can't really learn their craft. They can study like crazy, memorize, and learn new repertoire but they can't practice. Because practical experience is so important, my main advice to conductors is to conduct anything that will give them experience. I remember one young man at Tanglewood who was really very good, tell me that a road company that performed Broadway musicals had come through looking for a conductor and that of course he had said "No." I told him, "And of course, you are a certified idiot. Any place you face living breathing musicians can be a terrific learning experience. If you are going to wait until you are asked to do *Missa Solemnis* you have got a long wait. In the meantime, if a clarinet player wants to know about the phrasing of *Hello Dolly*, you can give it to him and learn something." All the students were shocked by my answer. I told them to conduct anything. I told them that it didn't matter if they conducted student orchestras, the circus, or the *Ice Capades*. The important thing was to get up and start doing it. I told them that my past was not very exalted and that I had worked in films for a very long time and had done some of the most revolting work possible. By God, it gave me a rehearsal technique, and I learned how to orchestrate very quickly and, if necessary, on a bus!

Some of those same students said, "Well, if we don't have a group we work from records." There seems to be a great fashion to learn the repertoire from records now. I see nothing wrong with playing a record of, let's say, Elliott Carter's *Concerto for Orchestra*. You can hear it once before you start studying because unless you are terribly experienced, there is no way to get through that kind of dense score. But many people even learn works like the *Eroica* from a record. This is a big mistake in my opinion. They are not learning the piece, they are learning someone else's performance. A piece just can't get into your blood that way. The best way to learn a score is to hammer your way through it on the piano. Then you find out how the piece is constructed, which is always an eye opener.

Another thing that I find symptomatic about many young conductors today is their reluctance to perform on their instruments. I feel that conductors should keep up their instruments; they should play chamber music or concertos as much as possible. It keeps them in touch with actual "playing" (which is what the orchestral musicians have to do all the time) and teaches them chamber and solo repertoire. You can learn a lot about composers by playing their chamber music which will help you when you conduct their symphonic works.

To illustrate this point I'll tell you about an experience I had at Tanglewood. Kurt Masur, Seiji Ozawa, and I watched a young man conduct Bartók's *Dance Suite*. He was absolutely terrific! He was completely at home with the music; he had no problems with the rhythms; he had memorized the work and he knew what to do and how to balance it. Masur then asked the young man to do the Schubert Fifth the following week. He came back and didn't have a clue. He had absolutely no idea what to do with it. His performance was bad and I mean really bad. Masur instantly said, "He has no talent." I said, "Now wait a minute I want to talk to him." Seiji and I took the young man aside and suggested that he go down to the vocal department and spend a week accompanying Schubert songs before trying the piece again. We felt that that way he could discover Schubert's phrasing and where his melodies breathed. Then the young man disappointed me. He asked, "What good will that do?" I didn't stay long enough that summer to know whether he took my advice or not. So, I'm always in favor of conductors not neglecting their instruments. First of all if you keep up your instrument, whatever it is, it will remind you how hard it is to play. This is something that players want you to know. I think it is extremely dangerous to stand on a box all your life telling people how to play if you don't occasionally play yourself. I also think that you use a completely different set of nerve ends when you play than when you conduct. To gamble in public as a performer is good for you. If you make a mistake as a conductor, presumably you will know, the players know, but very few in the audience will know. Even if something goes off the rails no one really knows what caused it. But if a clarinet player, or a cellist, or a trombone player makes a mistake, everyone in the auditorium will know who did it. If you go out and play in public as a conductor you will be taking the same risks that the players are taking every night and they will appreciate that. They will appreciate it and this will create a closer bond between you and the orchestra. I continue to play chamber music incessantly all over the world. This is primarily for selfish reasons, because I love it. It's my favorite thing to do and is the best kind of music making there is. If your ears have been stuffed with orchestral tuttis it is wonderful to suddenly be able to hear every strand and line separately. I also like to play concertos with orchestras occasionally. The players really respect that.

Another thing young conductors can do is to get a position as an assistant conductor and be ready to fill in at the last moment if someone gets sick. If you know what you are doing your career can take off. Many of us did that. Many young people are also competing in the conducting competitions. Personally, I don't believe in them. I have steadfastly refused to be on any juries because I don't think it's that clear cut. If someone conducts better on Friday afternoon it does not make him a better musician in my opinion. I also think so many competitions are just unreasonable. I once saw a list of prerequisites that Lorin Maazel put together for a conducting competition. The next time I saw him I asked, "Lorin, how could you have all the stuff you required in your head as a young man. Could you have done that at age twenty?" He said, "Probably not."

I believe empirical knowledge is the best. For instance, if you hammer your way through the first rehearsal of *Petrouchka* with an amateur orchestra you will have learned more about Stravinsky than if you read twenty books in a row. My manager, Ronald Wilford, who has been my manager since the very first day I ever picked up a stick, taught me this very important lesson after I had been working for several years. Somehow he got me, by hook or by crook (Columbia Artists managers are very powerful), a one night charity concert with the Philadelphia Orchestra. I got to do my first *Heldenleben* with them! I remember coming off the stage thinking, "I have just done the greatest Strauss performance that has ever happened on this continent." When Ronald called me in the hotel and asked how the performance had gone, I said, "It was unreal. It was sensational." He said, "Great, then you will have no trouble doing it next week in Kalamazoo." Well, I went to Kalamazoo and when I gave the first downbeat found that nobody knew the piece. I suddenly realized a very hard lesson. Any major orchestra will play well whether you are any good or not. If you are great they will play better, but if you are bad they will not allow themselves to fall to your level. So, I realized that very often it's not the conductor's performance at all; it is the orchestra's. If a rank beginner has a concert with the Berlin Philharmonic, the concert will go well in spite of him. However, if the same beginner went to a second-rate orchestra, he would suddenly realize how little he knew about the piece. Suddenly he wouldn't be standing up in front of some extraordinary machine but would be in front of a lot of people who are asking, "What do you mean and what do you want?" That's difficult! So I think it is invaluable for young conductors to conduct second-rate orchestras. I did for many years. If you are permanently based in a large city like New York, Chicago, Boston, or Los Angeles you will find endless regional orchestras. They are usually very happy to have conductors guest conduct them. You will be able to get a lot of experience that way.

It's also important where you live geographically. Recently someone came up to me for advice about conducting. When I asked him where he lived he said, "Long Beach." I replied, "Number One: move." I mean nobody's going to make it in Long Beach! You have to be geographically correct. I made my career, or at least most of it, in England. I had the classic case of being in the right place at the right time under the right circumstances. Also, my repertoire predilections were very much sought there at that time. I don't know whether it would happen now for me to the same degree. I've always known that quite apart from working and wanting a career, you have to have a tremendous amount of luck. However, and I hate pontificating, luck can run out if it isn't backed up with knowledge. If you back it up you can have slightly fallow periods and it won't hurt you. If it's not backed up the luck will run out. I know many people like this and I won't name names.

Of course, a conductor's ultimate goal is to get his own orchestra. Leopold Stokowski told a funny story years ago during a lecture to a bunch of young people at Tanglewood. Someone asked at that time, "How do we go about getting our own orchestra?" There was a general laugh from the kids sitting around the lawn, but old Stokowski, deadly serious answered, "That's not a funny question. It's a perfectly valid question and you cannot be a conductor without wanting your own orchestra. I'll tell you how to do it. Look around realistically at regional orchestras (not at the Philadelphia Orchestra or the New York Philharmonic) and find an orchestra that has a season that you can cope with. Go there and listen to them, find out what the political structure is, find out who their conductor is, and see if you can get him fired!" There was a horrendous pause and when people finally laughed he said, "Go ahead and laugh, it works." There was a certain amount of cynicism in that story but you have to admit it is funny. I'm also sure that his own advice had worked for him somewhere along the line.

JW: Many young conductors become music directors of college and university orchestras to gain conducting experience. Unfortunately, these positions often make it difficult for them to enter the professional conducting world. Why do you feel there is such a split between the professional and academic conducting worlds?

AP: I think academic conductors tend to become too localized. For instance, I know Daniel Lewis [conductor of the USC Symphony] is a very good conductor. He was always laudable and was often used as a last minute substitute with the Los Angeles Philharmonic. This was desperately unfair to him because he's a wonderful musician! It's the same way in London or Vienna. Academic conductors don't tend to be very honored in their home grounds. Also, they can't travel much because they are working fifty-two weeks a year and they don't have the time to go out and try elsewhere. They get kind of paralyzed in those positions. However, on the other hand, to impart knowledge is more than honorable. It's admirable and enviable. I'm not so sure that someone who spends his lifetime teaching is necessarily any worse off than somebody who's conducting some remote regional orchestra.

Actually, you can do a lot of repertoire with student orchestras. For instance, neither Strauss's *Don Juan* or Beethoven's *Fifth* is very difficult, but students tend to be frightened of them. The *Rite of Spring* is also supposed to be very difficult but by now most orchestras, even student orchestras, know how to play it. What you do need for the *Rite* is a very good timpanist. The orchestra can ricochet off of the timpanist. If he's right, nothing can happen. If he's wrong, you are screwed no matter what you do. Let me tell you a funny anecdote. We were looking for an assistant conductor when I was the music director for the London Symphony Orchestra. Part of their audition was to do the last stretch of *Rite*. I had done it the week previously in a concert so the orchestra had it under their fingers. I went to our timpanist and said, "Listen, I want you to do me a favor otherwise this will be a pointless audition. I want you to play whatever these young people are beating and not what you know to be correct." He looked at me and said, "You know, I've been waiting twenty years to do this." As a result, nobody got it. Nobody conducted it correctly!

Another thing young conductors have to cope with is a phenomenon that happens to all of us regardless of experience or age. Conductors can be very successful with some orchestras and failures with others. I really can't explain this though I have discussed this with many colleagues. For instance, I have been very successful with the Vienna Philharmonic. They genuinely look forward to my coming. On the other hand, the orchestra in Munich is not terribly happy to see me. Well, Colin Davis is extremely popular in Munich but isn't well liked in Vienna. Simon Rattle has terrible luck in Boston but here in Los Angeles they think he's absolutely great. You can see it happening within the first ten minutes of the first rehearsal and that is what is so mysterious. I never know what predicates it. I've discussed it with my colleagues and none of us know. We just accept it.

JW: Maybe certain personalities fit better within certain cultures and an orchestra is like a mini-culture.

AP: Yes. But that's very difficult on a young conductor. When you have a great many years experience, a big reputation, and a big repertoire and season to fall back on, you can go to place X and be unpopular. You can say, "O.K., go to hell." But if you are young and you really want to make it and find that you are not popular with an orchestra, it can be a very big blow to your career. Your popularity or unpopularity with an orchestra may have nothing at all to do with your inherent capability. This is a mysterious phenomenon and conductors have to cope with it.

JW: That is where luck is a factor.

AP: Yes. You have to hit the right places for you at the right time.

Biography

André Previn, former music director of the Los Angeles Philharmonic, held the post for three seasons. He began his tenure in October 1985 and succeeded Carlo Maria Giulini to become the ninth conductor to head the orchestra in its sixty-six year history.

Mr. Previn has been music director of the Houston Symphony, London Symphony Orchestra, Pittsburgh Symphony, and Los Angeles Philharmonic. He has been guest conductor of the orchestras of Boston, Chicago, Los Angeles, New York, Philadelphia, Amsterdam, Berlin, Copenhagen, Paris, Prague, Rome, and Vienna. Mr. Previn is also the principal conductor of London's Royal Philharmonic.

Born in Berlin on April 6, 1929, Mr. Previn moved as a child to California where he studied composition with Joseph Achron and Mario Castelnuovo-Tedesco, and conducting with Pierre Monteux. He began to earn his living in music as a teenager, working in Hollywood film studios as a conductor, arranger, and composer. His outstanding achievements in film include four Academy Awards. It was during this period that a personal and musical relationship developed with violinist Joseph Szigeti that was in large part responsible for what has become an abiding enthusiasm for chamber music. In 1960, Mr. Previn began to concentrate all his efforts on a symphonic conducting career.

Mr. Previn's recordings include performances with the London Symphony, Royal Philharmonic, Vienna Philharmonic, Chicago Symphony, Pittsburgh Symphony, Philadelphia Orchestra, and Los Angeles Philharmonic.

André Previn is also a recognized composer. His works include a piano concerto and two suites of preludes commissioned and performed by Vladimir Ashkenazy; a cello concerto; a guitar concerto; two quintets for wind and brass; a song cycle for British mezzo-soprano Dame Janet Baker; three orchestral works commissioned by the Pittsburgh Symphony, Vienna Philharmonic, and Philadelphia Orchestra; and a music drama called *Every Good Boy Deserves Favour,* on which he collaborated with playwright Tom Stoppard. This work, performed at the Metropolitan Opera House and Kennedy Center as well as abroad, had been staged by the Philharmonic during its 1986-87 season. He has also completed the composition of a piano concerto for Vladimir Ashkenazy.

André Previn Discography

Composer	Work	Orchestra	Soloists	Label	CD	LP	MC
Bartók	Concerto for orchestra	Los Angeles Philharmonic		Telarc	CD-80174		4AM-3718
Bartók	Violin concerto no. 2	London Symphony	Perlman	Angel			7748-4-RC9
Beethoven	Coriolan Overture	Royal Philharmonic		RCA	7748-2-RC	7748-1-RC9	4XG-60424
Beethoven	Creatures of Prometheus Overture	London Symphony		Seraphim			
Beethoven	Creatures of Prometheus Overture	Royal Philharmonic		RCA	7748-2-RC	7748-1-RC9	7748-4-RC9
Beethoven	Egmont Overture	Royal Philharmonic		RCA	7747-2-RC	7747-1-RC9	7747-4-RC9
Beethoven	Piano concerto no. 1	Royal Philharmonic	Ax	RCA	RCD1-7199		
Beethoven	Piano concerto no. 2	Royal Philharmonic	Ax	RCA	RCD1-7199		
Beethoven	Piano concerto no. 3	Royal Philharmonic	Ax	RCA	5930-2-RC		5930-4-RC
Beethoven	Piano concerto no. 4	Royal Philharmonic	Ax	RCA	5930-2-RC		5930-4-RC
Beethoven	Piano concerto no. 5	Royal Philharmonic	Ax	RCA	RCD1-5854		HRE1-5854
Beethoven	Symphony no. 4 in B flat	Royal Philharmonic		RCA	RD-60362		RK-60362
Beethoven	Symphony no. 8 in F	Royal Philharmonic		RCA	RD-60362		RK-60362
Beethoven	Symphony no. 5	London Symphony		Seraphim			4XG-60423
Beethoven	Symphony no. 5	Royal Philharmonic		RCA	RD-87894		RK-87894
Beethoven	Fidelio Overture	Royal Philharmonic		RCA	RD-87894		RK-87894
Beethoven	Leonore Overture no. 3	Royal Philharmonic		RCA	RD-87894		RK-87894
Beethoven	Symphony no. 6	Royal Philharmonic		RCA	7747-2-RC	7747-1-RC	7747-4-RC9
Beethoven	Symphony no. 7	Royal Philharmonic		RCA	7748-2-RC	7748-1-RC9	7748-4-RC9
Beethoven	Violin concerto	Royal Philharmonic	Swensen	RCA	7777-2-RC	7777-1-RC	7777-4-RC
Berlioz	Overtures (5)	London Symphony		Seraphim			4XG-60407
Bernstein	Chichester Psalms	Royal Philharmonic	A. Jones, Roberts	MCA	MCAD-6199	MCA-6199	MCAC-6199
Brahms	Academic Festival Overture	Royal Philharmonic		Telarc	DC-80155		
Brahms	A German Requiem	Royal Philharmonic	M. Price, Ramey	MHS	512318		
Brahms	Symphony no, 4	Royal Philharmonic		Telarc	DC-80155		

Composer	Work	Orchestra	Soloists	Label	CD	LP	MC
Britten	Gloriana: Courtly Dances	Royal Philharmonic		Philips	CD-80126	DG-10126	
Britten	Spring Symphony	London Symphony	Armstrong, Baker, Tear	Angel	CD-47667		
Britten	Young Person's Guide to the Orchestra	Royal Philharmonic		Philips	CD-80126	DG-10126	
Bruch	Violin concerto no. 1	London Symphony	Perlman	Angel		S-36963	4XS-36963
Chopin	Piano concerto no. 2	London Symphony	Licad	CBS	MK-39153		IMT-39153
Chopin	Piano concerto no. 2	London Symphony	Licad	Angel		SZ-3912	4X3S-3912
Debussy	Images	London Symphony		Angel	CDC-47001		4DS-37674
Debussy	La Mer	London Symphony		Angel	CDC-47028		
Debussy	Nocturnes	London Symphony		Angel	CDC-47028		
Debussy	Prelude à l'après-midi d'un faune	London Symphony		Angel	CDC-47001		4DS-37674
Dvořák	Symphony no. 7 in d	Los Angeles Philharmonic		Telarc	CD-80173		
Dvořák	Carnival Overture	Los Angeles Philharmonic		Telarc	CD-80238		
Dvořák	Symphony no. 8 in G	Los Angeles Philharmonic		Telarc	CD-80206		
Dvořák	Symphony no. 9 in e	Los Angeles Philharmonic		Telarc	CD-80238		
Dvořák	Scherzo capriccioso	Los Angeles Philharmonic		Telarc	CD-80206		
Dvořák	Notturno in B	Los Angeles Philharmonic		Telarc	CD-80206		
Elgar	Cello concerto	London Symphony	Ma	CBS	MK-39541		IMT-39541
Elgar	Enigma Variations	Royal Philharmonic		Philips	416 813-2		416 813-4
Elgar	Pomp and Circumstance Marches (5)	Royal Philharmonic		Philips	416 813-2		416 813-4
Elgar	Symphony no. 1	Royal Philharmonic		Philips	416 612-2		
Falla	Three-Cornered Hat (complete)	Pittsburgh Symphony	Von Stade	Philips	411 046-2		
Fauré	Requiem	Royal Philharmonic	A. Jones, Roberts	MCA	MCAD-6199	MCA-6199	MCAC-6199

Composer	Work	Orchestra	Soloists	Label	CD	LP	MC
Gershwin	An American in Paris	London Symphony		Angel	CDC-47161		4AM-34760
Gershwin	An American in Paris	Pittsburgh Symphony		Philips	412 611-2		412 611-4
Gershwin	Cuban Overture	London Symphony		Angel	CDC-47021		
Gershwin	Piano concerto	Pittsburgh Symphony	Previn	Philips	412 611-2		412 611-4
Gershwin	Piano concerto in F	London Symphony	Previn	Angel	CDC-47161		4AM-34760
Gershwin	Porgy and Bess (excerpts)	London Symphony		Angel	CDC-47021		
Gershwin	Rhapsody in Blue	London Symphony	Previn	Angel	CDC-47161		4AM-34760
Gershwin	Rhapsody in Blue	Pittsburgh Symphony	Previn	Philips	412 611-2		412 611-4
Gershwin	Second Rhapsody for Piano	London Symphony	Ortiz	Angel	CDC-47021		
Glinka	Ruslan and Ludmila Overture	Los Angeles Philharmonic		Philips	416 382-2		416 382-4
Goldmark	Rustic Wedding Symphony	Pittsburgh Symphony		Seraphim			4XG-60463
Goldmark	Violin concerto	Pittsburgh Symphony	Perlman	Angel	CDC-47846		
Grieg	Piano concerto	London Symphony	Lupu	London	414 432-2		414 432-4
Grieg	Piano concerto	London Symphony	Lupu	London	417 728-2		
Handel	Overture in d	Pittsburgh Symphony		Philips	411 047-2		
Handel	Royal Fireworks Music	Pittsburgh Symphony		Philips	411 047-2		
Handel	Water Music Suite	Pittsburgh Symphony		Philips	411 047-2		
Harbison	Ulysses' Bow	Pittsburgh Symphony		Nonesuch		79129-1	79129-4
Holst	The Planets	London Symphony		Angel	CDC-47160	AM-34761	4AM-34761
Holst	The Planets	Royal Philharmonic		Telarc	CD-80133	DG-10133	
Janacek	Sinfonietta	Los Angeles Philharmonic		Telarc	CD-80174		
Korngold	Violin concerto	Pittsburgh Symphony	Perlman	Angel	CDC-47846		
Lalo	Symphonie Espagnole	London Symphony	Perlman	RCA	6520-2-RG	6520-2-RG6	
Liszt	Piano concerto no. 1	London Symphony	Gutiérrez	Angel			4AE-34442
Liszt	Piano concerto no. 1	Pittsburgh Symphony	Dichter	Philips	420 896-2		
Liszt	Piano concerto no. 2	Pittsburgh Symphony	Dichter	Philips	420 896-2		
Maxwell Davies	Violin concerto	Royal Philharmonic	Stern	CBS	MK-42449		MT-42449

Composer	Work	Orchestra	Soloists	Label	CD	LP	MC
Mendelssohn	Fingal's Cave Overture	London Symphony		Seraphim			4XG-60468
Mendelssohn	Midsummer Night's Dream	London Symphony	Watson, Wallis	Angel	CDC-47163		
Mendelssohn	Midsummer Night's Dream	Vienna Philharmonic	Lind, Cairns	Philips	420 161-2		
Mendelssohn	Midsummer Night's Dream Overture	London Symphony		Seraphim			4XG-60468
Mendelssohn	Ruy Blas Overture	London Symphony		RCA			ALK1-9534
Mendelssohn	Ruy Blas Overture	London Symphony		Seraphim			4XG-60468
Mendelssohn	Symphony no. 4	London Symphony		RCA			ALK1-9534
Mendelssohn	Symphony no. 4	London Symphony		Seraphim			4XG-60468
Mendelssohn	Violin concerto	London Symphony	Perlman	Angel		S-36963	4XS-36963
Mozart	Arias	Royal Philharmonic	Battle	Angel		DS-38297	4DS-38297
Mozart	Concerto for 2 pianos no. 10 in E-flat	London Symphony	Lupu, Previn	Seraphim			4XG-60448
Mozart	Exsultate, jubilate	Royal Philharmonic	Battle	Angel		DS-38297	4DS-38297
Mozart	Piano concerto no. 17	Vienna Philharmonic	Previn	Philips	412 524-2		
Mozart	Piano concerto no. 20	London Symphony	Lupu	Seraphim			4XG-60448
Mozart	Piano concerto no. 24	Vienna Philharmonic	Previn	Philips	412 524-2		
Mussorgsky	Night on Bald Mountain	Los Angeles Philharmonic	Previn	Philips	416 382-2		416 382-4
Mussorgsky	Pictures at an Exhibition	Vienna Philharmonic		Philips	416 296-2		
Offenbach	Gaité Parisienne	Pittsburgh Symphony		Philips	411 039-2		
Orff	Carmina Burana	London Symphony	Armstrong, English, Allen	Angel	CDC-47411		4AM-34770
Ponce	Guitar concerto	London Symphony	Williams	CBS	M2K-44791		
Previn	Guitar concerto	Royal Philharmonic	Fernández	London	425 107-2		425 107-4
Previn	Piano concerto	Royal Philharmonic	Ashkenazy	London	425 107-2		425 107-4
Prokofiev	Alexander Nevsky	Los Angeles Philharmonic	Cairns	Telarc	CD-80143		
Prokofiev	Cinderella (excerpts)	London Symphony		Angel	CDC-47969		
Prokofiev	Lieutenant Kijé Suite	Los Angeles Philharmonic		Telarc	CD-80143		

Composer	Work	Orchestra	Soloists	Label	CD	LP	MC
Prokofiev	Lieutenant Kijé Suite	London Symphony	Previn	Angel	CDC-47855		4AM-34711
Prokofiev	Peter and the Wolf	Royal Philharmonic	Parker	Philips	CD-80126	DG-10126	
Prokofiev	Piano concerto no. 1	Royal Philharmonic		Telarc	CD-80124	DG-10124	
Prokofiev	Piano concerto no. 1	London Symphony	Ashkenazy	London	425 570-2		
Prokofiev	Piano concerto no. 2	London Symphony	Ashkenazy	London	425 570-2		
Prokofiev	Piano concerto no. 3	London Symphony	Ashkenazy	London	425 570-2		
Prokofiev	Piano concerto no. 4	London Symphony	Ashkenazy	London	425 570-2		
Prokofiev	Piano concerto no. 5	London Symphony	Ashkenazy	London	425 570-2		
Prokofiev	Romeo and Juliet	London Symphony		Angel	CDCB-49012		
Prokofiev	Symphony no. 1	London Symphony		Angel	CDC-47855		4AM-34711
Prokofiev	Symphony no. 1	Los Angeles Philharmonic		Philips	420 172-2		
Prokofiev	Symphony no. 5	London Symphony		Seraphim			4XG-60434
Prokofiev	Symphony no. 5	Los Angeles Philharmonic		Philips	420 172-2		
Prokofiev	Symphony no. 7	London Symphony		Angel	CDC-47855		4AM-34711
Prokofiev	Violin concerto no. 2	Royal Philharmonic	Mullova	Philips	422 364-2		
Rachmaninoff	Aleko: Intermezzo and Dance	London Symphony		Angel	CDM-69025		4AM-34741
Rachmaninoff	Isle of the Dead	London Symphony		Angel	CDM-69025		4AM-34741
Rachmaninoff	Piano concerto no. 1	London Symphony	Ashkenazy	London	425 576-2		421 270-4
Rachmaninoff	Piano concerto no. 2	London Symphony	Ashkenazy	London	425 576-2		
Rachmaninoff	Piano concerto no. 3	London Symphony	Ashkenazy	London	425 576-2	421 270-4	
Rachmaninoff	Piano concerto no. 4	London Symphony	Ashkenazy	London	425 576-2		
Rachmaninoff	Rhapsody on a Theme of Paganini	London Symphony	Ashkenazy	London	417 702-2		421 270-4
Rachmaninoff	Symphonic dances	London Symphony		Angel	CDM-69025		4AM-34741
Rachmaninoff	Symphony no. 2	London Symphony		Angel	CDC-47159	AM-34740	4AM-34740
Rachmaninoff	Symphony no. 2	Royal Philharmonic		Telarc	CD-80113	DG-10113	
Rachmaninoff	Symphony no. 3	London Symphony		RCA			ALK1-4974
Rachmaninoff	Symphony no. 3	London Symphony		Angel	CDM7-69564-2	AM-34764	4AM-34764
Rachmaninoff	The Rock	London Symphony		RCA	6801-2-RG	ALK1-4974	
Rachmaninoff	The Rock	London Symphony		RCA			6801-4-RG

Composer	Work	Orchestra	Soloists	Label	CD	LP	MC
Rachmaninoff	Vocalise	London Symphony		Angel	CDM-69025		4AM-34741
Ravel	Alborada del gracioso	Royal Philharmonic		Angel	CDC-47468		4DS-38323
Ravel	Boléro	London Symphony		Angel	CDC-47162		4ZS-37670
Ravel	Daphnis et Chloé (complete)	London Symphony		Angel	CDC-47123		
Ravel	Daphnis et Chloé (Suite no. 2)	London Symphony		Angel	CDC-47162		4ZS-37670
Ravel	L'Enfant et les sortilèges	London Philharmonic	Wyner, Augér, Berbié, Richardson, Taillon, Finnie, Langridge, Huttenlocher. Bastin	Angel	CDC-47169		
Ravel	La Valse	Vienna Philharmonic		Philips	416 296-2		
Ravel	Le tombeau de Couperin	Royal Philharmonic		Angel	CDC-47468		4DS-38323
Ravel	Ma mère l'oye	Pittsburgh Symphony		Philips	400 016-2		
Ravel	Pavane pour une infante défunte	London Symphony		Angel	CDC-47162		4ZS-37670
Ravel	Pavane pour une infante défunte	Royal Philharmonic		Angel	CDC-47468		4DS-38323
Ravel	Rapsodie espagnole	Royal Philharmonic		Angel	CDC-47468		4DS-38323
Ravel	Tzigane	London Symphony	Perlman	RCA	6520-2-RG		6520-2-RG6
Ravel	Valses nobles et sentimentales	Royal Philharmonic		Angel	CDC-47468		4DS-38323
Rimsky-Korsakov	Flight of the Bumblebee	London Symphony		RCA			AGK1-1330
Rimsky-Korsakov	Scheherazade	London Symphony		RCA	VD 60487		VK 60487
Rimsky-Korsakov	Scheherazade	Vienna Philharmonic		Philips	411 479-2		
Rimsky-Korsakov	Tsar Sultan Suite	Royal Philharmonic		Telarc	CD-80107	DG-10107	

Composer	Work	Orchestra	Soloists	Label	CD	LP	MC
Rimsky-Korsakov	Tsar Sultan: March	London Symphony		RCA			AGK1-1330
Rimsky-Korsakov	Tsar Sultan: March	Royal Philharmonic		Telarc	CD-80107	DG-10107	
Rodrigo	Concerto de Aranjuez	London Symphony	A. Romero	Angel	CDC-47693	AM-34716	4AM-34716
Rodrigo	Fantasia para un gentilhombre	London Symphony	A. Romero	Angel	CDC-47693	AM-34716	4AM-34716
Saint-Saëns	Carnival of the Animals	Pittsburgh Symphony	Jennings, Jennings	Philips	400 016-2		
Saint-Saëns	Piano concerto no. 2	London Symphony	Licad	Angel		SZ-3912	4X3S-3912
Saint-Saëns	Piano concerto no. 2	London Symphony	Licad	CBS	MK-39153		IMT-39153
Schumann	Piano concerto	London Symphony	Lupu	London	414 432-2		414 432-4
Schumann	Piano concerto	London Symphony	Lupu	London	417 728-2		
Shankar	Sitar concerto	London Symphony	Shankar	Angel	CDM-69121		
Shapero	Nine-Minute Overture	Los Angeles Philharmonic		NW	NW-373-2	NW-373-1	
Shapero	Symphony for classical orchestra	Los Angeles Philharmonic		NW	NW-373-2	NW-373-1	
Shostakovich	Symphony no. 5	London Symphony		RCA	6801-2-RG		6801-4-RG
Shostakovich	Symphony no. 6	London Symphony		Angel		AM-34764	4AM-34764
Shostakovich	Violin concerto no. 2	Royal Philharmonic	Mullova	Philips	422 364-2		
Sibelius	Violin concerto	Pittsburgh Symphony	Perlman	Angel	CDC-47167		
Singing	Violin Suite in a	Pittsburgh Symphony	Perlman	Angel	CDC-47167		4AM-34769
Smetana	Moldau	Los Angeles Philharmonic		Philips	416 382-2		416 382-4
Strauss, R.	Also sprach Zarathustra	Vienna Philharmonic		Telarc	CD-80167		
Strauss, R.	Death and Transfiguration	Vienna Philharmonic		Telarc	CD-80167		
Strauss, R.	Ein Heldenleben	Vienna Philharmonic		Telarc	CD-80180		
Strauss, R.	Four Last Songs	Vienna Philharmonic	Auger	Telarc	CD-80180		
Strauss, R.	Metamorphosen	Vienna Philharmonic		Philips	420 160-2		420-160-4
Strauss, R.	Sonatina no. 1 for winds	Vienna Philharmonic		Philips	420 160-2		420-160-4
Tchaikovsky	1812 Overture	London Symphony		Angel	CDC-47843		
Tchaikovsky	Manfred Symphony	London Symphony		Seraphim			4XG-60445

Composer	Work	Orchestra	Soloists	Label	CD	LP	MC
Tchaikovsky	Marche Slav	London Symphony		Angel	CDC-47843		
Tchaikovsky	Nutcracker (complete)	London Symphony		Angel		S-3788	4X2S-3788
Tchaikovsky	Nutcracker (complete)	Royal Philharmonic		Angel	CDCB-47267	DSB-3992	DSB-3992
Tchaikovsky	Nutcracker (excerpts)	London Symphony		Angel	CDM-69044		
Tchaikovsky	Nutcracker Suite no. 1	London Symphony		Angel		S-36990	4XS-36990
Tchaikovsky	Nutcracker Suite no. 2	London Symphony		Angel		S-36990	4XS-36990
Tchaikovsky	Piano concerto no. 1	London Symphony	Gutiérrez	Angel			4AE-34442
Tchaikovsky	Piano concerto no. 1	Royal Philharmonic	Parker	Telarc	CD-80124	DG-10124	
Tchaikovsky	Romeo and Juliet	Los Angeles Philharmonic		Philips	416 382-2		416 382-4
Tchaikovsky	Romeo and Juliet Overture	London Symphony		Angel	CDC-47843		4AE-34442
Tchaikovsky	Sleeping Beauty (excerpts)	London Symphony		Angel	CDM-69044		
Tchaikovsky	Sleeping Beauty (excerpts)	London Symphony		Angel		AE-34442	4AE-34442
Tchaikovsky	Swan Lake (excerpts)	London Symphony		Angel	CDM-69044		
Tchaikovsky	Swan Lake (excerpts)	London Symphony		Angel		AE-34442	4AE-34442
Tchaikovsky	Swan Lake (excerpts)	London Symphony		Angel		AM-34722	4AM-34722
Tchaikovsky	Symphony no. 4	Pittsburgh Symphony		Philips	400 090-2		
Tchaikovsky	Symphony no. 5	Royal Philharmonic		Telarc	CD-80107	DG-10107	
Tchaikovsky	Violin concerto	London Symphony	Chung	London	417 707-2		
Tippett	A Child of Our Time	Royal Philharmonic	Armstrong, Palmer, Langridge, Shirley-Quirk	MCA	MCAD-6202	MCA-6202	MCAC-6202
Vaughan Williams	Bass tuba concerto	London Symphony	Fletcher	RCA	6782-2-RG	AGL1-5872	6782-4-RG6
Vaughan Williams	Symphony no. 1	London Symphony	Shirley-Quirk	RCA	6237-2-RG		
Vaughan Williams	Symphony no. 2	London Symphony		RCA	6238-2-RG		

Composer	Work	Orchestra	Soloists	Label	CD	LP	MC
Vaughan Williams	Symphony no. 2	Royal Philharmonic		Telarc	CD-80138		
Vaughan Williams	Symphony no. 3	London Symphony	Harper	RCA	6780-2-RG	AGL1-5872	6780-4-RG
Vaughan Williams	Symphony no. 4	London Symphony		RCA	6780-2-RG		6780-4-RG
Vaughan Williams	Symphony no. 5	London Symphony		RCA	6782-2-RG		6782-4-RG6
Vaughan Williams	Symphony no. 6	London Symphony		RCA	6779-2-RG		6779-4-RG
Vaughan Williams	Symphony no. 7	London Symphony		RCA	6781-2-RG		6781-4-RG
Vaughan Williams	Symphony no. 8	London Symphony		RCA	6781-2-RG	6781-4-RG	
Vaughan Williams	Symphony no. 9	London Symphony		RCA	6779-2-RG		6779-4-RG
Vaughan Williams	The Lark Ascending	Royal Philharmonic	Griffiths	Telarc	CD-80138		
Vaughan Williams	The Wasps	London Symphony		RCA	7830-2-RG		7830-4-RG
Villa-Lobos	Guitar concerto	London Symphony	Bream	RCA	6525-2-RG		6525-4-RG
Walton	Belshazzar's Feast	London Symphony	Shirley-Quirk	Angel	CDC-47624		
Walton	Belshazzar's Feast	Royal Philharmonic	Luxon	MCA	MCAD-6187	MCA-6187	MCAC-6187
Walton	Cello concerto	London Symphony	Ma	CBS	MK-39541		IMT-39541
Walton	Crown Imperial	Royal Philharmonic		Telarc	CD-80125		
Walton	Henry V, film suite	Royal Philharmonic		MCA	MCAD-6187	MCA-6187	MCAC-6187
Walton	Imrprovisations on an Impromptu by Britten	London Symphony		Angel	CDC-47624		
Walton	Orb and Sceptre	Royal Philharmonic		Telarc	CD-80125		
Walton	Portsmouth Point Overture	London Symphony		Angel	CDC-47624		
Walton	Scapino Overture	London Symphony		Angel	CDC-47624		
Walton	Symphony no. 1	London Symphony		RCA	7830-2-RG		7830-4-RG

Composer	Work	Orchestra	Soloists	Label	CD	LP	MC
Walton	Symphony no. 1	Royal Philharmonic		Telarc	CD-80125		
Walton	Symphony no. 2	London Symphony		EMI	CDM-763269-2		
Walton	Viola concerto	Royal Philharmonic	Kennedy	Angel	CDC-49628		
Walton	Violin concerto	Royal Philharmonic	Kennedy	Angel	CDC-49628		

"I was never part of any school that existed for five or ten years and then crumbled down. I didn't follow the avant-garde of the sixties. I'd like to think that I was intuitively right about what was good. However, I always try to be extremely critical and try to find out the value, the real value of music of any style. Musical value for me has nothing to do with a period of time, intellect, form, or instrumentation . . . ."

Stanislaw Skrowaczewski

Stanislaw Skrowaczewski

JW: What is your musical background? When did you decide to become a conductor?

SS: Well, I never even thought about it. Music was always in my life. I started to study music when I was four. Piano and composition were my major interests, though my first love was composition. Piano went very well, however, and I started playing my first public concerts when I was eleven and thirteen. At thirteen I conducted an orchestra from the piano in a performance of Beethoven's Third Piano Concerto. Music was almost effortless for me. I played a lot of chamber music; many quartets as a violinist. Though piano was my best instrument I still tried to do something as a violinist. I was also involved in a lot of concerts as a performer both in concertos and in chamber music.

At the same time I was also pursuing my interest in composition. I began by studying the scores of Bach, Haydn, Mozart, and Beethoven and went on to the Romantics–Bruckner, Strauss, and Wagner. These composers were my gods. I studied their scores as a boy and learned them very well. I also studied the instrumentation very well because you know the most important thing is to learn how to write for instruments.

My career as a pianist was cut short, however, when my hands were broken by a bomb in the war. The house I was hiding under collapsed and some rubble fell on my hands. It was no longer realistic for me to become a pianist. I had to stop completely for one year and I never came back to it. I can still play but I would not play in a concert. After this happened, musicians I had been performing with came to me and asked, "Why don't you come with us, we have a small ensemble that we want you to conduct." Conducting was so automatic for me. This was the beginning of my career as a conductor and it became a very obvious goal to develop it especially since I knew the entire literature very well: all the Brahms and Beethoven symphonies, many symphonies by Haydn and Mozart, all the overtures, many works by Wagner, Strauss, Schumann, and Schubert and the symphonies of Bruckner. I especially loved Bruckner! He was really a god for me. So it was very easy for me to become a conductor, there was just no problem. When I began to conduct it was just a continuation of what I had been doing on a smaller scale for years. I always recommend this route to young conductors. They should play chamber music, conduct, or sing in a choir. It's important to be an active performer. That gives you not only experience in performing but the feeling for it and how to produce it. If you learn just with a score, records, or a mirror it won't go very well when you are in front of a orchestra. It won't go, unless you are very special. You know there are some exceptions, inborn talents that have this sort of, how do you say it, natural gesture that's accurate and proper for the music. There are some, but very few. I know the young Bernstein was like that. He always knew intuitively how to use his gestures. However, I've also seen conductors already working with orchestras who can't make a clear up-beat. They just can't even keep the orchestra together. You see immediately the hazardous feeling that comes from the orchestra in this situation. The orchestra's response is automatic.

JW: Did you follow both careers of composition and conducting simultaneously?

SS: Yes, for a long time. But when my conducting became more demanding and I began to get engagements not only in Poland but from London, Paris, Rome, and Germany, I found I didn't have time to compose anymore. At the same time I also had a crisis with composition; I just couldn't stand my own works and felt I had to change everything. So I would say to myself, "Well next summer I will have more time and I will start to compose again." However, years started to go without composing. I didn't compose anything for almost twenty years. I started again by accident, when there was a big strike in 1969 at the New York Met. They closed the house for half a year and of course my own contract with them was on hold. Suddenly I had four weeks free at the last moment. So I wrote an English horn concerto for Tom Stacy here in Minneapolis who had asked me to write something for English horn because there was virtually no literature for the instrument at that time. So I wrote the first contemporary concerto for this instrument. I realized at that time that I had missed composing all those years. I just shoved it away by thinking that since I'm a conductor I will not perform my pieces and I just don't have time to compose. It takes a lot of time and concentration and a completely different type of concentration from conducting. It's just the opposite. When composing I like to forget everything that I know about music. It's very hard to isolate yourself and to cut off your mind from the music of other composers and to be on your own. It's terribly hard if possible at all.

JW: Which career is more fulfilling for you?

SS: Both. Only one is not sufficient at this moment in my life. I can't imagine just composing and I can't imagine just conducting. Conducting still thrills me. The necessity to get the best performance I can is very exciting!

JW: I imagine they are two different worlds. When you are composing you are immersed in a twentieth-century language and as a conductor much of the literature is from the eighteenth and nineteenth centuries.

SS: As a conductor it doesn't matter whether I'm doing a work of George Crumb or Brahms. I always think it is exciting to perform a work and if I have the chance to do it again I always see other possibilities. I could never say, "Oh, I recorded Brahms, that's it; I never want to perform Brahms again." There is always something I'd like to change and this makes it very interesting. So I would suffer if I were just left to composing alone at my desk and performed only from time to time. I would like to continue both careers as much as possible. Definitely, what suffers though is composition. There's no doubt about it because what happens is that there is always a big compromise between my ideas and my time. I would always like to make the composition more perfect, more interesting, more refined, and well constructed, but there's no time. On the other hand, I don't think conducting suffers, because if I have to conduct, I'm exposed, and I have to do what I think is the best. You know, it's my responsibility toward people, orchestras, and the public.

So I started composing again after twenty years. Five or six years after the English Horn Concerto, which I wrote in 1969, I got a commission from St. Bennedict College for a work for saxophone and orchestra. I wrote the concerto for Perry Luedders, an excellent saxophonist. I wrote for three instruments: soprano, alto, and baritone sax, which is very interesting in the lower register. The performance and the composition were quite a success. The only problem with this work is that there are very few saxophonists able to play all three instruments in the same piece. So the piece has not been played too often. Another saxaphonist, Ivan Roth in Switzerland, also performed it very well. He was another player who could play all three instruments well within the twenty-five minute time span of the piece.

It took me another five years after the Saxophone Concerto to write the Clarinet Concerto. So within ten years I only wrote three pieces. And those pieces were commissioned by very special people and for special instruments which were interesting to me. I wrote the Clarinet Concerto for Joseph Longo. He was the clarinetist who premiered my Clarinet Concerto and he was the first clarinetist when I was here in Minneapolis with the Minnesota Orchestra. Then I wrote a Violin Concerto in 1984-85 which was commissioned by the Philadelphia Orchestra for Norman Carol. Then in the same year the Minnesota Orchestra commissioned the *Concerto for Orchestra*. So, within a period of fifteen years I wrote only five large pieces and a few other smaller pieces.

JW: Was this because your conducting career was so heavy?

SS: Yes. And then my concentration for composing, as I mentioned before, is the opposite type of concentration from conducting. This concentration just didn't work often enough to put something on paper that I'd keep. I was struggling to write music that I would consider completely stupid a week later. I threw tons of music paper into my garbage can!

•••••

JW: How do you program? What are your criteria in selecting works to be performed?

SS: I select works that in my opinion are worth being performed.

JW: From your viewpoint as both a conductor and composer, what are your criteria in programming twentieth-century music?

SS: Well, it's rather a simple answer. There are two situations in which I have to program: as a guest conductor and as a music director of an orchestra. As a music director I am in charge of programming, including guest soloists and conductors. In that situation I try to schedule something, first of all, that I consider worth studying. I would never program something I thought was rubbish. As for guest conducting, I only take something that really seems to me representative of either the United States or the country I'm guest conducting in. From my point of view I would program for Europe identifiable American music, for example, Charles Ives, George Crumb, Samuel Barber, William Schuman, Peter Mennin, Elliott Carter, and Copland. I only program music that I'm convinced about so that if audiences tell me this is rubbish I can defend the piece by my own conscience. So you see, there are dangers and difficulties in programming twentieth-century music. So I am very critical and have tough criteria. Even if I'm mistaken I have to be very convinced about a piece before I'll perform it.

JW: What is it that convinces you about a composition?

SS: Well this is a very complex matter. If the piece is great you just know it intuitively and by analyzing its several layers and parameters both technical and spiritual.

JW: Do you gravitate toward music of a particular school or style.

SS: No. I was never part of any school that existed for five or ten years and then crumbled down. I didn't follow the avant-garde of the sixties. I'd like to think that I was intuitively right about what was good. However, I always try to be extremely critical and try to find out the value, the real value of music of any style. Musical value for me has nothing to do with a period of time,

244

intellect, form, or instrumentation though my own taste is against non-economical use of large instrumentation.

JW: How do you approach huge scores with all the ensuing problems of balance, textural clarity, and intonation?

SS: It's a question of the amount of time for preparation and your knowledge concerning what instructions should be given to the orchestra. Another important factor is that even good orchestras need to perform large works more than once. If large works were programmed every year for five years the orchestra would be able to give a much cleaner performance.

JW: How long does it take you to learn a new score?

SS: It depends very much on the difficulty of the work, the complexity of the work. So the amount of time I spend on scores is dependent on numerous factors.

JW: How do you approach a new score? Do you have a technique for score study?

SS: I wouldn't say I had a certain technique; in my case I already knew most of the nineteenth-century repertoire before I started to conduct. When I started conducting, I just needed to review my knowledge of the score which I already had by memory. Then I would have new ideas of the type of color, texture, balance, or tempi I would use. For example, in Bruckner or Strauss, I would ask for a certain contrapuntal line to be brought out more or I would ask for a certain sound that could be produced by having the strings play more on the fingerboard. I would experiment with balance during the rehearsals. However, I tended to know exactly what I wanted to hear before the first run-through. The conductor by experience has to know the nomenclature of the music perfectly and to have in his mind the sound of the instruments and chord. You need to know how long the rests should be held. Even if the composition is written in tone clusters you need to imagine how they will sound. Then during rehearsal if suddenly you hear in the cluster one or two notes that are too strong, you know exactly what to say. You know how to correct these things. So you must know everything in your imagination ahead of time. The tempo must be set before you come to the orchestra. If you try to change a tempo faster or slower it's not good. Only unless you say, "Listen this is something that doesn't sound right. Let's try to do it a little faster, a little slower," something like that. That's different, especially when you are performing contemporary compositions that have never been played. For example when I was performing a new work by Carter I would ask, "Would you mind if we tried this or this in slower tempi?" The orchestra accepts this because it is necessary in the creation of a new work. But with the works from the standard repertoire the conductor must come absolutely prepared with an exact tempo and imagination of the sound he wants before he makes the upbeat. The upbeat must show exactly what he wants from the orchestra. You modify your upbeats depending on what you want.

So, you should study a score from all points of view. You should know the vertical sound you want, the continuity and development of crescendos and diminuendos. You should know the logical development of the phrase, any phrase over eight, ten or sixteen measures, whatever the composer writes. It should always breathe. You should know all these things before coming to the rehearsal. This prepares the conductor to react immediately when something is wrong. If you don't know exactly what is wrong it is very bad. You stop and you correct the right thing. You know when you get it.

JW: Do you study at the piano?

SS: Sometimes. Sometimes, especially with more complex scores, contemporary scores. And of course if you know them by ear you know them, but sometimes you find some interesting note which makes a chord more beautiful or better sounding that is not brought out enough by the composer in some chords. Even with the best composers you will sometimes find one note, for example, a minor or major third that would make a difference in making the chord sound fuller. At the end of the Funeral March in the *Eroica* Symphony there is a C minor chord. It's scored for a relatively big orchestra of winds and strings. The minor third, the E flat, is only played in the second clarinet and horn. So if they play too softly the chord doesn't have the necessary fullness. You have to discover these things. So, sometimes you find things you never hear such as some little rhythmic matter that you never hear at the concert because of the way in which it was written. There are places in the works of even the best composers that don't come out automatically clear. The conductor needs to know these things. And obviously, if they do not come out immediately you have to bring them out in the rehearsals. This is not correcting the composer, it is only putting things in the right balance. In all classical music you sometimes have a balance problem. For instance in the works of Haydn, Beethoven, Mozart, or even Schumann, the trumpets and horns are often written in such a way that you can't hear the woodwinds clearly enough for the composition of the chord to be correct. This type of rehearsal is possible only with a good knowledge of the score. Otherwise, it is all very superficial conducting. I'm sure you and I both have had the experience with young conductors who only listen to records and with a minimal knowledge of the score follow only the main voice. You know, it's not enough. So I insist on proper study. It means imagining the score by yourself. If you have problems seeing vertical harmonies in complex works, go to the piano and plunge into them.

JW: How do you study conducting gestures? Do you practice them or are they the natural outcome of your musical imagination?

SS: Well, if the gesture doesn't come automatically it will be very difficult to learn. Do you know the story about Victor Hugo who answered a lady who asked, "Is it difficult to write poems?" He answered, "Madame, if it is not easy, it is impossible." So, I would say, if conducting gestures aren't easy it's almost impossible to learn, almost. It's interesting; you would think that if you are a performer such as a pianist or violinist that conducting gestures would come easily. That's not necessarily true. You now have many "performer" conductors that have gestures that don't come naturally to them. I think that there is a natural talent for gesture that's inborn and hard to develop. It can in some cases be developed and all the best teachers such as Markevich, Swarowsky, or Ferrara in Italy insisted that their students have a precise and clear beat.

JW: Do you practice conducting gestures ahead of time while you are preparing a score?

SS: No, but you do have to decide how to beat rhythmically complex measures, major ritardandos connected to different tempos, duplets against triplets with ritardandos like you will find in Schoenberg, for example. I think the conductor should decide ahead of time the exact amount of ritenutos and accelerandos that he'll take so that when the orchestra asks how you beat something you can answer, "Here I conduct in four and later at measure such and such I conduct in two." After that, don't change. You'd better not change it. Otherwise you are likely to confuse the orchestra. These things should be decided ahead of time and so very often I don't beat through the work but I do decide certain things such as sub-divisions of the beat, for example, at my desk ahead of time. Sometimes if I didn't put in enough thought ahead of time I find that my conclusions are not so practical. So the next time I conduct the work I will change things which may also change the interpretation. However, I will not change what I do during the rehearsals for a certain concert. I will change it for the next performance at a different concert. If the concert is with the same orchestra I'll just tell them that this time we are going to do it differently. It is also important to mark bars clearly. You sometimes even have to exaggerate the gesture of up-down. Some conductors beat so unclearly that after a few bars the musicians don't know where to enter. I think that it's very childish not to mark the down-beat of each measure, particularly in rhythmically complex works. It helps those players who have rests. The musicians that are already playing don't have the problem but the poor ones that are counting bars do.

•••••

JW: How do you arrive at your interpretation of a score?

SS: I think it is in part connected with memory. Memory has many different levels. Some may have a photographic memory which means that you even know page numbers. You may have a harmonic or melodic memory. The melodic is wonderful because then you don't count the bars of a melody to know that in the fourth or fifth bar there is an entrance for the horns. You just know the music. You may have a memory that connected with the orchestration. For example, if something is more colorful, you know, "Aha, the clarinets have entered and after this in the next bar, the bassoons and horns enter." Everything helps. Of course the best memory is to know everything!

JW: Do you believe in conducting by memory?

SS: For me whatever is best for the performance is the most important thing. If I know the piece well and I mean really very well, I can tell you exactly at any moment what the third clarinet or the forth horn is doing. When I know the score at that level I go without the score because it absolutely bothers me to turn pages. Also, when you memorize a score you realize that your eye contact, your gestures when you conduct are much greater. If I have any doubts, if I'm getting nervous that I may have a blackout on a piece that I know well, if there is a special rhythm I may miss or if I'm afraid the orchestra will miss something and that they are not secure, I use the score. I always use the score with soloists, any of them, as a principle. This is just for safety. This is because I have had many strange accidents with soloists, even the best ones, and in such a case, you have to know exactly what to do which sometimes includes shouting a rehearsal letter to the orchestra, which may escape your memory. Also, some soloists feel more secure if the conductor has the score.

JW: How do you rehearse? Do you plan and organize your rehearsals or are they spontaneous?

SS: I do plan rehearsals though sometimes they go in another direction. Before the first rehearsal I know exactly what I want to hear. It doesn't matter whether or not the work to be rehearsed is contemporary or from the standard repertory. I want to put a certain stamp on the work from the very beginning. I want to make sure that it will not be just a routine playing through of Brahms or something. It must have a certain character. With the standard repertoire, if the movement is short, we will play right through it. In Beethoven or Brahms, for example, I'll play through the exposition so that the orchestra can get used to my gestures. When we reach the development section I will start again from the beginning, correcting certain things, place by place. In pieces which are less-known, I will repeat larger sections after I have corrected them. Then I will go to other sections which have different problems. With a good orchestra, if the reprise is very similar to the exposition, I will play through it and not bother the orchestra too much. You have to show the orchestra that you trust them. If certain things were changed in the exposition, you have to trust that they will change them in the reprise though they are in a different key.

With a complicated unknown work I start and play through the work even if it is played poorly. With shorter contemporary pieces that the orchestra doesn't know, it is always good to do run-throughs no matter what happens so that the orchestra knows more or less how the piece goes. After that you can start at the beginning and stop whenever. If you stop every four measures before this run-through the orchestra will have no concept of the piece, which can prove disastrous in the end. So if you correct details at the beginning you are losing time because a lot of mistakes will correct themselves. This is very important and also depends on how many rehearsals that you have. If you have only one or two rehearsals you have to concentrate on the most important things that will give a good orchestra the main idea. At the very least you will ask for a certain timbre or certain phrasing that the orchestra will need to pick up and do. Sometimes, you know, in the summer festival, you will have only one or one and a half rehearsals a program! With a good orchestra that already knows the work you can start the first subject, start the second subject, play through some of the development, and in a few minutes you will know whether the orchestra knows the work. You don't have to play all the way through because you know the performance will go. This makes them very attentive during the concert. Now if you have many rehearsals you can concentrate on the details the first day. Usually what I like to do on the first rehearsal is to play through the entire program, with the exception of the concerto, even if it's poorly played. This gives the orchestra an idea of what the problems will be. They will take the parts home or will practice them during the break. When we go through the pieces a second time they already know it much better and a lot of things will have been corrected by themselves. Why lose time and stop and correct those things immediately. Let them play through the work and see where the difficult things are. On the second day, I will pinpoint the most difficult things and we will practice until they are good. Even after that it's good not to concentrate too much on the details, but to include the details in playing through larger sections of the work. That is very important. If you start and stop and correct details every few measures the details will get worse in the run-through because the sense of the whole is lost. In playing through larger sections you can solve phrasing and dynamic problems in context, such as a very delicate pianissimo coming after a big forte. If they still don't remember you do have to stop and correct things until you have the feeling that they know what to do.

Then of course it's very important to play through the program at the dress rehearsal unless a symphony is so well known that you can just play through the exposition and development and don't need to play the recapitulation. You have to know when to trust the orchestra. In that case don't play through the work unnecessarily because you don't want them to expend the energy at the rehearsal instead of at the concert. However, most of the time I do complete run-throughs though I don't ask for big fortissimos and for a lot of tension. I want them to save themselves and usually they know how to do that themselves. It's also important to play through all four movements of a large symphony just like at the concert. Then if you need to correct things you can do it later. This is of course unless the work is so well known that you can just play through sections. So it depends on the quality of the orchestra, their concentration, how well they work with you and how much you can trust them. That's my method; it's not necessarily the best, but it seems to work for me.

JW: I'm sure that a lot of this depends on the experience of the conductor and on his knowledge of a particular orchestra.

SS: Yes, when I did the Brahms Second Symphony several weeks ago the orchestra knew the piece and we only played through certain sections using the same method I just described. However, with Barber's *Medea's Dance of Vengeance,* we played through the work and then corrected several things immediately. They had performed it three years ago and there had been some rhythmic difficulties. Some places at the end just didn't go. So I practiced those sections at a slower rhythm until they saw how it went and then cleaned up those spots. There were also some technical difficulties such as high positions which we had to work on. Sometimes you have places which call for very high positions in the horns and in the brass. You need to practice those spots, repeat them and correct the intonation. You know that it also helps to sometimes fix individual chords so that they can hear each other without the pressure of going through the piece. This always helps to clean up the orchestra. Then I think if you show concern, if the conductor shows concern for the beauty of intonation, the lightness of certain notes, it will certainly interest the better musicians, so that eventually they will repeat and practice along those lines by themselves. It also helps to ask the strings to play a quick passage slowly and pianissimo so that they can really put their fingers down and hear the intonation, which will help them at a faster tempo.

•••••

JW: What is your opinion on the early music performance practice research? Would you ever retouch a Beethoven score, for instance?

SS: I think that Beethoven's scores are already so meticulously perfect on their own. Beethoven worked very carefully and for a long time on his compositions. If you see sketches to his symphonies, especially the Fifth or the *Eroica* you will see pages and pages of themes, of developments and harmonies which he changes all the time. When he finishes a score it is so perfect that you don't need to change a thing! Some conductors add, for example, trumpets, horns, or timpani to the recapitulation if the exposition was orchestrated with them. I personally do not do it because I don't feel that the orchestration has to be repeated exactly in the recapitulation. Beethoven often writes material that is not meant to be identical. Very often the amount of measures of a crescendo, ritardando, or diminuendo are different in the recap. He often uses different dynamics and because the recap is in a different key will use different instruments.

There are different types of problems in some scores by Haydn, Mozart, Schubert, and even Schumann concerning dynamic markings. Often you will find fortissimo markings followed by more fortissimo markings with no dynamic sign in between. So you have to ask, "Well, which is louder and what happens in the middle?" You have to of course decide where the real climax of a certain section is and then balance the dynamics according to that decision. Also in Haydn, especially if you have a small string section, you will have to alter the dynamic markings if you find fortissimo in the trumpets. You have to balance them with the woodwinds and the strings. Some conductors will change the second trumpet to an octave lower than the notes found on the natural instruments at that time. I don't do that because it doesn't sound right to me. I usually leave the trumpets and horns in Beethoven and Haydn where I find them.

JW: So you would never add anything to a Beethoven symphony, not even doubling the woodwinds?

SS: Well, there are many things you could do in the *Eroica*, for instance. You could double the woodwinds with the strings if you have a large string section. I used to do it. Now it depends on the size of the orchestra, the hall, and on the occasion. If I play the *Eroica* with a major orchestra in the Summerfest outside in an open place, I will double the woodwinds. If the balance in a hall is better if I double, I will do it. There are always problems with doubling, though, because immediately the intonation goes down a little even with the best orchestras! It is just much more difficult to get true and beautiful intonation. So if I were to record the *Eroica* I would certainly not double the winds!

Now I think you can edit parts and put in your own bowings and articulations and maybe make small dynamic changes for the balance. If you use a chamber orchestra, which is done more and more, you don't even need to put in dynamic changes. You can easily ask that the two flutes or two oboes balance themselves with the orchestra.

JW: What do you think about Beethoven's metronome markings?

SS: Well, I think all this fuss about metronome markings is nonsense! We all know that doesn't mean that Beethoven's metronome didn't work. What I mean is that composer's themselves constantly change their own opinion about metronome markings. When I compose something (I'm sorry to put myself in such a distinguished group) I often find that I'll change the markings one year later. Then if I am conducting the piece again I might change them again in another situation, a different hall, and with a different orchestra. Composers are faced with music we put on paper. We write in metronome markings and then find when we start to rehearse the music with real instruments and real sound, often there is a difference between our abstract thinking and reality. Debussy compared the metronome marking to a beautiful rose in the morning that had a little mist and dew on it. In a few hours the dew is gone, the rose is developed and is not quite so fresh. Music is like this. You put a metronome marking on the rose in the morning and when the weather changes, the rose changes!

I have watched Robert Craft conduct rehearsals for Stravinsky, who was always very exact in his notation. I watched Stravinsky stop Craft and change his own markings as much as twenty or thirty points. So I think in the end it is absolutely nonsense to say you must follow Beethoven's markings. People are making names for themselves by saying that we must adhere to these markings. Then some critics write about how wonderful it is. I think the whole business is just one big misunderstanding!

•••••

JW: How would you suggest that young conductors break into the professional world?

SS: I simply cannot answer that question because I don't know. One of the main problems with conductor preparation is that it is not easy to have an orchestra. Conductors can't learn without one and can't get one without experience. It's a vicious circle. Of course talent is needed first and then great preparation: knowledge of music theory and instruments, experience, practice, composition; knowledge of not only the symphonic repertoire but the chamber music repertoire as well. Chamber music is very important because it gives you the proper perspective as to how certain composers should be interpreted. Conductors should also be excellent performers on an instrument and really must play the piano to be able to play the scores. Conductors should play in chamber ensemble, violin, viola, oboe, flute, bass, piano, or organ. Conductors need to get this feeling for ensemble playing which is so terribly important in the orchestra. Preparation at your desk even with a knowledge of the piano and scores is fine and necessary, but the jump from the desk to an orchestra is a dangerous one. So if you play instruments yourself and are used to ensemble playing conducting will come more naturally.

If you have an honest manager who really cares about you and your career and who gives you good advice, it will help. Then you need luck. Certain conductors and certain soloists have made their careers at a certain point because of a lucky break or because they had the image and background the public and managements were looking for. Ten years earlier or after and they probably would not have become stars. You see wonderful artists who never came at the right moment. They are still wonderful but they are not stars.

•••••

JW: In closing could you talk a little bit about the Hallé Orchestra where I believe you are conducting around twelve weeks a year?

SS: The Hallé Orchestra is one of the finest British ensembles. It's an orchestra which gives you excellent interpretations of any style you want.

JW: How do you find English audiences compared to American audiences?

SS: Conservative, very conservative. This is often a problem because it is difficult to create unusual programs since the English orchestras rely on ticket sales to survive. In Germany, orchestras can depend on governmental support and in the States you can count on the community and on private enterprise because contributions are tax deductible.

Biography

In 1984, following nineteen years as music director of the Minnesota Orchestra, Stanislaw Skrowaczewski was elected principal conductor of the Hallé Orchestra. With the Hallé he led tours to the United States, Germany, Austria, Switzerland, Scandinavia, Spain, and Poland and issued recordings for RCA, Chandos, and IMP.

Born in Lwow, Poland, in 1923, Skrowaczewski began piano and violin studies at the age of four. He composed his first symphonic work at seven, gave his first public piano recital at eleven, and two years later played and conducted the Beethoven Third Piano Concerto. An injury to his hands during World War II terminated his keyboard career, after which he concentrated on composing and conducting. In 1946 he became conductor of the Wroclaw (Breslau) Philharmonic, and he later served as music director of the Katowice Philharmonic (1954-54), Krakow Philharmonic (1954-56), and Warsaw National Orchestra (1956-59).

Skrowaczewski spent the immediate postwar years in Paris, where he studied with Nadia Boulanger and cofounded the avant-garde group known as Zodiaque. In 1956 he won the International Competition for Conductors in Rome and, invited by George Szell, made his American debut with the Cleveland Orchestra in 1958. This led to his appointment in 1960 as music director of the Minneapolis Symphony Orchestra (later called the Minnesota Orchestra, of which he is now conductor laureate). Since then, he has regularly conducted major orchestras throughout the world as well as the Vienna State Opera and the Metropolitan Opera. He has made international tours with the Concertgebouw, French National, Warsaw, and Hamburg orchestras. He has twice toured with the Philadelphia Orchestra to South America and with the Cleveland Orchestra to Australia.

Skrowaczewski's interpretations of the Bruckner symphonies have earned him the Gold Medal of the Mahler-Bruckner Society and his programming of contemporary music was acknowledged by five ASCAP awards. Skrowaczewski has recorded an extensive repertoire for RCA, Philips, CBS, EMI/Angel, Mercury, Vox, Erato, Muza, and other labels.

Many of Skrowaczewski's own works have received major international awards. Among his more recent compositions are the Violin Concerto (commissioned and premiered by the Philadelphia Orchestra), Concerto for Orchestra (Commissioned and premiered by the Minnesota Orchestra), Concerto for Clarinet, English Horn Concerto, and "Ricercari Notturni," the last receiving the 1979 Kennedy Center Friedheim Award.

Stanislaw Skrowaczewski Discography

Composer	Work	Orchestra	Soloists	Label	CD	LP	MC
Beethoven	Fidelio Overture	Minnesota		Vox			
Beethoven	Leonore Overture no. 1	Minnesota		Vox			
Beethoven	Leonore Overture no. 2	Minnesota		Vox			
Beethoven	Leonore Overture no. 3	Minnesota		Vox			
Beethoven	Overtures (6)	Minnesota		Vox			
Beethoven	Piano concerto no. 1	London Symphony	Douglas	RCA	7780-2-RC	7780-1-RC	
Beethoven	Piano concerto no. 5	London Symphony	Bachauer	Philips			
Berlioz	Symphonie fantastique	London Symphony		Chandos	CHAN 8727		
Brahms	Academic Festival Overture	Hallé		MCA	MCAD-25188	MCA-25188	
Brahms	Hungarian Dance no. 1	Hallé		MCA	MCAD-25230		
Brahms	Hungarian Dance no. 1	Hallé		MCA	MCAD-25230		
Brahms	Hungarian Dance no. 10	Hallé		MCA	MCAD-25230		
Brahms	Symphonies (4)	Hallé		IMP			
Brahms	Symphony no. 1	Hallé		MCA	MCAD-25188	MCA-25188	
Brahms	Symphony no. 2	Hallé		MCA	MCAD-25160	MCA-25160	
Brahms	Symphony no. 3	Hallé		MCA	MCAD-25857		
Brahms	Symphony no. 4	Hallé		MCA	MCAD-25230		
Brahms	Tragic Overture	Hallé		MCA	MCAD-25160	MCA-25160	
Brahms	Variations on a Theme by Haydn	Hallé		MCA	MCAD-25857		
Chopin	Grand Fantasy on Polish Airs, for Piano	Paris Conservatory	Weissenberg	Angel	CDM-69036		
Chopin	Krakowiak, for piano	Paris Conservatory	Weissenberg	Angel	CDM-69036		
Chopin	Piano concerto no. 1	New Symphony Orchestra of London	Rubinstein	RCA	5612-2-RC	VCS-7091	
Chopin	Piano concerto no. 2	Paris Conservatory	Weissenberg	Angel	CDM-69036		
Handel	Royal Fireworks Music	Minnesota		Vox			
Handel	Water Music Suite	Minnesota		Vox			

Composer	Work	Orchestra	Soloists	Label	CD	LP	MC
Mayer	Andante for strings	Minnesota		Desto		7126	
Mayer	Two Pastels	Minnesota		Desto		7126	
Mozart	Piano concerto no. 17	Minnesota	Klien	Vox			
Mozart	Piano concerto no. 27	Minnesota	Klien	Vox			
Ravel	Alborada del gracioso	Minnesota		Vox			
Ravel	Boléro	Minnesota		Vox			
Ravel	Boléro	Minnesota		Mobile	MFCD-802		
Ravel	Daphnis et Chloé, suites 1 & 2	Minnesota		Vox			
Ravel	La Valse	Minnesota		Vox			
Ravel	Le tombeau de Couperin	Minnesota		Vox			
Ravel	Ma Mère L'Oye (complete)	Minnesota		Vox			
Ravel	Pavane pour une infante défunte	Minnesota		Mobile	MFCD-802		
Ravel	Rapsodie espagnole	Minnesota		Vox			
Ravel	Rapsodie espagnole	Minnesota		Mobile	MFCD-802		
Ravel	Une Barque sur l'océan	Minnesota		Vox			
Skrowaczewski	English horn concerto	Minnesota	Stacy	Desto		7126	
Shostakovich	Symphony no. 5	Hallé		IMP	PCD 942		CIMPC 943
Wagner	Tannhäuser Overture and Venusburg Music	Minnesota		Vox			
Wagner	Tristan und Isolde: Prelude and Liebestod	Minnesota		Vox			

"A conductor has to know himself completely. This is important not only musically but psychologically as well. The persona of the conductor is only partly musical. The conductor also is a psychologist, a father and mother figure rolled into one. . . . You need to have the people skills necessary to treat individual strengths and weaknesses as well as know how to deal with an orchestra as a collective unit. . . . That takes knowledge of myself and others."

Leonard Slatkin

Leonard Slatkin

JW: Why did you decide to be a conductor? How did you get started? Do you have advice for other young American conductors?

LS: Everyone in my family is a musician. My father was a professional conductor and while he was around I didn't dare conduct. He died when I was nineteen. At that time I was playing viola in a youth orchestra in Los Angeles and during one rehearsal the conductor was called away for an important telephone call. He threw a score in front of me and said, "I'll be back in ten minutes." That's how I started. I loved the experience and decided to study conducting seriously.

After that I went and did some work at Aspen and got accepted at Juilliard. I began to really learn the repertoire and could be relied upon to jump in whenever I was needed. I also had a teacher who told me a simple fact about how to get started. He said, "If you really want to conduct, I assure you, know as much repertoire as early as possible so that when an opportunity is presented you are ready for it. Opportunities come around every so often for everyone."

Another thing I did that I suggest to everyone, especially if you live in a major city, is to go to rehearsals. Go to as many as you can. Watch for the mistakes conductors make because there is more to be learned from the mistakes other people make than from their positive qualities. I think that is because it is easy to avoid mistakes when you see them happen. On the other hand it is superficial to imitate the good things a conductor does. That's because they don't come from the inside. For me, it's important not to try to imitate. I always find it amusing now when I hear about some young conductors who try to look like me when they conduct. I hope that's not true; I don't want that.

Another thing about so-called "breaking in" is that people place too much importance on a manager or an agent. I don't think you need a manager at the beginning. I don't know why everyone thinks that it's a big deal to have a manager. I don't see many assistant conductors with managers. Gary Zimmermann didn't have a manager in St. Louis and neither did Catherine Comet. What you need to do is to be creative. Organize your own groups and draw attention to yourself in some way. For example, this year is

259

an anniversary year for Barber, Gould, and Bernstein. Look for things like that and plan a program around it and advertise it. When I was in Juilliard (which is a very competitive place) I would get odd nonmusical jobs at a company here and there, such as loading dress racks in the garment industry to pay for the little groups I organized and conducted. One summer I even worked at a piano bar! You usually need some money because these days even the students at the conservatories expect to get paid at a very early age.

Another thing a young conductor needs to ask is where he wants to be at the end of five years, *realistically*, and I hope that he won't say directing the Berlin Philharmonic. Lay out a plan. Try to get an affiliation with a major orchestra of any type. Look at the Exxon Affiliated Artist Program. Try to get into that. A lot of people find that door blocked off but it's the first one I would suggest. Try to get into that program and if nothing happens at least it can place you in an audition circumstance. You may not get the jobs for a bit, but you might get to audition for a few orchestras and have the real experience of being in front of that kind of ensemble.

In addition to that there are manners and methods of knowing where the openings are. For example, I got a call this morning; an acquaintance knew I was here (Minneapolis) and asked what they were doing for the assistant conducting job. I told him I didn't know. Now he had found out I was here and knew something was open (as far as I know that's true). He asked me if I could find out and get back to him. Dabble a little bit, get some information. Keep your ears open. That's one way of doing it. Send letters and resumes everywhere. What harm can it do?

Another thing a young conductor should do is get into a place of visibility like Tanglewood or Aspen. Don't let the amount or lack of repertoire deter you. Also, the American Symphony League Workshops are excellent. Take every opportunity that comes your way. Don't turn down anything that turns up. It's not easier in Europe. When I hear people say, "Well, I'm going to go to Europe," I feel they are giving up and it bothers me. A lot of people give up too early. There are enough of us Americans now to prove that it can be done. I was born here, trained here, so was Michael Tilson Thomas and Gerard Schwartz. None of us spent much time in Europe because things turned up here first. It's not impossible to have a career in the United States as an American conductor. Also, I'm seeing more women out there. Of course there's more competition too. Despite what people think, I don't think that the people in the business have a prejudice toward women conductors. I haven't seen one orchestra react negatively to a woman because she was a woman. It's still considered a bit of a novelty to the public, but it is getting to be less of a novelty, which is great. One of the problems was that a lot of women ten or so years ago were not very good. That made it harder on women today. Now there are a lot of good people who have solid backgrounds. Catherine Comet is a very good example of that. Catherine knows exactly what she is doing.

Also, keep as many doors open as you can. If the major orchestra door doesn't open one can go into the smaller orchestra route. I suspect there's enough orchestras there. But, if your real ambition is to get further along, I'd sort of stay away from that if you can. I would go for the assistant position of a big orchestra for a couple of years and see how it goes. I also think if one has ambition that it's probably not a good idea doing the university route. I don't know why but there is a big gap between the academic world and the professional world. They seem to be at odds with each other. People usually get out of academia and get into the professional world. However, people have to realize they should do what they do best. A lot of people are not prepared to say, "Hey, maybe this is what I should be doing. I do this well." Also, if you are in an academic situation you should use your time there to really hone in on pieces that will serve you later on. A lot of people in academia only program esoteric pieces. That's not the place to do that. First of all you wouldn't be teaching the kids stuff they are going to use when they get out and personally you would be learning things you wouldn't be able to use later. In a university situation it is not a waste of time to be practical. Program standard repertoire. You can balance it out so you combine the new and the old, but learn the standard rep! In this way you can find your strengths and weaknesses. I'm always asking myself even at this point what repertoire I do best and what I don't do very well.

Studying conducting itself has plusses and minuses. I think most of the outstanding conductors learn the elements that make them outstanding by themselves. You can study certain things at the technical end of it, certainly such as how to listen, but no one can teach the true communicative skill of conducting. No one can say, "Well you're going to teach your eyes to look in a particular way." If you are born with communicative skills they can be refined by a teacher but ultimately it's not something you really can teach. The teaching I've done tends to be on a very basic level. I can guide somebody through a score, and say, "Try this, here's a few ideas, but that's all." Another reason conducting is hard to teach is because every conductor is an individual physically. They need to approach conducting in their own individualistic way. Young conductors who try to imitate their teachers will probably wind up getting into very bad habits that go against the way they are built. I see a lot of women conductors who try to imitate men. That's the wrong approach. It goes against physical nature. Women should conduct like women. Also, don't try to make musical suggestions that go against musical nature. Conduct as you feel like conducting. Certain things look awkward for anybody, but there are ways of getting around those and they shouldn't be done by imitating someone. They should be done by doing what's natural for your own body. An orchestra will sense that kind of thing right away.

261

JW: So did you ever study your conducting gestures or did they just come to you naturally?

LS: They came naturally. However, I don't think it's wrong to look at yourself in the mirror. Or better yet have a friend look. The best thing a conductor can get is feedback. Very few conductors are honest with themselves to the point of being able to say, "Yes, that's wrong, this isn't right, I can't do that well." A lot of conductors have come up to me and told me that I'm very clear technically. I never think of myself like that. I just find that I'm relatively facile with technical problems. I don't think about solving these problems. I really don't. I don't think about where the arms and hands are. I have no interest in all of that. I can teach it, but at this point I find it's more helpful to teach practical things. The first trumpet here in Minneapolis has a metropolitan orchestra. He was doing *Petrouchka* and last summer I went through it with him. I told him, "Listen. You've been in the orchestra long enough. You have probably seen three or four people do this piece and you already know what works and what doesn't work. Use that information." However, I do know several little tricks for the piece and they're just tricks, that's all. They make things a little easier in certain places. I don't make things harder than they have to be, and if one has a little sleight of hand in a couple of these things (which don't alter the music at all), then there's no reason not to use them. I have one trick I use in the First Tableau. When the first violins, violas, and oboes go into three and everyone else is still in two [Rehearsal no. 25] I always go into three with them and tell the people still in two not to watch. It works. The other trick is in the Fourth Tableau at the end of the Suite [Rehearsal no. 243] where the time signature is marked 5/8. The tempo is fast and the rhythm is very syncopated. This creates ensemble difficulties if the 5/8 is conducted in one. However, what's two 5/8 bars together? A 5/4 bar. The conductor can combine these measures and conduct the quarter notes. That way you even get the upbeat correct. I also rewrite it for the people who need it. All I'm doing is making it easier for the players. I'm not compromising the music at all.

JW: Do you have any tricks for the Rite of Spring?

LS: *Rite of Spring* works fine as it is. I find all of the rhythms very natural. Now you have orchestras that know the piece very well. I've even done it in one rehearsal with the Los Angeles Philharmonic in the Hollywood Bowl. I find *Petrouchka* much harder to do. The structure is harder and the decisions are more complicated, such as the tempo relationships and transitions. The *Rite of Spring*, on the other hand, is basically straightforward. There's hardly any sudden tempo changes and when they are sudden they are with a rest beforehand and the orchestra has time to figure out the change. *Petrouchka* is in and out of different tempi constantly. The balances are also a problem in *Petrouchka*.

Now getting back to young conductors. When we have auditions for assistant conductors in St. Louis we use certain management techniques that you will find more commonly used in the business world than in this profession. Among the things we ask potential candidates is to talk about their strengths and weaknesses. It's quite amazing how many conductors acknowledge no weaknesses in these interviews. It's quite stunning. And usually if they do acknowledge a weakness they say something like, "Well, I don't have a big repertoire yet but this job will help me to get it." For them that constitutes a weakness! Very rarely will they talk about a personal weakness which of course is part of conducting as well. Conductors need to be honest with themselves. They need to count both their strengths and weaknesses. You can even make a list and say, "I don't do this, this, or that very well." They go in the "weakness" column. After you've done that you can decide which weaknesses from the "weakness" column can be made into strengths and which ones should be left alone. Not everybody has 100 percent strengths; at least I haven't met anyone yet who does! But it's very important to recognize what the weaknesses are. For instance, I know that I'm a lousy ballet conductor, terrible. I have a fantastic admiration for the people who can do this stuff well. I can't do it at all. I just don't feel the rhythm of the dancers, their bodies. I don't know what the tempo is when I'm looking at them.

A conductor has to know himself completely. This is important not only musically but psychologically as well. The persona of the conductor is only partly musical. The conductor also is a psychologist, a father and mother figure rolled into one. This doesn't mean that the conductor has to be nice, though. If you are the nice type you have to have enough passion so that you aren't too nice when you're conducting. On the other hand you need to have the people skills necessary to treat individual strengths and weaknesses as well as know how to deal with an orchestra as a collective unit. When I go to conduct a certain orchestra I usually know by now what type of situation I will encounter. I approach each orchestra in a different manner. That takes knowledge of myself and others. So, basically that is my advice for young conductors. What else would you like to talk about?

JW: Do you have a technique for score study and analysis? How do you approach a score you have never seen?

LS: There are two types of scores that I see. One is scores by composers and styles I know. The other is scores by composers and styles I don't know. If I am looking at a new Haydn symphony, for example, I compare it with the 25 other Haydn symphonies that I know. I can apply the same rules to the new Haydn symphony. If it's a new piece I look first at the instrumentation. I try to see what instruments are playing and how the score looks on the page. "Is this score legible? Can I read this thing?" That means a lot to me. That will influence decisions about performance. If I can't read it I may not want to do it. The studying process for me is to first of all get an overview of the work. I look at it and get an idea what the overall shape might be, the style it is in. I'm not concerned about details at all. I just want to get a rough impression. It's like getting a first look at a painting. Then I go back to it. I don't study in a vertical manner. I only study horizontally. I can take in pretty much a whole page. I try to hear the score in groups, in sort of a general overview. I ask myself, "What kind of writing is there for the winds, for the strings. Where is it homogenous? Where does it fuse?" So I begin to study that way first. Generally I tend to study by sonorities first.

JW: Do you do a harmonic analysis?

LS: No, I don't do any analysis. I look first of all for the blocks of sound. Of course I try to see where the exposition, development, and recapitulation are so I can have a rough idea of the form. I don't study at the piano even though I'm a pianist because I prefer to try to get as much of the sound of the score in my head just by looking at it. If I study at the piano I get the sound of the piano in my head. I don't want that, I want the sound of the orchestra. I learned score reading at the piano but before that I was a violinist and violist. I learned alto clef by playing Haydn string quartets and by just doing viola parts all by themselves. Eventually I learned the other clefs pretty much the same way. I got to be pretty good at that. However, sometimes it's a disadvantage because what you see on the page is sometimes not what you hear. I've gotten past that and can now look at a score and immediately see what key it's in no matter what the transpositions are. So I never learned scores on the piano, only clefs on the piano. I also don't advise people to learn scores written in C. For instance, Prokofiev scores have the English horn written in the alto clef. It's much more advantageous to have a score that shows you what the players have in front of them so that when you make a suggestion to a player you have what he has in front of you. Otherwise, if the clarinet asks you a question, "What do I have in this bar?" You have to say, "Well, my score is in C but your part is in A Clarinet, therefore you should have an. . . ." I'd rather have what they have in front of me. When I talk with them I don't even say the word "written." I just say, "You should have such and such a note in your part." Once in a while I get a harmonic question and I have to tell them how their note fits into a certain chord. Then I have to transpose. But composers shouldn't score in C. The other thing I don't like is when composers put a rehearsal number every ten bars instead of doing it by phrases. That takes up rehearsal time because you always have to count ahead or back to rehearse the actual phrase.

JW: So you don't do any harmonic analysis.

LS: No, I don't. For instance when I was conducting the Brahms Second Symphony yesterday I felt that a certain measure going into D flat was so lovely that I didn't want to think about anything except the beauty of that D flat. There are many ways to learn a score, that's all. I find that as I get a little older I just have less time for analysis. I would just rather get to the music. I don't want to deal with all this other stuff. I keep wondering if part of the minimalist school of writing is a reaction to all the analysis they had to go through when they were students. Now they just want to stay in F major for four hours!

I really have to call Philip Glass a fraud, though, that's been perpetrated on the public. On the other hand a composer like Elliott Carter is certainly not a fraud, though his style bothers me as much as the minimalists. Our home critic was very upset that I didn't program any Carter this year. I have very little patience for music that is so complicated that it becomes just an intellectual exercise instead of a musical experience. I'm equally bothered by pieces that are so simplistic that I don't even have to look at them.

JW: That's very courageous of you to express such strong personal opinions!

LS: I think ultimately you have to be public about what your likes and dislikes are. It's foolish to get out and do something you don't like. When you're learning and studying, yes, you do everything you can just to get the experience. But you get to a certain point where you have to be honest and if other people don't like what you think and what you feel, too bad. You can't go through your life satisfying other people all the time, the critics especially. You just can't do that.

JW: What is your opinion on the performance practice research that is being done now?

LS: That's another interesting subject! Most of us are products of how we grew up and I grew up in a household during a time which was not very concerned with performing practices of different eras. I think the research is very interesting. Some of it I even find fascinating. However, I have no interest whatsoever in trying to do this myself. It goes completely against my own instincts. It doesn't allow for the hypothesis of what the composers might have thought if they heard their pieces now. Also, I don't care what anybody says, there's no way of knowing how this stuff sounded back then. There just isn't. You can get a rough idea, but that's all. I don't know any of these people in the early music groups who didn't start out learning their instruments in the mid to late twentieth-century manner. So they themselves have to regress from what they learned. Already that presents a problem to me.

JW: What do you think about Beethoven's metronome markings? What about the Roger Norrington performances?

LS: Nonsense. I'll tell you why. I can't understand the fuss about this. Everyone is making a big deal about Beethoven's original markings. First of all there are letters of Beethoven talking about the flexibility of his markings. Secondly, the majority of the Beethoven metronome marks were put in by Beethoven when he was deaf and put in many years after the majority of the works had been written. They were put in at the time of the Eighth Symphony. He put markings in for his earlier symphonies and for his earlier sonatas at this time as well. Leaving that argument aside, just think about modern composers such as Copland, Stravinsky, and Britten. We have audio documentation of them not obeying their own metronome markings. If they don't why should we assume that the deaf Beethoven did? An even more striking example is Bernstein. When you look at early recordings he made of his own works the tempos are much faster than he performs them today. What happened? So I have a lot of problem with this trend. I think even if you look at the relationship of the metronome marking in the Fourth Symphony for example, you will see the same marking for the opening *vivace* as for the last movement *allegro non troppo*. Do you mean to tell me that the *allegro non troppo* is the same tempo as the *vivace?* Also, Beethoven's *presto* markings sound extremely rushed. Maybe it sounds rushed because I'm used to hearing it a certain way. Fine, then it's my fault. However, I'm not so sure that the people who insist on following the exact markings really feel it that way. I'm really not sure about that. I don't tackle most Baroque music now because of all this academic research. I'm just put off by it all. However, I remember a couple of years ago I decided to do the Bach B minor Mass. I'd never done it and it was a piece I'd always been frightened of. It's an enormous work and a supreme masterpiece. I was also confronted by all the current research and scholarship. What should I do? I wound up approaching it as I remember hearing it when I was younger. That's the sound that stayed with me. I made it into a very impressive work. I used vibrato and open strings where I needed them and I didn't use boy choristers. I have great respect for the scholars in this but I wonder honestly that when it's all said and done if they actually feel it that way and if that's really their gut feeling for how it should be performed. I don't like that all we get on the back of album covers now are metronome marks. It's nonsense. I'm sorry but I don't think you can dismiss certain historical traditions. Traditions are passed down. If all this music has been passed down to us and has been allowed to develop in a certain way why should we look backward instead of forward?

JW: Do you retouch the Beethoven symphonies? For instance do you double the woodwinds and add horn parts in the Eroica?

LS: I add a lot of stuff for the horns.

JW: How many horns do you use?

LS: I use three but I love to get an assistant when I need it. I also double the woodwinds. I use those doublings because with the full modern string section the wind parts get obliterated. I did the Schubert Ninth last week as well. Not only do I double but I use the four horns to help some of the other wind parts. In the Coda you never hear the tune unless you give it to the horns. I do the same thing in the Trio. You have to throw in two horns to hear the tune. In the Coda I even have the trombones help out the lower string parts. I also change phrasings a bit here and there. I even make changes in Tchaikovsky. Some things that are written down an octave I put up an octave so that they're heard. I can't think of too many pieces where all of us conductors don't do something. Even if you're switching a dynamic marking around you are doing something. Usually we are changing phrases that don't work. But the minute you start as a conductor and say "Let's have a little less horn here" you are changing what's been written. Hopefully we only change to clarify what we think were the composers intentions. Look at Mahler, for instance. Every six bars or so we get instructions from Mahler, who was also a conductor. These instructions were probably based on his own performances of the work and were related to what went wrong the first times he performed them. When he writes *geschleppen* every few bars, what does he mean? Does he mean that we should move ahead or is it a caution against the tendency of the orchestra to slow down in these passages? We don't know. We can only guess. Also, I always thought it strange that the modern public or critics can accept very extravagant opera productions that clearly go against the grain and time frame of the composer and author. However, if conductors add a horn part here and there it is thought to be a terrible transgression. I also find it hard to believe that all the great conductors of the past such as Toscanini and Furtwängler were completely wrong in their musical instincts. It's ridiculous! Suddenly only the musicologists are correct.

JW: Do you have a special technique for achieving balance in new halls while you are on tour?

LS: In our hall the orchestra knows what to do. In new halls I let the orchestra experience the hall for themselves before I make suggestions. For instance, we had our first experience last year playing in Avery Fisher Hall [Lincoln Center, New York]. In the past we had always played in Carnegie. So, I decided to see what would happen. Well, I found that all I had to do was to put the winds up on risers and to ask the basses and cellos to come out towards the audience. The orchestra didn't find any problem with that arrangement and adjusted immediately. I know we sounded pretty good in there. We also sounded good in Davies Hall [San Francisco] which is a really tough hall. I was very surprised. It's a little muddy acoustically for us but we felt comfortable in there, mostly because my orchestra is not a brass-dominated orchestra. St. Louis has a good brass section though it's more low-key than most American orchestras. It's my idea of a brass sound.

When I guest conduct I take care of most of the balance problems on stage. I know what I want by now and what I don't want. I know most of the halls also. But when it's a hall I don't know I can pretty much rely on the players' instincts. The orchestras I conduct at this point in my career have very good instincts. However, if I ever get into trouble I sometimes use the ears of the assistant conductor. Sometimes I ask him to conduct while I go listen. I don't expect every orchestra to sound like mine when I get there. Few conductors have that ability. Eugene Ormandy could do it. He would show up and after the first rehearsal every orchestra sounded like the Philadelphia Orchestra. It was amazing, just amazing.

JW: How do you develop your own specific type of wind, brass, or string sound?

LS: I inherited very good players. I didn't have to do very much. What I tried to do was to blend the brass with the strings and to only let them fly when they need to fly. I let the soloists keep as much individuality as possible. Very rarely will I impose something on someone unless it's not matching what someone else is doing. I just say, "First oboe is not playing it the same as the first clarinet. Let's try it so we at least agree on how to do it." Otherwise I leave them alone. They know the hall and all the pieces well enough that I don't have to deal with it. You have to be a little careful when you are on the road guest-conducting. It's like being invited as someone's house guest. You don't rearrange the furniture while you are visiting. However, you do make yourself comfortable. So, when I'm guest conducting I consider it sort of like a few nights in a friend's house. I expect them to accommodate me but I also respect their own way of doing things.

JW: Do you rehearse differently with your orchestra than you do with other orchestras?

LS: Absolutely. At home we automatically know what sound we're looking for. I'm not one of those conductors who tries for different sounds in different styles. At the same time I also don't try for the same sound but if I do a Beethoven symphony it won't sound radically different than the [Mozart] *Jupiter* Symphony. If I do a Brahms symphony it's not going to sound radically different than a Schumann symphony. They know these things at home. It's clear because they know what I want and I know that they can produce it. So, when you are dealing with the musical aspects of a work there's never any question as to the kind of sound you need to achieve. On the road it's different. I usually tell the strings to vibrate or the brass to take it easy. At home they already know exactly what I'm going to say at any given moment on that subject. So a lot of times I'll stop and just look at them and they already know.

JW: Do you enjoy guest conducting?

LS: Yes because you get a different perspective on the repertoire from other good orchestras. Also, you can bring your own ideas of a certain repertoire to another orchestra. Rehearsing another orchestra from a different perspective is very illuminating. When I'm home and a guest is conducting I love to sit out in the audience and listen to the type of sound the guest conductor is accomplishing. I'm also very interested in the type of interpretation the guest is doing. It's fascinating!

JW: How do you plan repertoire for your orchestra and as a guest conductor?

LS: That's two very different things! The music director is responsible for the city and community he serves. The music director guides the people in their tastes because he is the cultural arbitrator. You have to go with your strengths, however. I have a particular passion to get the American repertoire before the public both as a guest conductor and as a music director. At home the community hears a lot of American music! I'm doing the Copland Third Symphony here in Minneapolis. Can you believe that it hasn't been done since 1958? That's ridiculous! So that's my programming mission. As a music director you cover a wide gamut of things. I conduct many things in St. Louis that orchestras on the road don't know me for. I only conduct the works I feel I can bring something to. If somebody suggests Bruckner Nine at home for instance, I'll say. "That's a piece for a guest conductor!" Sometimes I'll try out a piece I didn't do very well five years ago to see if I have something to bring to it now. I find that sometimes I do and sometimes I don't! So my choice of repertoire is wide at home. I also try to do certain works several times during the same season. For instance this year I'm doing the Copland Third Symphony here in Minneapolis, at home in St. Louis, and in New York.

JW: How do you rehearse when guest conducting in Europe?

LS: I usually get more rehearsal time. For instance, with radio orchestras you get six or seven three hour rehearsals.

JW: That's a lot of rehearsal time!

LS: Yes, but actually after three rehearsals I'm bored. The thing about European orchestras is that they don't come to the first rehearsal as prepared as they do here in the States. We're not talking about the very good orchestras such as the Vienna Philharmonic or the Berlin Philharmonic. They are always very prepared in their repertoire.

JW: What about when they are doing works outside of their standard repertoire?

LS: They struggle quite a bit with repertoire they don't know! I remember doing the Rachmaninoff Second Symphony with the Berlin Philharmonic. It was really a struggle for them. It's not a piece they normally play. It came out all right. I think if I were doing Brahms or something like that I would feel right at home with only one rehearsal.

JW: Do you think they enjoyed doing the Rachmaninoff?

LS: No, I don't think so.

JW: Do you find Europe more conservative than the United States?

LS: Yes, in general Europe is much more conservative though there are contrasts. For instance, London is extremely conservative but France is crazy. In Germany you have different groups. One group likes contemporary music and another group hates it. Both groups show up at everything so you get a lot of booing. There are always fights breaking out in the audience between certain pieces. I try to be very careful about what I do in Europe and where I do it. I spend a lot of time in London now. I'll be spending a lot of time in Munich also. I go over about twice a year or so. I also do one opera a year now. One year it's in Europe and the next year it's in the States. But one opera production a year is enough!

JW: Do you enjoy conducting opera?

LS: Yes, but not as much as the symphonic repertoire. The operas I do are carefully chosen. I just did *Salome* in Chicago, which was great fun! Next year it will be *Tosca*. A lot of work! I don't plan to do too much Verdi. Maybe *Otello* and *Aida*. I don't really think I could do the other Verdi operas very well. It's just not for me!

JW: What are your criteria for programming twentieth-century works?

LS: They are the same criteria I use for any other repertoire. I ask myself if I was in the hall listening to it would I enjoy it? Would it make me think, would I be stimulated by it, or would I be bored? If I'm bored by a piece I won't do it!

JW: Do you have a composer-in-residence who helps sort through the scores for you?

LS: What happens is that we get about forty scores a month. First the composer-in-residence looks at them, gets rid of the amateur ones, and then discusses the other ones with me. We talk about it though he knows by now which ones will stimulate me stylistically. Once in awhile he will say, "Look,

270

this is a piece you probably don't want to do but look at it anyway." If it's a good piece we'll see if someone else wants to do it. Occasionally I'll take it up and say maybe we should do this piece! At home I try to have as broad a taste as I can. It's important for the audience. It's important for the orchestra!

JW: Is there an area in conducting that we haven't discussed that you would like to talk about?

LS: Yes. I think a lot of people get caught up in the technical end of things. If you really have the opportunity to watch very fine conductors you will see that their techniques are not very clear. It's just the presence of their personalities that communicates to the orchestra what is going on. I had a teacher who had a very interesting piece of advice. He said, "You know, if you happen to see a concert on television, you should turn the sound off and watch. You should be able to tell what piece the conductor is conducting by the way they use their gestures. The way they communicate through their expressions." I remember I was watching TV in Estonia about twelve or thirteen years ago when a concert came on and the sound was jammed. It was [Rafael] Kubelik conducting, and in around 10-15 seconds it was clear he was conducting the Dvořák G major Symphony. It was absolutely clear! Yet I watched and saw that Kubelik didn't have a precise technique at all. However, the phrasings were clear and it was obvious what work he was conducting! I think if we have the music inside our bodies it doesn't matter if the first beat isn't straight down. It doesn't matter if the left hand doesn't operate quite as independently as we would like it to. What's important is that the essence of the music be conveyed through the gesture. Technique is only a means to achieve the kind of expressive gestures we use. So my advice is, yes, learn the basics, learn the rules, but know that in this case the rules were made to be broken. Be only in the service of music, not in the service of technique. That's important. Most people say that I have a terrific technique. I don't even think about it. I don't watch myself. The couple times I have seen myself on video were interesting because what I thought was good was the fact that I did use gestures that conveyed what the music was about.

Biography

Leonard Slatkin has been the music director of the Saint Louis Symphony Orchestra since 1979. He began his long association with the orchestra first as assistant, and then as associate conductor, and as the music director of the newly formed Saint Louis Youth Symphony. He established a reputation as a "multifaceted conductor" and "an expert orchestrator/illustrator." Throughout his tenure with the Saint Louis Symphony, Mr. Slatkin has received unanimous praise from audiences and critics alike. As music director, he has led the orchestra on two highly acclaimed overseas tours – to Europe in 1985 and the Far East in 1986. Annual tours in this country have included stops in Chicago, Washington, D.C., Boston, San Francisco, Los Angeles, and New York. Mr. Slatkin recently signed an exclusive, five-year, thirty-disc recording contract with BMG Classics. Among the works to be recorded are symphonies of Mahler, Shostakovich, and Tchaikovsky, as well as American repertoire from Aaron Copland and Walter Piston.

Born in Los Angeles, California, in 1944, Mr. Slatkin was surrounded by a musical family as a boy. His parents, conductor-violinist Felix Slatkin and cellist Eleanor Aller, were founding members of the famed Hollywood String Quartet. After beginning his musical career on the piano, Slatkin first studied conducting with his father before continuing with Walter Susskind at Aspen and Jean Morel at the Juilliard School.

Mr. Slatkin's early career was filled with regular engagements with many American orchestras. After firmly establishing himself in this country, he made his European debut in 1974 with the Royal Philharmonic in London. Currently, Mr. Slatkin is a frequent visitor with major orchestras in Boston, Cleveland, Philadelphia, Los Angeles, London, Vienna, Amsterdam, Paris, and Israel.

Mr. Slatkin has been the recipient of many honors including ASCAP awards in 1984 and 1986 for adventuresome programming of contemporary music with the Saint Louis Symphony Orchestra; the prestigious Declaration of Honor in Silver from the Austrian ambassador to the United States for outstanding contributions to cultural relations between the two countries; the Lamplighter Award from the Saint Louis chapter of the Public Relations Society in January 1988; and an honorary doctorate from the Juilliard School of Music, which he attended. The recordings he has released with the Saint Louis Symphony Orchestra have been nominated for Grammy Awards for twelve consecutive years, winning two in 1985 for their recording of the Prokofiev Symphony no. 5.

Leonard Slatkin Discography

Composer	Work	Soloists	Orchestra	Label	CD	LP	MC
Bach	Fantasia and fugue, BWV 537		London Philharmonic	RCA	7862-2-RC		7862-4-RC
Barber	Adagio for Strings		St. Louis Symphony	Telarc	CD-80059	10059	
Barber	Adagio for strings		St. Louis Symphony	Angel	CDC-49463		4DS-49463
Barber	Essays 1, 2, & 3		St. Louis Symphony	Angel	CDC-49463		4DS-49463
Barber	Medea's Meditation and Dance of Vengeance		St. Louis Symphony	Angel	CDC-49463		4DS-49463
Barber	Overture to School for Scandal		St. Louis Symphony	Angel	CDC-49463		4DS-49463
Barber	Violin concerto	Oliviera	St. Louis Symphony	Angel	CDC-47850	DS-47850	4DS-47850
Bernstein	Candide Overture		St. Louis Symphony	Angel	CDC-47522	DS-37358	4DS-37358
Bernstein	Facsimile		St. Louis Symphony	Angel	CDC-47522	DS-37358	4DS-37358
Bernstein	Fancy Free		St. Louis Symphony	Angel	CDC-47522	DS-37358	4DS-37358
Bernstein	On the Town		St. Louis Symphony	Angel	CDC-47522	DS-37358	4DS-37358
Bizet	Carmen Suites 1 & 2		St. Louis Symphony	Telarc	CD-80048	10048	
Bolcolm	Session I		St. Louis Symphony	NW	NW-356-2	NW-356-1	
Bolcolm	Symphony no. 4	Morris	St. Louis Symphony	NW	NW-356-2	NW-356-1	
Borodin	In the Steppes of Central Asia		St. Louis Symphony	Telarc		DG-10072	
Borodin	Nocturne		St. Louis Symphony	Telarc	CD-80080	DG-10080	
Brahms	Academic Festival Overture		St. Louis Symphony	RCA	7920		
Brahms	Haydn Variations		St. Louis Symphony	RCA	7920		
Brahms	Serenade no. 1		St. Louis Symphony	RCA	6247-2-RC		6247-9-RC9
Brahms	Serenade no. 2		St. Louis Symphony	RCA	7920		
Bruch	Concerto no. 1 for violin	Lin	Chicago Symphony	CBS	MK-42315		IMT-42315
Bruch	Scottish Fantasy for violin	Lin	Chicago Symphony	CBS	MK-42315		IMT-42315
Castelnuovo-Tedesco	Guitar concertos nos. 1 & 2	K. Yamashita	London Philharmonic	RCA	RD 60355		RK 60355

Composer	Work	Orchestra	Soloists	Label	CD	LP	MC
Castelnuovo-Tedesco	Concerto for two guitars	London Philharmonic	K. Yamashita, N. Yamashita	RCA	RD 60355		RK 60355
Colgrass	Déja vu	St. Louis Symphony		NW	NW-318-2	NW-318	
Copland	Symphony no. 3	St. Louis Symphony		RCA			
Copland	Music for a Great City	St. Louis Symphony		RCA			
Copland	Billy the Kid	St. Louis Symphony		Angel	CDC-47382	DS-37357	4DS-37357
Copland	Rodeo	St. Louis Symphony		Angel	CDC-47382	DS-37357	4DS-37357
Debussy	Dances sacrée et profane	St. Louis Symphony	Tietov	Telarc	CD-80071	DB-10071	
Debussy	La Mer	St. Louis Symphony		Telarc	CD-80071	DB-10071	
Debussy	Prélude à l'apres-midi d'un faune	St. Louis Symphony		Telarc	CD-80071	DB-10071	
Del Tredici	In Memory of a Summer Day	St. Louis Symphony	Bryn-Julson	Nonesuch	Nonesuch 79043-2	79043	79043-4
Druckman	Aureole	St. Louis Symphony		NW	NW-318-2	NW-318	
Dvořák	Mazurek	St. Louis Symphony	Luca	Nonesuch	Nonesuch 79052-2	79052	79052-4
Dvořák	Romance	St. Louis Symphony	Luca	Nonesuch	Nonesuch 79052-2	79052	79052-4
Dvořák	Symphony no. 9	St. Louis Symphony		Telarc		10053	
Dvořák	Violin concerto	St. Louis Symphony	Luca	Nonesuch	Nonesuch 79052-2	79052	79052-4
Elgar	Cokaigne Overture	London Philharmonic		RCA	60073-2-RC		60073-4-RC
Elgar	Enigma Variations	London Philharmonic		RCA	60073-2-RC		60073-4-RC
Elgar	Froissart	London Philharmonic		RCA	60073-2-RC		60073-4-RC
Elgar	Serenade for strings	London Philharmonic		RCA	60072-2-RC		60072-4-RD
Elgar	Symphony no. 2	London Philharmonic		RCA	60072-2-RC		60072-4-RD
Elgar	The Kingdom	London Philharmonic	Kenny, Hodgson, Gillett, Luxon	RCA	7862-2-RC	7862-4-RC	
Erb	Prismatic Variations	St. Louis Symphony		Nonesuch		79118	79118-4
Fauré	Pavane	St. Louis Symphony		Telarc	CD-80059	10059	
Gershwin	"I Got Rhythm" Variations	St. Louis Symphony	Siegel	Vox		CT-2122	
Gershwin	An American in Paris	St. Louis Symphony		Angel	CDC-49278	DS-49278	4DS-49278
Gershwin	Cuban Overture	St. Louis Symphony		Angel	CDC-49278	DS-49278	4DS-49278
Gershwin	Lullaby	St. Louis Symphony		Angel	CDC-49278	DS-49278	4DS-49278
Gershwin	Piano concerto	St. Louis Symphony	Siegel	Vox			CT-2122

Composer	Work	Orchestra	Soloists	Label	CD	LP	MC
Gershwin	Porgy and Bess	Berlin Radio Symphony	Alexander, Estes	Philips	412 720-2		412 720-4
Gershwin	Porgy and Bess: Catfish Row Suite	St. Louis Symphony		Angel	CDC-49278	DS-49278	4DS-49278
Gershwin	Rhapsody in Blue	St. Louis Symphony	Siegel	Vox			CT-2122
Glière	Russian Sailor's Dance	St. Louis Symphony		Telarc		DG-10072	
Glinka	Russlan and Ludmilla Overture	St. Louis Symphony		Telarc		DG-10072	
Grainger	Irish Tune	St. Louis Symphony		Telarc	CD-80059	10059	
Grieg	Peer Gynt Suites 1 & 2	St. Louis Symphony		Telarc	CD-80048	10048	
Handel	Overture in d	London Philharmonic		RCA	7862-2-RC		7862-4-RC
Hanson	Symphony no. 2	St. Louis Symphony	Oliviera	Angel	CDC-47850	DS-47850	4DS-47850
Kabalevsky	The Comedians	National Philharmonic		RCA	5661-2-RC9	5661-1-RC	5661-4-RC9
Khachaturian	Sabre Dance	National Philharmonic		RCA	5661-2-RC9	5661-1-RC	5661-4-RC9
Mahler	Symphony no. 1	St. Louis Symphony		Telarc	CD-80066	GD-10066	
Mahler	Symphony no. 2	St. Louis Symphony	Battle, Forrester	Telarc	CD-80081/2	DG-10081/2	
Mussorgsky	Night on Bald Mountain	St. Louis Symphony		Vox			CT-2109
Mussorgsky	Pictures at an Exhibition	National Philharmonic		RCA	5661-2-RC9	5661-1-RC	5661-4-RC9
Mussorgsky	Pictures at an Exhibition	St. Louis Symphony		Vox			CT-2109
Pachelbel	Kanon	St. Louis Symphony		Telarc	CD-80080	DG-10080	
Paganini	Violin concerto no. 1	London Symphony	Midori	Philips	420 943-2		420 943-4
Prokofiev	Cinderella (excerpts)	St. Louis Symphony		RCA	RCD1-5231	ARC1-5231	ARK1-5231
Prokofiev	Symphony no. 1	London Philharmonic		RCA	5661-2-RC9		5661-4-RC9
Prokofiev	Symphony no. 5	St. Louis Symphony		RCA	RCD1-5035	ARC1-5035	ARE1-5035
Rachmaninoff	Piano concerto nos. 1-4	St. Louis Symphony	Simon	MH			C-85767
Rachmaninoff	Rhapsody on a Theme by Paganini	St. Louis Symphony	Simon	MH			C-85767
Rachmaninoff	Symphonic Dances	St. Louis Symphony		MH			C-85767
Rachmaninoff	Symphony no. 3	St. Louis Symphony		Vox			CT-2312
Rachmaninoff	Vocalise	St. Louis Symphony		MH			C-85767
Ravel	Boléro	St. Louis Symphony		Telarc	CD-80052	DG-10052	
Ravel	Daphnis et Chloé Suite no. 2	St. Louis Symphony		Telarc	CD-80052	DG-10052	
Ravel	Pavanne	St. Louis Symphony		Telarc	CD-80052	DG-10052	

Composer	Work	Orchestra	Soloists	Label	CD	LP	MC
Rimsky-Korsakov	Russian Easter Overture	St. Louis Symphony		Telarc		DG-10072	
Rouse	Infernal Machine	St. Louis Symphony		Nonesuch		79118	79118-4
Satie	Gymnopédies 1 & 3	St. Louis Symphony		Telarc	CD-80059	10059	
Schwantner	Distant Runes	St. Louis Symphony		Nonesuch		79143-1	79143-4
Schwantner	Rainbow	St. Louis Symphony		Nonesuch		79143-1	79143-4
Schwantner	Sudden Rainbow	St. Louis Symphony		Nonesuch		79143-1	79143-4
Shostakovich	Symphony no. 10	St. Louis Symphony		RCA	6597-2-RC		6597-4-RC9
Shostakovich	Symphony no. 5	St. Louis Symphony		RCA	5608-2-RC	5608-1-RC	5608-4-RC9
Stravinsky	Fireworks	London Philharmonic		RCA	5661-2-RC9		5661-4-RC9
Tchaikovsky	Marche Slav	St. Louis Symphony		Telarc		DG-10072	
Tchaikovsky	Nutcracker	St. Louis Symphony		RCA	RCD2-7005	ARC2-7005	ARE2-7005
Tchaikovsky	Nutcracker (suite)	Minnesota	Douglas	ProArte	CDD-184		PCD-184
Tchaikovsky	Piano concerto no. 1	London Symphony		RCA	5708-2-RC	5708-1-RC	5708-4-RC
Tchaikovsky	Serenade	St. Louis Symphony		Telarc	CD-80080	DG-10080	
Tchaikovsky	Swan Lake (excerpts)	Minnesota		ProArte	CDD-184		
Tchaikovsky	Sérénade Mélancolique	London Symphony	Midori	Philips	420 943-2		420 943-4
Tchaikovsky	Valse-Scherzo for violin	London Symphony	Midori	Philips	420 943-2		420 943-4
Tower	Sequoia	St. Louis Symphony		Nonesuch		79118	79118-4
Vaughan Williams	Tallis Fantasia	St. Louis Symphony		Telarc	CD-80059	10059	
Vaughan Williams	Fantasia on Greensleeves	St. Louis Symphony		Telarc	CD-80080	DG-10080	
Vivaldi	Four Seasons	English Chamber Orchestra	Garcia	RCA	RCD1-5827	HRC1-5827	HRE1-5827
Vivaldi	Violin concerto	English Chamber Orchestra	Garcia	RCA	RCD1-5827	HRC1-5827	HRE1-5827
Walton	Portsmouth Point Overture	London Philharmonic		Virgin	VC-970715-2	VC-970715-1	VC-970-715-4
Walton	Symphony no. 1	London Philharmonic		Virgin	VC-970715-2	VC-970715-1	VC-970-715-4

"When I feel strongly about a piece, the conviction is there. One of the main factors that contribute to interpretation is time; there are no short cuts. Real insight comes only after doing the pieces over and over and over again, and daring to go further each time. Everytime I pick up a score, I see new things. Now what makes that happen? First of all, I don't live my life carefully, I don't believe in the status quo, and I don't believe I know it all. If anything, I think that I know too little. I have thousands of questions and not many answers, but by posing the questions to myself and to fellow musicians, I can perhaps come a little closer to the core."

_____ Edo de Waart

Edo de Waart

JW: When did you decide to become a conductor and what course has your career followed?

EdW: The real decision to make conducting my life came after I won the 1964 Mitropoulos Conducting Competition in New York. Until then I had played the oboe and was a member of the Concertgebouw Orchestra. Although I had wanted to be a conductor for a long time, I didn't have any grand ideas about whether I would be able to make it my life. The first proof that I might really have a chance came when I was one of the winners of that competition. It decided my fate completely. When I returned to Amsterdam I played oboe for only one more month with the Concertgebouw before they offered me an assistant conductorship. Soon afterward I went to New York as an assistant to Bernstein. When I came back from that I knew I would continue as the assistant conductor with the Concertgebouw and I had an offer as well from the Rotterdam Philharmonic to become staff conductor the following season, 1966-67. As such I was second in command and conducted thirty-five concerts a year. My career took off very quickly from there, maybe too quickly, and I never looked back.

I stayed with the Rotterdam Philharmonic for twelve years, six years as on staff and then six years as music director. In 1975 I was named principal guest conductor of the San Francisco Symphony and a few months later, when Seiji Ozawa left San Francisco for Boston, the position was offered to me. I accepted and was the music director in San Francisco until 1985. After that there was a hiatus for one year in which I was to be the music director of the Netherlands Opera. Things didn't work out there because all kinds of signals were crossed. In the meantime an offer came from the Minnesota Orchestra, which I took, and now I am in my fifth season here. Altogether I have been music director of an American orchestra for twelve years and music director of a Dutch orchestra for six years. Eighteen years in all.

JW: What are the main differences being a music director in the States and in Europe?

EdW: Though there are many differences, in the end the job boils down to the same thing: one's rapport with the musicians, the ability to work with them, and the ability to motivate them so that all can give the best performance. Of course, you work under very different circumstances. One of the major differences is that in Europe the orchestras are largely subsidized by the government while American orchestras are funded by private and corporate support. The European government subsidy gives you more freedom and flexibility than the American system. Also, in Europe there is more communication between the management and the musicians, and in general you find a more amicable way of working. In the United States there is less talk and less communication. The unions and management are not necessarily tuned to the same goals. It took quite a while for me to get used to this in San Francisco and to get used to the much more rigid structure of an American orchestra. However, with an American orchestra you know very clearly where you stand and that is an advantage. So, there are merits to both systems.

Another thing that is quite different is the amount of rehearsal time. In Europe you usually have more time and the pace towards the concert is slightly less frantic. You have more leisure to sort out things out. Often in the United States you have too little time, but on the other hand, American musicians are very fast workers. In Europe you have more rehearsals but you also need those rehearsals because the musicians know they have the time and don't need to learn so fast. So again, ultimately you get the same result here or in Europe. You just use a different approach and a different way of getting there, but once you are there it's basically the same.

•••••

JW: You have a reputation as an orchestra builder. In San Francisco I watched the orchestra improve dramatically while you were there and I've watched the same thing happen with the Minnesota Orchestra. How do you do it?

EdW: This aspect of conducting has always interested me because I don't think I am capable of expressing my deepest inner thoughts when the tools I am working with aren't good. However, my initial goals are never to build an orchestra. I just have certain standards that I insist on – standards that were instilled in me by excellent teachers who came from the Mengelberg and Concertgebouw tradition. They taught me, for instance, that the orchestra should attack and release chords together and in the same way, and that they should be beautifully in tune with the overtones right. These are very simple things, but a lot of my colleagues aren't very interested in them. Some of them seem solely interested in emoting which is only part of the job. So, I think that some conductors are real music directors and others are not. I think a real music director has to work on many things that may not be immediately apparent. A real music director doesn't only rehearse for the opening Wednesday night concert!

I feel that the first couple of years with your own orchestra is very much like redoing a house. Are you just going to spray paint on everything or are you going to take the walls down, fix the leaks and wiring, and put in new pipes? You also have to realize that while you are doing this the house won't look very pretty. But in this process you are constructing a new and healthy structure from the inside out; a structure that will be able to hang together whether you are conducting it or not. I left my successor in San Francisco a very healthy orchestra. Blomstedt didn't have to do a whole lot of housecleaning. He went on from where I left off and since he is very thorough in his work, the San Francisco Symphony is doing extremely well.

But going on using the same analogy, you have to realize that before you furnish the house it has to be able to hold out the wind and the rain. It has to be solid and strong and in the shape you want. Only then can you put your beautiful paintings on the wall and make the house come alive. So, you see, mine is not a quick-fix approach and never has been. The older I get the less I can do that sort of thing, which doesn't make me very suitable as a guest conductor. I find that I can't just come in and try to make something special happen in four days unless it is a splendid orchestra and we happen to click, looking for the same things.

JW: So you much prefer being a music director instead of guest conducting?

EdW: It's not a preference. I am a music director and could not do the other. I'd spiritually die.

JW: Do you find yourself guest conducting less and less?

EdW: I only do five or six weeks a year now.

JW: How do you program as a music director versus as a guest conductor?

EdW: The difference is again very obvious. As a music director you program works that you know will leave something with the orchestra and will build up a style of playing over the years. As a guest conductor you are not worried about those things. You just come in with a piece that you like and do well and that you know the orchestra will do well. You don't worry about whether it will have an effect on their playing. As music director I plan a season with the orchestra in mind. I want them to go through a certain amount of music in different styles, knowing that if we apply ourselves we will be better next year and can build on that. Finally we may arrive at the point where the orchestra will play everything they do extremely well. So for me, it's all very simple because I think in this way. For someone else it would be different.

JW: How much freedom do you have in your programming?

EdW: Far less than it seems. You have to make many compromises because you need to take ticket sales into account. You want the hall as full as possible. It is like walking a tightrope between putting on audience favorites every year and the things you feel need to be played and belong in an artistically viable and alive season. This tightrope doesn't give you a lot of freedom. Also, you can only plan about forty hours of music per season. That's what twenty-four programs times an hour and a half are worth. Not everybody realizes how little music you can actually do in a season. So it is more a matter of discarding all the time while trying to balance out the programs. You end up saying things like, "Well, there is no French music, why? Let's put in a little baroque music; there's too much German music, so let's take some out and put in some Russian music. No English music, why not? Should we play Elgar or Vaughan Williams this year?" Then when your orchestra starts touring and recording there are different types of demands. You will have to play the repertoire that you will be playing on tour and you will have to play the repertoire that you will be recording. So, it's a challenge every year to come up with programs that will sell tickets, will be good for the orchestra and still will have a character of their own. Of course, as a guest conductor you have none of those problems.

JW: How do you select your twentieth-century literature?

EdW: That's another challenge. The best way is if you know and believe in a composer and his or her work. Or you may hear a tape and feel that the work speaks to you. I feel that it is very important that we play music from our own time, though audiences increasingly have come to dislike most of it. That's a very sad comment. But on the other hand, I also find that certain pieces go over better with the audience than I thought. It's really a matter of being open-minded and curious.

JW: How do you select your premieres?

EdW: Well, when you look at a score you look at the whole picture. You look at the compositional language, the instrumentation, at the structure, and even then it's hard to say why a work is good or not. You have to rely on your intuition. I often ask myself, though, what I would have done in 1910 if someone had put a Mahler score on my desk. Would I have recognized the greatness in the work? Maybe not.

JW: Does your staff help you in selecting scores?

EdW: Yes, and our world is very small and we hear about a lot of composers. However, it is very difficult for an unknown composer to get his music played. Many pieces are chosen from word-of-mouth recommendations.

JW: Some composers that I have talked to think that the symphony orchestra is dying and they don't want to compose for it any more.

EdW: That's baloney!

JW: I think maybe they are afraid to write for it because it's so difficult to get a performance.

EdW: Well, one reason it is difficult to get a performance is that we are all stymied by the need for an audience. There are hardly any music education programs in the schools right now. The audience is not getting any richer culturally. This poses a big problem and I have no answer for it at the moment. That's a whole other interview.

•••••

JW: What do you think of the early music performance research going on?

EdW: It interests me very much. I really admire people like Bruggen, Norrington, John Eliot Gardiner, and Harnoncourt, and I love their performances. However, I think that it would be extremely difficult for me or someone in my position to become a specialist in any one area because of the amount and variety of music done each season. Even so, if I were to become a specialist it would probably be in the area of the late romantic composers rather than the baroque or classical composers. But when we do older music like the Mozart we did this week (Mass in C Minor and Symphony no. 40), we work very hard to clean it up and to lighten it up. Our work may not be really audible yet to the audience, but we are trying to make our performances closer to how this music might have originally been played. Next week we will go through the same process with the Beethoven *Eroica*. I really try to adhere to the metronome markings that Beethoven wrote because they give me an indication of how he felt his music should be played. I don't think that you should just go past them with the excuse that his metronome was broken. You need to try his tempos and one try is not enough. You have to try many times, and they will grow on you, and make sense.

JW: Do you reduce the strings as well?

EdW: I usually do to a certain extent, except you have to realize that we are in a different situation now. We play in a big hall and not in a little palace room, which those works were originally written for. We play for 2,500 people and those works were often played with audiences of 500-1000. So, I think that you can play with the full orchestra if you play lightly and more transparently.

JW: Would you ever retouch a score? It used to be such a widespread practice.

EdW: Most of the retouching fad was done before World War II. After the War most conductors have adhered more to the score. Before that though, major retouching was done by a lot of conductors. Mahler, for instance, totally rewrote part of Beethoven's Ninth Symphony. Personally, I don't believe in retouching, though I might change a dynamic marking here and there or a slur or a dot.

JW: But you wouldn't change the instrumentation?

EdW: No, never.

JW: What about doubling the winds?

EdW: Well, doubling is not retouching. Doubling is a search for a bigger and meatier sound. Some of my older colleagues still do that when they do Beethoven. They like the fatness of the sound. I have never done it, and certainly never will, unless we play in the Metrodome!

••••

JW: How do you approach a score you are learning for the first time? How long would you like to live with it before performing it?

EdW: It totally depends. I am not at all convinced that one has to live with a score forever to give a good performance. In Bach's or Mozart's time, works were played with the ink still wet on the page and I'm sure those were wonderful performances. A good performance depends on things like intuition, taste, and innate musicianship and culture. A conductor who doesn't have those things won't get a good performance even though he spends five hundred hours on a score! On the other hand, someone who has an alert mind and great intuition can quickly learn scores and give excellent performances. I have given good performances of scores I've only looked at once because I understood the piece. And since I didn't want to learn it from memory I didn't have to put in an extra twenty hours. I understood the tempi, I understood the structure, and the rest I did in rehearsal. In some scores there isn't much to find so when you perform them you just open the gates and let the music pour out. I feel that we have lost the ability to improvise. Charles Munch never rehearsed that much, yet he gave wonderful performances. He would tell the orchestra, "You know this piece and I know this piece so let's see each other in a few days." And they would give fantastic concerts! On the other hand, I have spent months on a Beethoven or a Mahler score because there was so much to find in them. So, it's a highly personal matter.

When I was a student I would ask my teachers how to learn a score. They replied that they didn't know. They told me to just go and learn it. So, that seems to be the answer. Trust that your way will work and if it doesn't, change your way. Some people work a lot with recordings or only with recordings. Other people swear that they never hear a recording and then you visit them in their home and they have an elaborate sound system with thousands of records on the wall. You may wonder why they have all of those records if they never listen to them. I personally think it is very good to listen to other people's performances to find out what makes a performance special or boring. I can't go to Erich Kleiber anymore, he's dead, or to Klemperer or to Furtwängler to ask them questions or to sit in their rehearsals. The second best thing you have is their recordings. You listen not to copy but to analyze. As you can see this is not a subject I'm very enthusiastic talking about.

JW: Can you comment on rehearsal techniques?

EdW: You work from the inside out. I know that I sometimes nitpick too much, but I also feel that the growth of an ensemble depends on a lot of detail work. Also, I feel an obligation to the musicians not to work in a way that obliterates their refined qualities. This could happen if you just played through a work all the time. So I work, for instance, on putting dots on things, or in getting the strings to play on the same part of the bow, in the same way and at the same time. Rehearsal technique reflects a conductor's good qualities or lack of them. But even after twenty-five years in this profession, some of the rehearsals just don't take off. You end up grinding through them without being able to get them going. Often a piece inspires you tremendously and you can communicate that inspiration to the orchestra. Other times it just doesn't go. So, there are no set answers in this profession. I have learned through the years not to fight it. You just get the work done and the orchestra ready and hope that the lights will come on at night.

JW: You are a very strong interpreter. I know that it's mysterious business, but can you describe how you reach your interpretations?

EdW: When I feel strongly about a piece, the conviction is there. One of the main factors that contribute to interpretation is time; there are no short cuts. Real insight comes only after doing the pieces over and over and over again, and daring to go further each time. Everytime I pick up a score, I see new things. Now what makes that happen? First of all, I don't live my life carefully, I don't believe in the status quo, and I don't believe I know it all. If anything, I think that I know too little. I have thousands of questions and not many answers, but by posing the questions to myself and to fellow musicians, I can perhaps come a little closer to the core. You also can't be deterred by failure. Unfortunately, our Western civilization is mainly geared for success. You have to realize that a lot of art is about failure. You fall and you have to

285

climb up again. You keep struggling, striving, and digging into yourself. I'm sure Mozart didn't think his music was as divine as we think it is. I'm sure he was often highly unhappy with what he did. Interpretation is what you are and what you think the composer is and what he wants to say. It is one of the great mysteries of this profession. Some evenings you will look in a score and it won't say a word to you because you are not receptive to it. Many evenings you will be completely wide open to it. You won't know whether this is because you ate something particular that day, or because the weather changed, or that the stars were standing in a particular constellation. You have no idea where or when this type of inspiration will hit and this is the miracle. Thank God, though, the older you get the more often scores speak to you. I see things that inspire me more often now than I did earlier in my life. I also don't get so hung up when things are not working. You will always have evenings when you think you or your players did something incredibly beautiful or incredibly ugly. This can inspire or turn you off. There is no telling why that happens or whose fault it is. The only thing you know is that you have to go on and not look back.

•••••

JW: What is your advice to young conductors?

EdW: Trust yourself, trust your instincts and your intuition. Keep your ears and eyes open. Go and listen a lot to your fellow musicians, whether they are conductors, singers or violinists, or what have you. It doesn't matter. Be patient. There are no short cuts, no tricks, no pills to take to get there quicker. I think that after composing, conductors have the hardest profession in music because we have to span such an incredibly wide repertoire. We are not playing an instrument; we have to go through a hundred people to make our feelings come out and be heard. Our ideas are expressed through and with other people. It's a difficult and demanding profession, but fantastically rewarding, and totally worth all the blood, sweat and tears that it requires.

Biography

Edo de Waart was appointed the eighth music director of the Minnesota Orchestra in 1986. Artistic highlights since his arrival have been critically acclaimed concert performances of Wagner's *Das Rheingold* and Mussorgsky's *Boris Godunov*, successful tour appearances throughout the Eastern United States, the signing of a multiyear recording contract with the Virgin Classics label, the on-going series of performances of symphonies of Gustav Mahler, and world, American, or subscription season premieres of works by, among others, Paul Hindemith, John Adams, Stephen Paulus, and Walter Piston.

Born in Amsterdam in 1941, Edo de Waart studied oboe and conducting in that city at the Music Lyceum. Upon graduating he was appointed associate principal oboe of the Concertgebouw Orchestra. At age twenty-three he took first place in the Dimitri Mitropoulos Conductors Competition and became assistant conductor to Leonard Bernstein with the New York Philharmonic Orchestra for the 1965-66 season.

Returning to the Netherlands, he was named assistant conductor of the Concertgebouw under Bernard Haitink. He held that post until 1967, when he became conductor of both the Rotterdam Philharmonic Orchestra and the Netherlands Wind Ensemble, which he founded. Six years later de Waart assumed the music directorship in Rotterdam, retaining the position until 1979.

De Waart turned his attention to the United States in 1975, when the San Francisco Symphony Orchestra engaged him as principal guest conductor. Only two years later he was named music director, a post he held for eight seasons.

Mr. de Waart has been a guest conductor with many of the world's greatest orchestras including the Berlin Philharmonic, the Concertgebouw, the Hallé Orchestra, the New York Philharmonic, the Philadelphia Orchestra, the Pittsburgh Symphony Orchestra, the Cleveland Orchestra, and the Toronto Symphony. His opera engagements have included performances with the Bayreuth Wagner Festival, the Netherlands Opera, the San Francisco Opera, the Santa Fe Opera, and the Royal Opera at Covent Garden.

Edo de Waart Discography

Composer	Work	Orchestra	Soloists	Label	CD	LP	MC
Adams	Harmonielehre	San Francisco Symphony		Nonesuch	79115-2	79115-1	79115-4
Adams	Harmonium	San Francisco Symphony		ECM	821465-2	821465-1	821465-4
Adams	Nixon in China	St. Luke's	Sylvan, Maddalena, Hammons, Opatz, Friedman, Dry, Duykers, Page, Kraney	Nonesuch			
Adams	Shaker Loops	San Francisco Symphony		Philips	412 214-2		412 214-4
Adams	The Chairman Dances	San Francisco Symphony		Nonesuch	79144-2	79144-1	79144-4
Bach	Violin concerto in a	New Philharmonia	Grumiaux	Philips		6500.119	
Bach	Concerto in d for two violins	New Philharmonia	Grumiaux, Toyoda	Philips		6500.119	
Bach	Concerto in d for violin and oboe	New Philharmonia	Grumiaux, Holliger	Philips		6500.119	
Beethoven	Marches	Rotterdam Philharmonic		Philips		9500.080	
Beethoven	Romances for Violin	New Philharmonia	Grumiaux, Holliger	Philips	420 348-2		
Bruch	Violin concerto in g, no. 1	Minnesota	Salerno-Sonnenberg	Angel			
Debussy	La Damoiselle Elue	San Francisco Symphony	Ameling, Taylor	Philips	410 043-2	6514.199	7337.199

Composer	Work	Orchestra	Soloists	Label	CD	LP	MC
Duparc	Chanson Triste	San Francisco Symphony Ameling		Philips	410 043-2	6514.199	7337.199
Duparc	L'Invitation au voyage	San Francisco Symphony	Ameling	Philips	410 043-2	6514.199	7337.199
Dvořák	Serenade in d	Netherlands Wind Ensemble		Philips		6570.205	
Dvořák	Symphony in d	Concertgebouw		Philips		9500.605	
Franck							
Gershwin	I Got Rhythm Variations	Monte Carlo Opera		Philips	420 492-2	6500.118	420 492-4
Gershwin	An American in Paris	Monte Carlo Opera		Philips	420 492-2		420 492-4
Gershwin	Concerto in F	Monte Carlo Opera	Hass	Philips	420 492-2	6500.118	420 492-4
Gershwin	Rhapsody in Blue	Monte Carlo Opera	Hass	Philips	420 492-2	6500.118	420 492-4
Gounod	Petite Symphonie in B-flat	Netherlands Wind Ensemble		Philips		6570.205	
Grieg	Peer Gynt (excerpts)	San Francisco Symphony	Ameling	Philips	411 038-2	6514.378	7337.378
Haydn, M.	Violin concerto in A	Concertgebouw	Grumiaux	Philips		839.757	
Jongen	Symphony concertante	San Francisco Symphony	Murray	Telarc	CD-80096	DG-10096	
Mahler	Symphony no. 1	Minnesota Orchestra		Virgin	VC7 91096-2		VC7 91096-4
Mahler	Symphony no. 4	San Francisco Symphony	M. Price	Philips		6514/201	7337.201
Mozart	Arias	Philharmonia	von Stade	Philips		9500.098	
Mozart	Oboe concerto in C	New Philharmonia	Holliger	Philips		6500.174	
Mozart	March in D, K. 249	Dresden State	Ughi	Philips		6500.966	
Mozart	Marches	Rotterdam Philharmonic		Philips		9500.080	
Mozart	Masonic Music	New Philharmonia	Hollweg, Partridge, Dean	Philips		6570.063	
Mozart	Opera and Concert Arias	English Chamber Orchestra	Ameling	Philips		6500.544	

Composer	Work	Orchestra	Soloists	Label	CD	LP	MC
Mozart	Serenade in B-flat, K. 361	Netherlands Wind Ensemble		Philips	420 711-2	839-734	
Mozart	Serenade in D, K. 250	Dresden State	Ughi	Philips		6500.966	
Mozart	Serenades nos. 11 & 12	Netherlands Wind Ensemble		Philips		802.907	
Mussorgsky	Pictures at an Exhibition	Rotterdam Philharmonic		Philips		6500.882	
Prokofiev	Romeo and Juliet (excerpts)	Rotterdam Philharmonic		Philips		6500.640	
Rachmaninoff	The Rock	Rotterdam Philharmonic		Philips		9500.302	
Rachmaninoff	Caprice Bohemien	London Symphony		Philips		6500.362	
Rachmaninoff	Piano concerto no. 1	San Francisco Symphony	Kocsis	Philips	412 881-2	6514.377	7337/377
Rachmaninoff	Piano concerto no. 2	San Francisco Symphony	Kocsis	Philips	412 881-2		412 738-4
Rachmaninoff	Piano concerto no. 2 in c	Royal Philharmonic	Orozco	Philips		6570.046	
Rachmaninoff	Piano concerto no 3.	San Francisco Symphony	Kocsis	Philips	411 475-2		
Rachmaninoff	Piano concerto no. 4	San Francisco Symphony	Kocsis	Philips	411 475-2		
Rachmaninoff	Rhapsody on a Theme of Paganini	Royal Philharmonic	Orozco	Philips	6570.046		
Rachmaninoff	Rhapsody on a Theme of Paganini	San Francisco Symphony	Kocsis	Philips			412 738-4
Rachmaninoff	Symphonic Dances	London Symphony		Philips		6500.362	
Rachmaninoff	Symphony no. 1	Rotterdam Philharmonic		Philips		9500.445	
Rachmaninoff	Symphony no. 2	Rotterdam Philharmonic		Philips		9500.309	
Rachmaninoff	Symphony no. 3	Rotterdam Philharmonic		Philips		9500.302	

Composer	Work	Orchestra	Soloists	Label	CD	LP	MC
Ravel	Boléro	Rotterdam Philharmonic		Philips		6500.882	
Ravel	Sheherazade	San Francisco Symphony	Ameling	Philips	410 043-2	6514.199	7337.199
Reich	Variations for orchestra	San Francisco Symphony		Philips	412 214-2		412 214-4
Respighi	The Birds	San Francisco Symphony		Philips	411 419-2	6514.202	7337.202
Respighi	The Fountains of Rome	San Francisco Symphony		Philips	411 419-2	6514.202	7337.202
Respighi	The Pines of Rome	San Francisco Symphony		Philips	411 419-2	6514.202	7337.202
Rossini	Arias	Philharmonia	von Stade	Philips		9500.098	
Saint-Saëns	Symphony no. 3 in c	Rotterdam Philharmonic	Chorzempa	Philips	420 899-2		
Saint-Saëns	Symphony no. 3 in c	San Francisco Symphony	Guillou	Philips	412 619-2		
Schubert	Minuet and Finale in F	Netherlands Wind Ensemble		Philips		6570.205	
Strauss, R.	Oboe concerto in D	New Philharmonia	Holliger	Philips		6500.174	
Strauss, R.	Der Rosenkavalier	Rotterdam Philharmonic	Lear, von Stade, Welting, Bastin, Carreras, Hammond-Stroud	Philips		6707.030	
Strauss, R.	Eine Alpensinfonie	Minnesota Orchestra		Virgin	VC7 91102-2		VC7 91102-4
Strauss, R.	Serenade in E flat major	Minnesota Orchestra		Virgin	VC7 91102-2		VC7 91102-4
Stravinsky	Concerto for Piano and Winds	Netherlands Wind Ensemble		Philips		6500.841	
Stravinsky	Ebony Concerto	Netherlands Wind Ensemble		Philips		6500.841	
Stravinsky	Octet for Winds	Netherlands Wind Ensemble		Philips		6500.841	

Composer	Work	Orchestra	Soloists	Label	CD	LP	MC
Stravinsky	Symphony for wind instruments	Netherlands Wind Ensemble		Philips		6500.841	
Tchaikovsky	Francesca da Rimini	Concertgebouw		Philips		9500.745	
Tchaikovsky	Romeo and Juliet	Concertgebouw		Philips		9500.745	
Viotti	Violin concerto no. 22 in a	Concertgebouw	Grumiaux	Philips		839.757	
Wagner	A Faust Overture	San Francisco Symphony		Philips		6514.380	7337.380
Wagner	Der Fliegende Holländer: Overture	Concertgebouw		Philips	400 089-2		
Wagner	Die Feen: Overture	Concertgebouw		Philips	400 089-2		
Wagner	Symphony in C	San Francisco Symphony		Philips		6514.380	7337.380
Wagner	Tannhäuser	Concertgebouw		Philips	400 089-2		

Index

293

Author

Jeannine Wagar received her doctorate from Stanford University in orchestral conducting. Dedicated to excellence in both conducting and education, she has held the positions of conductor of the Stanford University Chamber Orchestra, music director/conductor of the University of Santa Cruz Orchestra, and principal guest conductor of the San Francisco Bay Area Women's Philharmonic, and is currently assistant professor of Music at Carleton College and music director/conductor of the Carleton Orchestra.

Wagar has received wide critical acclaim in Mexico City as guest conductor with the Sinfonica Nacional de Bellas Artes, with the Orquesta del Estado de Mexico, and in performances on Mexican national television. She has a special interest in contemporary music, has conducted numerous premiere performances, and has frequently been a guest conductor in international new music festivals.